# For Yankee Fans Only

**By Rich Wolfe**

Published by Lone Wolfe Press

ISBN: 0-9729249-0-6

Cover Photos: Courtesy of *The Sporting News*
Cover Design: Dick Fox
Photo Editor: Dick Fox
Cover Copywriter: Dick Fox
Interior Design: The Printed Page, Phoenix, AZ

www.fandemonium.net

# DEDICATION

## To Pat Solon

In memoriam
to an absolutely wonderful person and friend

# Chat Rooms

# PREFACE

Babe Ruth, Yankee Stadium, Mickey Mantle, and the New York Yankees—any discussion of great sports personages, edifices or dynasties must begin and end in the Bronx.

This made it easy to select Yankee fans as the first subjects in an 81-volume series of books on passionate fans that will be published in the next 15 months. From Green Bay to Austin, from Notre Dame to Boston and 76 other places, loyal followers will trumpet their neatest stories about their favorite teams. Once again, the Yankees and their fans lead the parade.

As stated on the dust jacket, there have been over 1000 books written about the Yankees but not a single one has been in regard to Yankee fans—the very people who are the reason for the team's existence. After all, only the fans buy the merchandise, fill the seats, and watch/listen to the broadcasts.

For some of us, baseball recalls broken glass, broken bats and broken dreams with lingering reflections of a simpler, more innocent time of riding your bike—with the glove on the handlebars—to a ball diamond where you were sure that you would deliver a game-winning hit.

For many of us, baseball defined our youth, still overly-impacts our adulthood and is one of the few things, other than grandchildren, that can make you feel young and old at the same time.

And for all of us, it is—most of all—a game of memories: the transistor under the pillow, sitting outside a small store feverishly opening newly purchased baseball cards, our first uniform, learning to keep score, the dew and mosquitoes, the sounds of the radio or the PA announcer at our first big league game. Little did many of us know that baseball would be the best math and geography teacher we would ever have…and none of us knew that the vibrant green of the field during our first major league game would be the lushest green, the greenest green and the most memorable green that we would ever see in our entire lifetime.

As Yankee fans share their memories with you, it is my hope that you will smile as these stories bring back your pleasant childhood and Yankee recollections.

Since the age of ten, I've been a serious collector of sports books. During that time—for the sake of argument let's call it 30 years—my favorite book style is the eavesdropping type where the subject talks in his or her own words—without the "then he said" or "the air was so thick that you could cut it with a butter knife" waste of verbiage that makes it so hard to get to the meat of the matter. Books such as Lawrence Ritter's *Glory of Their Times* and Donald Honig's *Baseball When the Grass was Real*. Thus, I adopted that style when I started compiling oral histories of the Mike Ditkas and Harry Carays of the world. I'm a sports fan first and foremost—I don't even pretend to be an author. This book is designed solely for other sports fans. I really don't care what the publisher, editors or critics think. I'm only interested in Yankee fans having an enjoyable read and getting their money's worth. Sometimes a person being interviewed will drift off the subject but if the feeling is that baseball fans would enjoy the digression, it stays in the book.

In an effort to get more material into the book, the editor decided to merge some paragraphs and omit some of the commas which will allow for the reader to receive an additional 20,000 words, the equivalent of 50 pages. More bang for your buck...more fodder for English teachers...fewer dead trees.

Jim Bouton, who graciously gave of his time at his beautiful abode for an interview for this book, perhaps said it best, "For years, we hold a baseball and it ends up holding us the whole time."

And Marty Appel, in his interview, appropriately opined: "Some say the beauty of baseball is that it isn't played by a clock. But there is a timepiece governing it, and it's the timepiece of our lives."

As this book jogs your memory, you might reflect how sweet it would be to have a "do over." Unfortunately, the sun doesn't back up for anyone. It just seems that sometimes, as you get older, the things that you want most are the things that you once had.

Go now.

*Rich Wolfe*

Celebration, Florida

# Chapter 1

# Leading Off

## Yankee Fandemonium

# CALLING STEINBRENNER "GEORGE" IS LIKE CALLING ATTILA THE HUN "TILLY"

Jim Copacino

*Jim Copacino, 53, grew up in Connecticut but changed loyalties when he moved to the Pacific Northwest.*

I was born in Torrington, Connecticut, where every young person had to make a great choice. The town was equally divided between Red Sox and Yankee fans. We'd get the Yankee games on a New Haven station and the Red Sox games out of the Hartford station. So every kid at about six or seven kind of declared his "major." I chose the Yankees. My father was a Red Sox fan, and my twin brothers, who are fifteen months younger than I, were Red Sox fans. My brothers and I were really like triplets growing up. We were very close, but they probably became Red Sox fans just because I wasn't. As we got older and a little more sophisticated, my father, brothers, and I would argue all the time. I felt very superior because I adopted the Yankees.

My brother, Bill, and I used to stand in our little yard and throw fly balls to each other. I'd be Mickey Mantle and he'd be Ted Williams. We'd keep throwing until one of us missed ten and had ten errors. We were convinced that as a result of whoever made the most errors that day, his team would win or lose the next day. It wasn't reliable, but we used to think we could will the outcome. If Ted Williams made the ten errors, dropped the ten balls, before Mickey Mantle did, surely the Yankees would win the next day. We weren't right very often because the Red Sox never won back in those days, and the Yankees always won. I think it was my brother's way to try to change fate.

One time, Ted Williams came to Torrington to do a fundraiser for the charity called the Jimmy Fund. It was a big deal. My dad was involved in something like the Rotary Club, so we got to go. He might have been involved in the planning, too. I was eight or nine-years old, and it seemed like the biggest gathering I'd ever been to. There were two or three hundred people there.

Somehow, my dad arranged for me to shake hands with Ted Williams. I was very sensitive to poison ivy, and during the summer we'd go play in the woods. I had poison ivy at that time, and I still remember going and shaking hands with Ted Williams—his big callused paw around my hand, and it was quite exciting. He was not wearing a tie—I do remember

> **"What if he gets poison ivy and can't hold a bat? Can they trace it back to me?" I thought I'd be in trouble.**

that. He wore a checkered sports jacket with flyaway collar. He was like John Wayne. I do remember that big hand and the strength he had.

Anyhow, on the way back in the car, I became very anxious and concerned that I may have given Ted Williams poison ivy, and even though I was a Yankee fan, I had a lot of respect for Ted Williams. I said, "What if he gets poison ivy and can't hold a bat? Can they trace it back to me?" I thought I'd be in trouble. I remember looking at the box score of the next game Ted played, and he went three for four with a home run.

I was too young to remember Joe DiMaggio, but my father loved him, even though he was a Red Sox fan, because Joe D. was Italian. My father's favorite players were first, Italian, and second, Red Sox players. My father was born in 1919, and the Red Sox last won the World Series in 1918. He's been really sick but he's promised he's not going to die until the Red Sox win another World Series. We're sure he'll live to be about a hundred and thirty.

He and I were going on a drive somewhere and he explained that all the great players he admired so much were Italian and had really changed their names: Mickey Mantelino, Whitey Fordetta—he had all these Italian names for these guys. I bought it completely for a couple of months. I told some of my friends, and they said, "You're full of crap. What are you talking about?"

My dad was also under the impression that Billy Martin was Italian, or, at least, partially Italian, and he liked Billy because of that.

On rare occasions, our CYO went to Yankee Stadium as a group. The trip was about a hundred and twenty miles. Torrington was not a metropolitan area of Connecticut. It was a little industrial town, not a terribly sophisticated place. Driving into New York was a big deal and, of course, negotiating the Bronx was an even bigger deal. My dad would take our family once or twice a year, and then maybe we'd go on the bus with the Little League once every two years. It was a really big deal and lots of fun.

> **I was stunned that my father had this power, this ability, to send telegrams to Gods!**

I was probably eight or nine years old, and my family was ready for one of our annual trips to Yankee Stadium. Though we lived about halfway between Fenway Park and Yankee Stadium, we tended to go to Yankee Stadium more often. I don't know why that was, but maybe it was my influence. This was my birthday so my dad said we would go to the Yankee game. We are all ready to go, and my dad said, "Come on inside with me for a minute." This would have been about nine in the morning. He picked up the phone and called Western Union. He said, "Operator, I want to send a telegram. I want to send it to Mr. Mickey Mantle, Yankee Stadium." I was sitting there with my mouth open. My dad dictated the telegram, "Dear Mickey, I'll be at the game today. Please hit a home run for me. Jimmy Copacino." I was stunned that my father had this power, this ability, to send telegrams to Gods! I knew that my father must be a very important man if he could do this.

Now, Mickey Mantle struck out three times that day and popped up. He didn't hit a home run. My father said, "He must not have gotten the telegram." That was his only explanation. But just sending a telegram to Mickey Mantle was a birthday gift enough.

As a kid, I was intoxicated by the voices of Mel Allen and Red Barber. They were a large reason I became a Yankee fan in the first place. I remember sitting in front of the black and white TV and hearing these southern voices come out of the television set. It was so exotic and interesting. I loved the words. Here you had the New York

Yankees in the Bronx and yet you had all this southern language, not only from Allen and Barber but from Mickey Mantle, too.

When I was about nine or ten, I figured out a way to get into my grandmother's car and turn on the key to just hear the radio. I listened to a whole Yankee doubleheader in the car in the garage and then the battery died. I got into a lot of trouble for that. I was sitting there on a Sunday afternoon in my grandmother's 1952 Ford listening to Mel Allen talk about these nondescript games with the White Sox. It was a very peaceful place to be. My father explained to me that we don't turn on the car—ever, for any reason, when you're nine or ten years old. He said we had televisions and radios in the house and that's where I should listen to baseball games.

At that time, the Yankees meant everything to me. My wall was covered with pictures. I don't know what it is, but some chemical, emotional thing happens with pre-pubescent boys where baseball becomes so important, like a spiritual or religious experience. I remember that in grade school it was common practice during the World Series to listen to the games played over the PA system. Today, we're all realists about marketing and the economics of modern baseball, but one thing I am nostalgic for are those beautiful fall afternoons, mid-week, when the radio sounds of the World Series would be on from two to five, or one to four. The way people followed the game back then was really special.

I remember clearly the 1960 World Series that ended with Bill Mazeroski's home run. I got home just in time to see the home run. When I'd left school, the score was 7-7. I got home and the Yanks were leading 9-8. Then Mazeroski hit the home run and it was over. I remember seeing the ball sail over the wall in Forbes Field. Tony Kubek had gotten hit in the neck with a ball, and he was badly hurt. I remember reading that Mickey Mantle was crying in the locker room afterwards. I really wept after that loss. The Yankees fired Casey Stengel right after that game because they thought he was too old. Yeah, that was very painful.

Then a crazy friend of my father's came to the house and brought a little pebble. He said, "Here, I got you the pebble from Forbes Field where the ball took a bad hop and hit Tony Kubek in the throat." For about a day, I thought I had this real relic of the game. He had just picked up a rock off our driveway and gave it to me, teasing me. I don't remember if he was a Red Sox fan or not, but he just knew how much this Series had meant to me so he said, "I want you to have a little part of it." After a while I figured out that there was no way he could get this pebble from Pittsburgh.

In 1968, in the middle of my senior year of high school, my parents moved back East from Youngstown, Ohio, to Murray Hill, New Jersey. I was captain of the baseball team and editor of the newspaper and was really involved in school so I wanted to stay behind and graduate with my class. So I lived with a friend's family, and then literally the day after graduation, I moved to New Jersey.

After we moved to New Jersey, I could go see the Yankees play. In 1968, I had one of my best experiences ever in the ballpark. The Detroit Tigers were flying high. They won the pennant and beat the Cardinals in the World Series. This was the year baseball expanded to ten teams in each league and there was no East-West division so a team could finish in tenth place. The Yankees were ninth. The high-flying first-place Tigers came to town and the hapless Yankees improbably beat them on Friday night and Saturday. My friend and I had tickets for the doubleheader on Sunday.

The Yankees won the first game, and in the second, they were behind something like 8-2 in the late innings, when they rallied and came back. Mickey Mantle was still playing, and he hit a double. In the bottom of the ninth, they scored a bunch of runs, took the lead like 10-9, and were about to sweep the Tigers. The problem was that they were out of pitchers.

Ralph Houk waved to the **bullpen**. In those days, the pitchers used to come out in a little car. My friend and I were looking at our rosters and looking at our scorecards and saying, "Who is this?" Well, out of the car came Rocky Colavito. He was from the Bronx. He had had a

> The Yankees once had a bullpen car (Toyota) that fans threw trash at constantly. The trash attracted rats that ate through the engine cables. The car was scrapped in favor of a golf cart.

very distinguished career with the Indians and the Tigers, and in 1968, in the twilight of his career, he finished with the Yankees. He was a right fielder and a power hitter, but he had a great arm. So, Rocky Colavito, the reserve outfielder, came in, pitched the last inning against the fearsome Tigers lineup, and got the win. He had only pitched three innings in his entire career before this, and that was ten years earlier. The Yankees swept the four games. For a Yankee fan in 1968, this was like winning the World Series because the Yankees were so terrible.

I had a girlfriend back in Ohio, and I had her come visit me in 1969. Together we went to Yankee Stadium for Mickey Mantle Day. It was right after Mickey retired. The Yankees had a big ceremony, and he drove around on a golf cart. Bobby Murcer, who was kind of his descendant in baseball, because he was from Oklahoma and played center field, hit a home run that day which was very poignant. The Yankees were terrible back then. I remember just standing and clapping for ten minutes, with tears streaming down my face. That was the end of my relationship with this woman. She said, "Why are you crying over this guy riding around in a golf cart?" So I realized it could never work between us.

The following summer I was home from college, living with my parents in New Jersey, when I got a real appreciation of the continuity of generations through baseball. That summer, I'd take the bus from Scotch Plains to the Port Authority Bus Terminal, then take the D train to Yankee Stadium and sit in the bleachers. In those days, I think a ticket for a doubleheader in the bleachers cost seventy-five cents, and I'd bring my own lunch. This one day, I was sitting in the bleachers next to a man who told me he used to see **Babe Ruth** play at Yankee Stadium all the time. This was 1969, so the man had been coming to Yankee Stadium for forty-some years. I was twenty, and he was sixty or sixty-five. It wasn't amazing, but just the fact that I was sitting next to someone who saw Babe Ruth play really struck me.

In Babe Ruth's first major league game in 1914, he was removed in the seventh inning for a pinch hitter.

In 1971, I was at Ohio University in southeast Ohio. At spring break, a bunch of us would jump in a car, scrape together gas and food money, and drive to Ft. Lauderdale. The Yankees trained there in those days so naturally I wanted to go and see spring training. Spring training was much less formal in those days, very accessible.

This was a few years after Mickey Mantle retired, but he used to be at spring training as a batting instructor. So here I was at the railing, twenty-one or two-years old, and there's Mickey about fifty or sixty feet away from me. I'd been trying to get a Mickey Mantle autograph all my life. I had waited outside Yankee Stadium after games with the other kids for him to come out and he never seemed to come out before my father would say it was time to go. I was always trying to be like Mickey Mantle when I played baseball. Isn't it funny? Of people my age, there must be millions of us who used to stand in front of the TV and try to stand like Mickey Mantle and talk like Mickey Mantle. Billy Crystal tells that great story about how he did his Bar Mitzvah with an Oklahoma accent. I actually wrote an essay in school in seventh or eighth grade about my hero. The teacher sent it to the Yankees, and I got a Mantle picture with an autograph on it, but I was never quite sure it was the real thing. The essay has been misplaced over the years, but I clearly remember getting a letter back on Yankee stationery, probably written by some PR intern, which said, "Dear Jim, Thank you very much for your essay. Mickey appreciated it very much. He'd like you to have this autographed picture."

So here I was, standing against the rail at the ballpark in Ft. Lauderdale, and Mickey Mantle was about fifty or sixty feet away from me talking to a couple of sports writers. It was a very quiet moment in spring training. There was no game going on at the time. I thought, "This is it. This is my chance." I noticed a guy who was either a sportswriter or a member of the front office, and I assumed he had credentials. I called him over and said, "Look, I've been a Mickey Mantle fan all my life. This is a big thing for me. Can you ask him for his autograph for me?" He said, "No, I can't do that. I don't want to bother him. I don't know Mickey that well." I said, "He won't mind. He's not doing anything." I handed the guy the program I had and my pen, and finally talked him into going over to Mickey.

He stood outside the little circle of people Mickey was talking to, and finally I saw him talking to Mickey and then he gestured over to me. I saw Mickey scowl, take the program, put it on his thigh, and bend over to write. He started to write, then he shook the pen. He started to write again and shook the pen again. Then in disgust, Mickey handed the program back to the guy, and the guy came over to me and said, "Your pen ran out of ink." For years, I had this program with "M-i-c" written on it. In a way, it makes for a better story than if I had gotten his full autograph.

I often thought about Mickey Mantle during my twenties and thirties when I realized what a complicated and tortured individual he was. So this blond Oklahoma god became, as you got a little older and you began to see what he was, an object to be pitied, and it was really sad. You could see how little self-esteem he had and the sort of demons he fought with and that was tough to

**I always wondered growing up what life would be like when Mickey Mantle dies? I thought it would mark a point of passage where I'd no longer be young.**

accept. I always wondered growing up what life would be like when Mickey Mantle dies? I thought it would mark a point of passage where I'd no longer be young. I often thought about that even when he was healthy, before he got sick. You think about those things in your thirties as you pass out of youth. You think about your parents of course, and you think about the big influences on yourself as a child. You come to grips with these issues of mortality and time passing and all that other stuff. There were the Beatles and the Yankees, and these guys start to die. What will life be like afterwards? It's a wonderful thing really to be able to have this conversation, which is so intimate, with a stranger across the country. Baseball's one of the few things that can bring people together. It's the miracle of the game.

In the 1970s, I would pay $2.50 for a seat. I had my favorite row right behind the box seats. In those days, the Yankees would draw twenty-five, thirty thousand fans on a weekend; seventeen, eighteen thousand during the week. You could go up to the box office and say, "Section 27, row A or B," and they'd usually give you the ticket. I spent a lot of time at Yankee Stadium when the team wasn't very good.

I remember the Yankee "joints" and Manny's Baseball Land and the Stadium Grill. For years, Manny's Baseball Land was the great souvenir place. It was right across from the Stadium underneath the El on 161st Street. It was an old storefront that had a plywood front that flipped open. This was before the days when baseball merchandising became so sophisticated that these trinkets appear in every J.C. Penney's in every mall in the country. Manny's sold T-shirts, autographed baseballs, pictures, little bats. It was a small place, but they did a great business.

In 1978, I moved to Seattle. It was tough moving away from New York, especially at that time when it was terribly exciting to be a Yankee fan. I did consider having to leave my Yankees, but it was one of those lifestyle decisions. I knew, though, that my wife and I had to move to a city that had major league baseball.

The first game I went to in Seattle at the Kingdome was against Cleveland. After a lifetime of going to games in the Bronx, where the excitement is at fever pitch and the Stadium is sold out every night, and New York fans are passionate and crazy, I come to the Kingdome, where the team plays on plastic grass, and there are four thousand people in this gray cave, and they're all well behaved. In fact, the last game I went to before moving west was a Yankees-Red Sox game, and the fans were nuts. Fights broke out in the stands.

That first game in Seattle, I brought my Yankee Stadium manners. I went up to the hot dog vendor and said, "Gimme a dog." He looked at me and said, "Sir, you'll have to wait in line behind these other people." Here were these people politely waiting for their hot dogs so I went to the back of the line and began to learn to be "Seattle polite." I thought, "Why have I moved to where nobody cares about baseball?" Fortunately, that changed when **Lou Piniella** managed the team. He had been such a key part of that 1978 Yankees pennant drive.

When Lou Piniella played minor league baseball in Aberdeen, S.D. in 1964, the team's batboy was Cal Ripken, Jr.

# THE REASON MANY PEOPLE ARE RED SOX FANS IS THEY CAN'T AFFORD WORLD SERIES TICKETS

### George Philippides

*George Philippides, 42, is a respected Boston cardiologist and a rabid Yankee fan dating back to his childhood days in Garden City, Long Island.*

My parents emigrated from Greece to Brooklyn, where I was born, and they were **soccer fans** so the neighborhood kids turned me into a Yankee fan. When I was about five years old, we moved out of Brooklyn and into what seemed to be a "Mets neighborhood": Garden City, New York, on Long Island. At that point, being a Yankee fan marked you as being "different." From the get-go, my brothers and I took pride in being the "Yankee kids" on the block. For the longest time, until the Yankees became champion caliber again, which wasn't until the mid-to-late 1970s, we were always putting up with the obnoxious Mets fans who had won a championship in the interim.

The kid across the street from us was a Mets fan, but his dad had it right—Mr. Watson was a Yankee fan. In a failed effort to try to turn his kid into a Yankee fan during the late 1960s, early 1970s, Mr. Watson would take us to the old Yankee Stadium. My first memory was of him throwing us all in his station wagon and driving up into the Bronx to go to the Stadium. As a matter of fact, I saw Mickey Mantle about three or four times before he retired, thanks to Mr. Watson. His son, Ken, Jr. was a perfectly nice guy, but I don't know

> More U. S. kids play soccer today than any organized sport, including youth baseball. The reason so many kids play soccer is so they don't have to watch it.

where he went wrong. Ken, Jr. would talk Ron Swoboda and Ed Kranepool, and I would talk Tom Tresh and Joe Pepitone. When we would play Wiffle Ball or stick ball, we would each be our favorite Met or Yankee.

The car rides to Yankee Stadium were great because Mr. Watson would regale us with stories about the Yankees in the 1950s, talk about that heyday of baseball when there were three teams back then in New York. Actually, Mr. Watson turned me on to reading a lot about baseball history, which I still love. I would read everything I could about the Dodgers, the Giants, and the Yankees of the 1950s. I always felt that I was born about ten years too late. Mr. Watson was somebody in my sports development who was integral in getting me to like the Yankees even more than I had.

Mickey Mantle was my favorite player, and I begged for the Number 7 when I played ball. I first really became a fan when the Yankees were having their worst years in the late 1960s and Mantle retired. It was traumatic for a little kid.

There were a lot of differences between my family, being Greek, and the other families in our Garden City neighborhood. I think we were the only family of immigrants, and we also seemed to be politically to the left of many of the families. It seemed like everybody was a Republican and a Mets fan. My brothers and I rooted for the Yankees, and my family voted Democrat. We were the only kids on the bus who actually would admit that our parents were voting for McGovern and not Nixon.

At the same time, I distinctly remember being the only kid in my fifth grade class who wanted **Muhammad Ali** to beat Joe Frazier. As a matter of fact, I made small bets with everyone. When Ali lost, I could not believe it. I went in to school late the next day, hoping I would be left alone, but I was picked on all day. Part of the reason for that, also, was that I was one of the "Yankee guys." This friction went all the way through the evil Mets years when they were much better than the Yankees.

In 1979 Muhammad Ali beat football player, Lyle Alzado, in an eight round bout.

I still make fun of my junior high and high school friends who came back over to the boat when the Yankees picked it up again in the 1970s. They won't admit to it, but they were all Mets fans back then. I felt there was a badge of honor to be one of the few guys who hung with the Yankees until they got good again.

By my last years of high school, the Yankees were great. I took off from school with some friends and my brothers and went to see the last playoff game of the 1976 season, the day Chris Chambliss got the home run that put the Yankees in the World Series for the first time in twelve years. One of the boys somehow got his dad's car, and we had gotten tickets and took off together. We sat up behind home plate and watched Chris Chambliss hit that homer. It was one of the greatest celebrations I've ever been a part of. Fifty thousand people were in the stadium screaming and hugging each other. When are New Yorkers ever openly affectionate? But strangers were just hugging each other.

I'll never forget going out to find our car, which was somewhere deep down Jerome Avenue. Cars were jam-packed, parked back-to-back, and we took to walking on the cars, which was okay with everyone. People would reach out—I'll never forget this—and hand you beers. They would also hand you other things to smoke, if you wanted to. It was just this big New York party, and I'd never seen New Yorkers be so nice to each other. It was a great event.

After college, I went to medical school at Albert Einstein College of Medicine in the Bronx. At the same time, my middle brother, Menas, was going to **Fordham University**. He's my brother, but he's also a good friend, so I went to Fordham a lot to watch him play soccer, and we also went to a lot of baseball games. I thought, "This is great. I'm in the Bronx. I've got my brother, and we go to a lot of baseball games." We actually devised this one scam together:

The dean's secretary at Einstein was named Camella, and she was dating Gene Michael, who, in the early 1980s was the general manager of the Yankees. Somehow, Camella was always getting tickets.

> The St. Louis Rams, previously the Los Angeles Rams and before that, the Cleveland Rams, got their nickname from the Fordham football team.

Camella and my buddies at Einstein and I became friends. We liked Camella, but we also enjoyed the fact that she was always throwing us tickets.

So we had these tickets, but we had no way to get to Yankee Stadium. Then we figured out that the driver of one of the vans that was supposed to take us to our clinical rotations at the different hospitals was a Yankee fan.

We chatted with this guy, and convinced him that instead of taking us to the hospital, to keep the van going past Bronx-Lebanon Hospital and drop us off at the Stadium. After he would drop us off, he'd return to his route. He would listen to the games on the radio and when he would hear it was the ninth inning, he would head back and pick us up at the Big Bat. So we had this system whereby we got free tickets and free transportation from our dorm to Yankee Stadium, all paid for by Albert Einstein College of Medicine. We just thought we were Gatsby. This was like manna from heaven for us.

In medical school, as part of your sub-internship, you're given your own patients for the first time. I had this one patient, Edward, who I became very close to. He had a seven-year old boy, Manuel, who he adored. Edward would page me every four hours to find out his lab results, but he was a sweet guy, and I got tight with him to the point where he and his wife invited me over to their house for dinner. Not to get overly dramatic, it became apparent that Ed's cancer was not going to be treatable, and he ended up dying. One of the things I remember from my time in the Bronx was Ed and his son and I going to a Yankee game together. Manuel was all decked out in the Yankee cap and jacket. Ed's death hits home now because I have an eighteen-month-old son. Going to Yankee games together is what you fantasize about doing with your kid. Edward died two years after I left the Bronx, when I was training in Boston. His wife sent me a very nice letter when he passed away, and every Christmas she would send me a picture of their family. In the pictures, the kid always had the Yankee cap on. It was sort of their way of thanking me for the time I spent with them and for getting the tickets. Clearly, our love for the Yankees was an important part of our bond.

Throughout the Einstein years, we went to a ton of Yankee games, and were just really into the Yankees. I went to the final World Series game in 1981 when they lost to the Dodgers, which was painful because we sat back up in the nosebleed seats in a section full of criminals. Sitting there reminds you that as great as Yankee Stadium is, there are some really aggressive drunk fans up there and you have to be careful.

Certain old friendships and family relationships have been cultivated and certainly maintained, in no small part, because we're Yankee fans first. My brothers, Menas and Nick, still live in Garden City, New York, and I'm up in Boston, so I'm sort of removed from their day-to-day lives. But if I'm watching a great game, and the phone rings right after something amazing happens, it's a fair bet that it'll be one of my brothers or my friend Leo.

> **Certain old friendships and family relationships have been cultivated and certainly maintained, in no small part, because we're Yankee fans first.**

Back in the 1980s, Don Mattingly would make a play, and the phone would ring. I would instinctively pick it up and say, "Hello Leo," or "Hello Nick," because I knew those guys were watching the game. To this day, when something intense happens with the Yankees, I know I'll get a call, either while the game is happening or the next morning. Then Leo and I will spend an hour, not doing what we're being paid to do, to talk in depth about why Derek Jeter is really the best shortstop we've ever seen.

I moved up to Boston to attend Boston Medical Center for my internal medicine training. I quickly found out there are enough displaced New Yorkers in Boston that you can easily find Yankee fans. After a few years, another doctor and I went "in" on Fenway tickets. He was from Detroit, so he would use the tickets for Detroit games, and I would use the Yankee tickets.

When I go to a game at Fenway Park, I often wear a Yankee shirt and a Yankee cap so people throw beer at me all the time. I really like being a Yankee fan at Fenway Park—I'm sorta strange that way. I feel that the best place to watch a baseball game in America is Fenway Park. As much as I love Yankee Stadium and the history it's got, Fenway is so small, so cozy, and the views are great. Most of the seats are close enough to home plate that you can really hear the ball hit the catcher's mitt. There's just nothing like it. And going to a Yankees-Red Sox game is just the best baseball game you can go to. The stadium is packed. Yankee fans there are very intense. And Red Sox fans—every big play everyone's going crazy and yelling at each other. I love being there.

> **If you want to be a Yankee fan and be open about it at Fenway, you've just got to be prepared for people just standing up and yelling in your face...**

If you want to be a Yankee fan and be open about it at Fenway, you've just got to be prepared for people just standing up and yelling in your face, "The Yankees suck," from the seat right behind you, in your ear, when they've had enough of your cheering. You've got to accept that when Bernie Williams hits a homer, and everyone's hushed in your area and you get up and start cheering that you're going to be glared at for the next two innings. Or have people from the section above throw beer down on your head.

One time there was a guy behind me and a bit over who kept throwing solid objects at me. It was less than funny. He was pretty drunk. That wasn't happy. But for the most part, I've not had the kind of near-violent experiences at Fenway that I've seen at Yankee Stadium. I hate to admit that, but it's true.

I just truly love rooting for the Yankees, and don't feel like I want to back down when I'm in Red Sox territory. The Red Sox fans, they're no shrinking violets. They give as good as they get. When the Yankees lose a big game, I hear about it.

A few years ago, a patient of mine had an infectious disease problem so I called the infectious disease physician on call. He came to the unit, examined the patient, and we got to talking. For some reason, the talk switched from medicine to baseball. It became apparent that we both had Red Sox tickets for that evening. We traded ticket numbers, and he looked at me with a horrified expression. He said, "You're the —— Yankee fan that's been sitting behind me and ruining my afternoons for the last ten years." He knew who my brother was. He remembered that my brother is also a fairly obnoxious vocal fan. That's how he recognized me, from my voice screaming in his ear for ten years. I said, "I remember now the back of your head and you guys cringing, but I didn't know it was you, because I couldn't see you." So, in a way we'd known each other since 1988 but didn't realize it until 1998. We've been friends ever since, though he really hates the Yankees. I think the Red Sox fans can take the grief, and that's sort of why I do it. And they like to give it back.

When I was doing my internship in Boston, I had a patient in the coronary care unit who came in with unstable angina, chest pains not controllable with medicines. I was in the CCU when the Red Sox were playing the Mets in the 1986 World Series. This guy got so riled up about the Red Sox on TV that we had to take his TV privileges away, and this guy ended up basically saying, "Screw you." He pulled off his EKG monitor, and he signed out against medical advice. He walked out of the hospital. He walked to a bar down the street, had a cigarette, watched the end of the World Series game, and then re-admitted himself. That's a Red Sox fan. When he came back in, he said, "Look Doc, I'm not even gonna apologize. This is what I did." I said, "Fine." I re-admitted him and we took care of him.

Mets fans just seem like superficial fans to me. There's less substance there than in Yankee fans and Red Sox fans. I think the Yankees, in a way, capture the essence of New York more than the Mets do. The Yankees and their fans, to a certain degree, are about being brash and saying, "We're gonna beat the best. We're gonna be the best. We're gonna be the richest." Be whatever. And they're not afraid to call that shot and then to go out and try to do that. I think the Yankees are a perfect fit for New York. It doesn't surprise me that at the end of each Yankee game, especially when they win, they play that Frank Sinatra song, "New York, New York." It truly is who the Yankees are.

# MOM, THAT'S EXACTLY THE WAY IT HAPPENED...GIVE OR TAKE A LIE OR TWO

### Mark Jurkowitz

*A child of the 1960s, Boston Globe media writer Mark Jurkowitz, 48, grew up in Scranton, Pennsylvania, equidistant from New York City and Philadelphia.*

We used to be able to pick up the **Phillies** on a local ABC affiliate. Those were the days of the old TV sets, so you'd turn on the TV, and it would take about three minutes for the picture to come in. In the meantime, you could hear sound. You could always tell if you had tuned into a Phillies' game because there would be so few people in the ball park that while you waited for the picture to come on, you could actually hear individual conversations. You'd hear people say, "I'll have some popcorn." It was a metaphor for how bad the Phillies were in those days. I became a Yankee fan because the choice between Pancho Hererra and Mickey Mantle was easy.

Two or three times a year when I was a kid, I would take a group trip with the Boy Scouts or our synagogue to Yankee Stadium for the old Sunday **doubleheaders**. It was always the same thing: You'd watch the first game, and then about the fifth or sixth inning of the second game, the adult chaperones would come around and say, "We're

> P.K. Wrigley and Milton Hershey were bitter business rivals. When Wrigley bought the Chicago Cubs, Hershey tried to buy the Philadelphia Phillies... and sell chocolate gum. Hershey failed in both efforts.

> In 1943, the Chicago White Sox played 44 doubleheaders.

leaving after Mantle's next at bat." You always got to see Mickey's next at bat. To this day, I still have a ball autographed by Mickey that Nestor Chylak, a long-time American League umpire who was a friend of my father's, got for me.

My father was not a Yankee fan. He liked the San Francisco Giants. He also liked the Detroit Tigers, who in the early 1960s were among the Yankees key rivals. He was always saying things like, "Oh Mickey Mantle. He can't carry Willie Mays' jock strap." He respected Mickey Mantle, but it was a grudging respect.

I can remember being in the back yard at our house fooling around, playing ball, and listening to the Yankee game on the radio. This was during the 1962 season when Mantle missed sixty-one straight days with a broken foot. In those days, teams didn't announce disabled lists like they do now, where they say a player is going to be out for fifteen days. The Yankee announcers would never say how long Mantle was going to be out with an injury, so every day they'd say something like, "Well, Mickey is day-to-day." This went on for two months.

Well, he finally came back and pinch hit in the eighth inning of a game against the Baltimore Orioles, which I think the Yankees were losing by one run. So here Mantle was, his first at-bat in sixty-one games, and he hit a pinch-hit homer. I remember running around my back yard, sort of delirious. Even my father, who was outside with me, said, "That's not human." So even a non-Mantle admirer like my father was forced to acknowledge the miracle of Mickey Mantle.

In late 1976, a couple of friends and I were on a cross-country trip, and we stopped in an Oklahoma City bar for a few drinks. I said, "I'm not leaving here without talking to Bobby Murcer." I knew he was born or lived in Oklahoma City, and I desperately thumbed through the Oklahoma City phone book looking for his number. I tried to call him from a pay phone. I wasn't successful. I wasn't very clear-headed at the time.

The following year, I attended my first World Series game, which was also the three-homer, Reggie Jackson game. I was about twenty-two, living in Arizona, but for a brief time I was staying in my hometown of Scranton. A friend and I took a group bus to the ballpark and went to the game. I think it's fair to say that we consumed about two quarts of liquor during the course of the game. I can't remember how we sneaked it in. We were young and healthy so we were pretty wired. The Yankees won the World Series. It was an unbelievable event.

After the game, emboldened by the alcohol coursing through my veins, I decided to run onto the field and get a piece of Yankee Stadium turf. We were sitting fairly high up in the stands so it took us a while to get down, but I was determined to get on the field. Everybody was running around like crazy, and the Yankees had hired a bunch of "rent-a-cops" to police the situation. The reality was that about ninety-five percent of the people on the field were running around with impunity, getting away with whatever they wanted. The other five percent that the rent-a-cops caught took an awful thrashing.

I was drunk and had taken about three or four steps onto the field when I was hit by a flying tackle and went face down on the ground. I was a smaller man then; I probably weighed only about a hundred forty, hundred fifty pounds. I was quickly lifted by two very burly men. They carried me parallel to the ground and one of them said, "Let's break this ———'s neck." Now that scared me a little bit.

They ran me back to the stands and threw me head-first about eight rows. You know the old saying about when you're inebriated, your body actually tends to be a little loose. Well, rather than tightening up and landing head first, and fracturing my skull or my shoulder, I landed with a clatter. I wasn't badly hurt, but I hadn't gotten my piece of turf, so I unceremoniously picked myself up and tried to survey the situation. The guy right in front of me, now in the stands, who had been running around the field had gotten a big chunk of turf and was waving it in his hand. I came from behind and ripped it out of his hand. My friend and I high-tailed it back to the bus, which was waiting in the parking lot to take us back to Scranton. I guess I should say that I think I stole somebody's batting helmet during the game so I had that on to help protect my head. My friend was a lot stronger than I was and had a lot more physical courage, but he stayed back in the stands and just stood there laughing at me the whole time.

It turned out that the battery from the bus had been stolen during the game. We waited nearly three hours for the battery to be replaced. The entire time, about sixty drunken Scrantonians chanted "Reggie," "Reggie," "Reggie."

The best part of the experience was that I got home very, very late, and the next morning I said two things to my mother: "There's a patch of brownish green stuff in a cellophane bag in my top drawer. It looks like dope. It's not. Don't throw it out." Then I told her the story of the brutality I'd suffered at the hands of the Yankee Stadium rent-a-cops. My mother actually wrote a letter to then-Mayor Ed Koch, complaining about how her nice little boy had been mistreated.

Two years later I was at one of the most nerve-racking games of all time. It was the Bucky Dent home-run game that ended with two outs in the ninth inning and with the Red Sox tying and winning runs on base, and Carl Yastrzemski popping out to Graig Nettles, the Yankees third baseman. I can remember when it was over, literally, each hand was shaking like a leaf. I went to a nearby liquor store and bought a pint of J&B Scotch and chugged it until I stopped shaking. I didn't finish the whole bottle, but I took a nice healthy shot. It was like a scene right out of the movie *Lost Weekend* where Ray Milland is shaking and swigging alcohol until he finally stops.

I called my great Red Sox friend. I didn't say a word. My friend said, "I'm leaving town," and he hung up the phone. He didn't really leave town, but I knew we weren't going to have any conversations about the subject for at least a few days. Eventually he healed.

A few years later, about 1983, I was working at a weekly newspaper in Boston. One day, I got a press release that there was a shipbuilders' convention in town and that **George Steinbrenner** was going to be there. I figured, "Every sports reporter in the city is going to know about this. They're gonna be all over him. There could be a million people there." I called and found out that the sporting press had not

John Elway, Deion Sanders and Billy Cannon, Jr. were signed by George Steinbrenner and given $100,000 bonuses. All three quit baseball for the NFL.

been alerted. I asked if there was going to be press availability. I was told, "Well, if you're interested, sure he'll make himself available."

So I went down to Hynes Auditorium where the convention was being held. Literally, there was one other reporter and myself. We were in a small room off the auditorium. So I got about ten or fifteen minutes of face time with George Steinbrenner. I really wasn't planning to write a story; I just wanted to meet him. I said, "I'm a journalist, but I'm really here as a Yankee fan. I wanted to meet you and I want to ask you one question."

After Bobby Murcer had been traded straight up for **Bobby Bonds**, he ended up in the National League with the Giants and the Cubs. Late in his career, he had come back to the Yankees. This was at the tail end of his career. I asked Steinbrenner something to the effect of: "Is Bobby Murcer going to stay a Yankee?" He looked at me and said, "Son, as long as Bobby Murcer wants, he has a job in this organization." And Murcer did. He became the Yankee announcer. Instead of laughing, Steinbrenner looked me right in the eye and promised the guy a job for life.

My love for the Yankees has never waned. It was, however, once tested, when I had a true crisis of faith. That was when there was a rumor that Steve Garvey, the former Los Angeles Dodger first baseman, was going to be traded to the Yankees. I hated the Dodgers, one of the most despicable teams in baseball, and I hated Garvey. I actually spent some time thinking about that possibility and decided that if the trade happened, I might not be able to be a Yankee fan anymore. I probably hated the Dodgers so much because when they were in Brooklyn they beat the Yankees in the 1955 World Series. I even hated Sandy Koufax, though he's a nice Jewish boy.

Garvey was this sort of good-looking "Jack Armstrong All-American Boy" type. People called him "Popeye" because he had this gigantic set of forearms. He was this milk-drinking, squeaky-clean guy with some kind of problem because his wife eventually left him for Marvin Hamlisch, the songwriter. Garvey epitomized those

> In 2002, Barry Bonds received 68 intentional walks…
> Eight came when no one was on base.

sanitized Dodger teams I hated, and just the thought of him coming to my team! Frankly, when Don Zimmer first came to the Yankees, I found that disconcerting and annoying because he'd been a Red Sox manager, but I got over that.

My wife, Linda, is a huge Red Sox fan. She's a big believer in the Curse of the Bambino mythology. A couple of years ago, she set up a Babe Ruth shrine in our kitchen. It consisted of a photo-

**She's a big believer in the Curse of the Bambino mythology.**

graph of Babe as a pitcher in a Red Sox uniform. Underneath she set a little candle and every Friday she would light the candle. Every Friday she would also go buy the Babe a cigar. These weren't cheap cigars either. After about six months, I told her that the man had been dead for over half a century, and I really didn't feel like spending five bucks a week on cigars for him anymore.

I never worried about my wife's sanity. All Red Sox fans are mentally ill. They can't help it. They're tormented. They're tortured. They're self-pitying. They're angry. I totally respect her for her feelings. She hates the Yankees as much as I hate the Red Sox. I would be less impressed with her if there were any equivocation in her hatred of the Yankees.

We used to go to Mickey Mantle's restaurant when we'd visit New York. I saw Mantle there on a couple of occasions. One time, when I was on my way to the bathroom I saw this incredible photograph of him that I'd never seen before. It was taken around 1960 in the win-tertime at Yankee Stadium with snow on the ground and Mick was wearing a three-piece suit and swinging a bat at a snowball that somebody had thrown at him. The photo captures the moment of impact, as the snowball is fragmenting and Mantle's eyes are closed. It's incredible. He's dressed to the nines and there's about two inches of snow on the ground, and you can see Yankee Stadium in the back-ground. It was a huge, incredible picture.

My wife later called the manager of the restaurant and bought the pho-tograph right off the wall for my birthday. It was terribly expensive. That proved that even though she hates the Yankees, she loves me.

# HERE COMES THE JUDGE

Bill Manger

*The Honorable Judge William Manger, 57, didn't move from Paterson, New Jersey to Oklahoma in search of Mickey Mantle's soul, but he might have. Bill had the good fortune to become like a son to Yankees pitching star Allie Reynolds, "The Chief." Their closeness allowed Bill the opportunity to meet many Yankee greats.*

As kids we'd play softball on the school playground. I tried to imitate Mickey Mantle's switch-hitting and his walk. Mantle had a very identifiable walk when he came to the plate. He walked like he was in two pieces because he had such leg problems. I always knew when Mantle was coming up to the plate whether it was on radio or TV or whether I was at Yankee Stadium in person. There was kind of a buzz that always went through the Stadium. There was more excitement when Mantle was coming up.

The second game I ever went to was in 1954. I was eight years old. Allie Reynolds was pitching against the Boston Red Sox. The Sox had Ted Williams in those days. This was Allie's last year. It was a big game. My dad said, "Listen. We have to leave early. They're playing the Red Sox, and Reynolds is pitching. There's going to be a bigger crowd than normal so we have to leave a good thirty-forty minutes earlier." That's what we did. We went to Yankee Stadium and it was a great game. The bases were loaded. Ted Williams was up and Reynolds was pitching. There were two outs. I remember everyone in the Stadium on their feet. He had two strikes on him. I was so small I had to stand on the seat so I could see. Reynolds struck out Ted Williams with the bases loaded. I never forgot it. The place went crazy. I remember my father hugging me and saying, "Wasn't that fabulous? Gee, Reynolds gets better with age. Why is he considering retiring?" Years later, I got to meet my hero, Allie Reynolds here in Oklahoma City. I told him about being at that game. He said, "I do remember the game, but let me tell you. I can count on one hand how many times I struck out Ted Williams. He was that good of a hitter."

When it was World Series time and the Yankees were playing the Dodgers, my school, P.S. 26, in Paterson, would transmit the radio over the PA system into the individual classrooms so we could hear the games. That's how I actually heard Don Larsen's perfect game before school let out and I could race home and see the end of the game. I lived three or four blocks from school, and I ran like heck.

If the teachers were hesitant about putting the game on the loud speaker, I would sneak a radio into the classroom and keep it hidden in my desk. It was a little transistor radio. One teacher caught me and confiscated it till the end of the game. I remember that real well. I was in about the sixth grade. That didn't discourage me. I kept bringing it with me and I'd try again.

I first met Allie Reynolds around 1988 because of my job at AT&T. AT&T had a campaign to raise funds for United Way. They called it the World Series of Giving. We wrote to ballplayers asking them for autographed baseballs that we could place in a lottery. Allie was on the committee. I had met him earlier, but this was when I really got to know him. If we needed an autograph for a fundraiser, I would call him up and say, "Can I come by your office and get a couple of items signed?"

Allie was a very successful businessman. His company, Atlas Mud Company, serviced oil wells and was actually bought out by a major oil company. He was a very, very bright, interesting man who was well versed on many subjects. He was one of the few college graduates in his time who played baseball. He was just an enjoyable person. The longer I knew Allie Reynolds as a personal friend, ex-baseball player, and businessman, the less our conversations were about baseball.

As time went on, he would say to me, "Kid, I got this minor legal question. Would you handle this for me?" So I said, "Sure." Allie was from the old school. If he wanted you as his attorney, you had to be his friend first so he could really trust you. After he was widowed, he didn't want to go by himself on trips, for instance, to receive an award in New York City or to attend an autograph show. He would say, "Come with me. I may need my attorney with me." But really he just wanted the company. So I'd go and that's how I met a lot of his teammates.

As an attorney for AT&T, I had many occasions to go to the corporate headquarters in Basking Ridge, New Jersey. I said to him, "Allie, if you get an opportunity when I'm up there, can you call Yogi so I can get some stuff signed?" So he called Yogi on the phone and Yogi said, "Yeah, send your friend over. Have him call me, and we'll arrange a time, and he can come by and I'll sign a dozen items. I'll be done in five minutes and we'll visit. No problem." So I called Yogi, and he agreed to such and such a time to come by his house in nearby Montclair.

> **I about died. I had my own Yogi story to take away.**

I went to his house, had a very nice visit, and met his wife, Carmen. Yogi said, "Carmen, would you come in here? I want you to meet Allie's friend from Oklahoma City. This is Bill Manger. He's an attorney with AT&C." Mrs. Berra said, "What?" I said, "No ma'am, I'm an attorney with AT&T." She said, "Well that's okay. He's like that all the time." Yogi never cracked a smile, never changed his expression at all. He said, "What's the problem? Two out of three ain't bad." I about died. I had my own Yogi story to take away. I had such a nice visit with them. He wanted to know how Allie was doing because Allie's health was declining at that time. This was 1992 or '93. It was a nice experience.

Allie also sent me to Gil McDougald's house in 1989 or '90. At that time, he and his wife lived in Spring Lake, New Jersey. McDougald had lost most of his hearing by that time, and that's the reason Allie and I had to make the arrangement with Mrs. McDougald. Gil had written me a note in the mail and given me directions how to get to his house from the Parkway. I had the nicest visit with the two of them. We had so much fun. By the time we were done talking, three hours had passed. We just talked about everything: baseball, what Allie was doing now, what my kids were doing in Oklahoma City, their kids, and their grandkids. It was a great experience. I was impressed with how bright and nice both of them were.

Gil McDougald said, "You know, I loved the Chief. The Chief was one great player. He should be in the Hall of Fame." That was our discussion. I sat right at his kitchen table with him. They had a very nice house about a block from the beach. Their children grew up and they adopted others and raised them and sent them to college and had a lot of grandkids so they always had a lot of kids in the house. It was a big old two or three-story house. They just sold it in the last year or two because Mrs. McDougald's knees were bothering her. They bought a split-level house where they didn't have so many stairs. He's a wonderful man. He had surgery to have cochlear implants and he now hears. What a man.

One story he told me was about **Phil Rizzuto** when he was a rookie in 1941 and Gomez was pitching. It was Opening Day. Gomez called Rizzuto over to the mound about the first inning. There was a runner on first or something, and he called time out. He said to Rizzuto, "Is your mother here today?" He said, "Yes, she is." He said, "Well that's good. She's in the Stadium. She's in the seats over there, and she's probably saying right now, 'that's my son out there talking to the Great Gomez.'"

All these players I met, guys who played for Stengel, referred to him as the "Old Man." Most of them were quite in awe of him with his platoon system and how he just seemed to have a knack for making the right move to win games and put the right player in at the right time. This was a common theme among these players. They would say, "The Old Man just a had a feeling that so and so was going to hit today, and so he played him."

I met Mickey Mantle for the first time about 1988 or '89. He was here in Oklahoma City for a dinner. At that time, Mantle was drinking heavily. I was disappointed. I was really thrilled when he finally recognized that he had this problem. He admitted it to the world and became cured. During the last year of his life, he was completely sober and was a wonderful guy. He was like a different personality when I met him then. It was like meeting two different people.

The first time I saw Mickey Mantle really drunk I couldn't sleep afterward. I had waited thirty-five years to approach my boyhood hero and

> Phil Rizzuto is the only baseball person to earn a Gold Record…his game calling was in the background of Meat Loaf's *Paradise by the Dashboard Lights*.

ask him for an autograph, and he cursed at me. He said, "I'm tired of this ——. I don't want to sign any of this crap anymore."

He would give a speech and use obscene language at a black-tie dinner. It was quite an experience. I'd rather not quote some of the things he said. I was shocked. And if you read the newspaper, read the quotes from Mickey Mantle's speeches, none of this stuff ever came out. The press really protected him. But the word had gotten out. His hosts would meet him at the airport and they'd try any way they could to keep him away from bad influences.

> **The other players liked him, but they also recognized his faults, and they protected him.**

One time, I was at a dinner where Mickey was at the head table with the then-governor of Oklahoma, Governor George Nigh. Governor Nigh was a very articulate speaker, and he gave a very comical speech, a great speech. Mantle came up to the stage next—and I'll never forget this—before he got started, he said, "Is that guy really the governor?" People said, "Yes, he is." He said, "No ——. I'd vote for that ——." How's that? People laughed, and yet they put their heads down in embarrassment at the same time.

I ran into Governor Nigh, who's now retired, at a restaurant one day, and we were waiting together at a cafeteria line. I said, "Governor, I remember you so well when we were at this dinner with Mickey Mantle." He said, "Yeah, remember when he said he'd vote for me—'vote for that ——.'" George didn't forget it. I'm glad I wasn't just hearing things.

After that dinner, I went home and told my wife, "I'm gonna have to stay up a little while before I go to sleep." I'll never forget it. I think that was the time I asked him to sign my copy of Peter Golenbock's wonderful book on the Yankees, *Dynasty*, and he said he was sick of signing things, but he did anyway. The other players with him at the table, guys like Bobby Brown and Moose Skowron, told him to sign it and shut up. The other players liked him, but they also recognized his faults, and they protected him. They said, "Sign that and don't make a big deal over it."

I'm still glad that Mickey Mantle was my boyhood hero. He took his problem straight on and conquered it. He went to the Betty Ford Clinic, and then he was like a different person. I really enjoyed visiting with him after he became sober. I think it was almost a year after that when he was diagnosed with cancer. I saw him again at an Old Timer's game at St. Louis. I took my son to meet him. He was just fine. He talked to me, and asked, "How's Allie doing?" He shocked me to death. He had a great memory. He was okay. I really have to say that I'm sorry alcohol got the best of him for a lot of years because without the alcohol he was a very nice man.

I remember being at Mickey Mantle's golf tournament near Tulsa in 1993. Yogi was there and he was supposed to be interviewed by the local radio station when somebody came by and said, "Have you seen George?" Yogi turned absolutely green. He said, "If Steinbrenner's here, I'm leaving." Here we were in the middle of nowhere in Oklahoma, and Yogi didn't want to be around if Steinbrenner was there. That's how bad it was. I'll never forget that.

Remember, Yogi stayed away from Yankee Stadium for fourteen years. In his last go-round as manager in 1985, Steinbrenner fired him sixteen games into the season. People went crazy. After that, Yogi wouldn't even go to Old Timers' Day. Some people said things like, "Can you imagine anybody being that reckless to do that to the Yankees and do that to a man like Yogi Berra." I had people say to me, "That's un-American to do that to Yogi Berra, a guy who's a hero and to be treated like that."

I've totally come full circle. I'm as big a Yankee fan as ever. If I can possibly get a Yankee game on TV here in Oklahoma, I will cancel what I have scheduled for that evening and watch the game. If I take a trip to New Jersey, I try to work in a Yankee game. I love to watch the Yankees play in their **pinstripes** at Yankee Stadium. I don't know what it is, maybe just the aura from growing up. I think it goes clear back to my first experience. I never stopped being fascinated by that uniform and the greatness that went along with it.

The Yankees' pin-striped uniforms were designed by owner Colonel Jacob Ruppert to make Babe Ruth look skinnier.

# WIT HAPPENS

## Barry Crimmins

*Forty-nine-year-old Barry Crimmins, a stand-up political comedian/satirist, believes rooting for the Yankees long distance as a child taught him there was a big world outside his small, upstate New York town.*

I've loved the Yankees since I was a little kid growing up in upstate New York. My parents are both from New England. My mother was a Red Sox fan and my father was a Boston Braves fan. Once the Braves moved to Milwaukee in the early 1950s, my father's interest in baseball waned. My parents never discouraged me being a Yankee fan. Particularly my mother, the Red Sox fan, didn't want her child to suffer the way she had. And the Yankees were great. They were just this tremendous team.

I first started following baseball around 1958, right at the time when there was no National League team in New York, so the Yankees were the "local" team. The games were transmitted on the radio, and even when the Mets came along, they weren't on the radio or TV, so the Yankees were the only New York team you could follow.

But living in Skaneateles, on the easternmost Finger Lake, Yankee Stadium seemed like a million miles away. My father used to take me to Cooperstown all the time because it was close to where we lived. I saw all the greats like Jackie Robinson, Casey Stengel, and Ted Williams inducted into the Hall of Fame.

Skaneateles was such a small place that it didn't seem a real possibility that I could go to games. I dreamed of it, and that made the Yankees even more mythical to me. Yankee Stadium was this place you could hear Mel Allen and Phil Rizzuto and Red Barber talk about on the radio, and you'd get to see the players on TV once a week, then later twice a week. The local Syracuse TV station would pick up the Yankee games on Sunday, and they would generally be the Game of the Week.

By 1968, Mantle's last year, the Yankees were pretty bad. My father told me he'd gotten some tickets and we were gonna go down to see the Yankees. We got up very early in the morning and drove down to New York. It was a beautiful drive, down through the beautiful pastoral countryside of upstate New York. After five or six hours, we eventually arrived. YANKEE STADIUM!! My father had gotten mezzanine box tickets, which are the modern equivalent of a club seat or even a luxury box, and before we took our seats, we had lunch at the Yankee Stadium Club. We walked in, and it was beautiful. I could hardly touch my food because I knew in a minute we were gonna see the stadium.

We walked out, and there it was in front of me. I couldn't believe it. It was just green and lush and amazing and we had these amazing seats right by the broadcast booth, and it was just unbelievable. It was just unbelievable. The seats were like theater seats. I was so overwhelmed being there the first time that I didn't notice that they were pulling the tarp out onto the field and the only Yankee within sight was Ruben Amaro, whose son is now the assistant general manager of the Phillies, who was playing catch with the batboys. That was all the Yankee baseball I saw that day. The game was rained out.

I didn't cry. I made sure to be as thankful to my father as possible for having taken me. At least I'd gotten into the park. But it really did set off a sort of depression because I felt like I was never going to see the Yankees play in Yankee Stadium.

Several weeks passed, and one night I had just come home from playing a ballgame. I was rushing to change my clothes, trying to hustle out of the house. I think I was going to the movies to meet some girls. The phone rang. It was my father's friend, Ralph Cheche, and he wanted to talk to me. He said, "What are you doing tomorrow?" I said, "I don't know." "Well, if you could go to any game, what would you go to?" I said, "Well, the Chiefs are in town," meaning the Syracuse Chiefs, the Yankee Triple A farm team. He said, "If you could go to any game, you'd go to the Syracuse Chiefs? I guess that means you wouldn't want to go to Old Timers' Day at Yankee Stadium." I said, "Of course, I'd go to Old Timers' Day at Yankee Stadium." Ralph said, "Well, be ready at eight o'clock." I said, "Mr. Cheche, we won't have time to get there." He said, "Well, we will if we fly."

His brother was a private pilot and they had tickets, so I flew down with Mr. Cheche and his brother. My father didn't go. He had given up his ticket for me. It was Old Timers' Day, and they were all there, literally. There were players from the 1927 Yankees there that day. Everybody was there, so the first Yankees I ever got to see play were the best. The seats were amazing, too.

The 1968 Yankees weren't good. Stan Bahnsen, who the Yankees later idiotically traded for Rich McKinney, who was just a horrible third baseman, was pitching for the Yankees. They were playing the Twins who were pretty good in those days. They had won the pennant in 1965, and had been just edged out by the Red Sox in '67. Mickey Mantle was playing, and he hit two homers in one game for the last time in his career, but the Yanks lost 3-2.

But I had made it. I saw Mantle play. I was so thankful to Ralph Cheche and his brother, and my father.

After that, it wasn't many years later before I went again to Yankee Stadium. In a way, it sort of describes what happened in the rest of my life. Within a few years of realizing big places are somewhere I could actually go out and function in and be part of, I decided I could do comedy. Up until that point, I had thought in order to be funny I had to be some urban guy who knew about minority groups, which I didn't know anything about. I learned I didn't have to be this scared little kid from a small town.

I love the fact that I've been able to attend a lot of games when I travel all over the country as part of my job. I particularly like the fact that I'm a Yankee fan who bucks the negative stereotype. I really believe in sportsmanship. I believe in showing respect to fellow fans. A fan is just another person. When I was five years old, I was a little kid with my Yankee hat on, and basically, I'm still that five-year-old kid with my Yankee hat on, and everybody else is just a five-year-old kid with a hat on. And five-year-old kids with hats on are people you should be nice to. They just happen to root for a different team. If a person's some front runner, okay. You can usually figure that out quickly and then you can be indifferent to him. But for the most part, if you can establish that a person's a life-long fan, then you should be nice to them and show respect.

I baffle fans by sitting at their stadiums with my Yankee hat on rooting for the Yankees, but knowing about their team, being literate about it, being complimentary and not screaming about balls and strikes when I'm sitting by the left-field foul pole. Actually, I probably enjoy rooting for the visiting team more than the home team because inevitably the majority of the people are wrong.

> **Actually, I probably enjoy rooting for the visiting team more than the home team because inevitably the majority of the people are wrong.**

I moved to Boston in 1979. I had been doing comedy around the country, and when I came to Boston, I got a job at this place called Springfield Street Saloon, which later became The Ding Ho, the first full-time comedy club in the city. At the time, they were only doing comedy shows one night a week. The place had been taken over by Chinese people who tried to keep the music business going but they were losing their shirts. They were serving Chinese food with a western décor. The owner took a shine to me, and I was hired to do comedy two nights a week, to do some bouncing, whatever they needed.

The Saloon was in one of those long, first floor, former Boston apartments, and as I was getting ready to work the very first night, I noticed Thurman Munson's face on the little black and white TV all the way at the end of the room. It was the news update toward the top of the hour where they give you about one minute of news. I saw Munson's picture, and I said to myself, "Uh-oh, he's either been arrested or he's dead. Man, do I hope he was arrested." And he was dead. I had to go out to work, and I was really upset. I was bouncing. I was standing at the door, taking the money, collecting cover charges, handling whatever, when this big burly guy, probably in his early forties, came in. He said, "I never paid a cover here. You ask him." Shen Li, the owner, told me to let him in, but he looked sheepish.

The guy came in, and he was clearly drunk, and I could see Shen Li doesn't like him. Then the guy said, "Hey, Thurman Munson's playing for the Angels now," and he gave a big laugh. The guy was a big dude, and I picked him up and threw him out of the building. Shen Li said to me, "That was great. I hate that guy."

**Here was something we could talk about where obnoxious boosterism didn't matter.**

From that point on, Shen Li and I were great friends, and from that place, the Boston comedy scene really emerged. When I went home that night, I watched Carlton Fisk on TV weeping, talking about Munson. To me, that showed the ultimate truth that ballplayers really do get past the petty stuff—"I'm for this team. You're for that team." When it really mattered, Fisk had complete respect for Munson, and was extremely eloquent in his despair over his death. I'll never forget it.

In a way, Munson's death provided a way for me to begin talking Yankees-Red Sox with people in Boston because I had just arrived. Here was something we could talk about where obnoxious boosterism didn't matter. It was inappropriate. So we'd start with something else. Immediately I would talk about how impressed I was with Fisk, about how he became much more likeable to me from that point on. I was in my late twenties and was starting to grow up and have a sense of proportion about sports. The great thing was if even if that big drunk guy had been a good friend of Shen Li's, I still would have thrown him out of the building on his head.

From 1994 until last year when we moved back to New York State, I was stuck out in Cleveland because my girlfriend, Karen, who is an attorney, had a case that was supposed to end within a year but lasted seven more. A year in Cleveland is like dog years. Nineteen ninety-four was the year Clevelanders acted like they invented baseball at Jacobs Field. Karen wasn't really a baseball fan, and she couldn't believe what I would go through to listen to a Yankee game. I'd literally stand on the refrigerator, flat on my back, holding the radio, trying to find a place where I could get reception. Eventually, I found guys on the Internet who would give me the play-by-play as they were watching the game. Then RealAudio came along and that was heaven. Then at one point, the Yankee games came on TV in Cleveland. Karen became a good Yankee fan just because she was impressed that someone could have that kind of devotion to a team.

In September 1995, I left Boston via train at about four in the afternoon, knowing I would be traveling through New York State and would be able to get most of the Yankee game. I was still traveling back and forth to Boston to do comedy, and I had taken a train out from Cleveland just so I could test radio stations along the way in anticipation of the Series. The Yankees had played a day game against the Tigers on the way out, and I heard most of the game. They were next going up to Toronto and had to do well there because if they lost any games, they weren't going to make the playoffs. I figured out that if I had a little Walkman radio right next to the window, I could just barely get some reception, though the transmission was kinda loud.

Then it was October, and the radio beam was higher than before. It's night. The Yankees game started and the train was about at Springfield and I could pick up the game on WABC radio. I was leaning so weirdly against the window, holding the radio right up to the window and sort of leaning up being the antenna. I looked like a lunatic.

This guy was looking at me funny, and I said, "I've got the baseball game on, but I can only get it this way." "Is it the Yankee game?" "Yeah." "I'm a Yankee fan. Can you tell me what's going on?"

So I began doing play by play and built up a little following over a couple of innings. The Yankees weren't doing well. They were losing. The train was making record time, and I was worried that we were going too fast and were gonna pass where I could get Yankee radio reception. We cut through the Berkshire Mountains, and reception got pretty dicey a few times, but I could still hear the game, and I was giving the grim details.

Since we had left out of Boston, there were Red Sox fans on the train. That year, the Red Sox were going to the playoffs. Of course, at this point, all the Red Sox fans were saying, "This wild card thing is terrible." They since have become very big advocates of the wild card. They were all cheering as I gave my bad reports on the Yankees. Finally, we got to Albany, and all of a sudden, the train stopped. We sat there for about fifteen minutes, and they announced, "We've got a big problem. We've got to get a new engine in here. We're gonna have a rather lengthy delay. You can get out and walk around. Don't go too far." I immediately thought to myself, "All right, I can get out and get good reception." As soon as I stepped off the train, the Yankee game came in clearly on my headphones. Now I had a huge crowd around me.

It was so wonderful because here we were at a train station just the way "The Babe" traveled. All these baseball fans were huddled around this poorly lit platform in Albany just like in the old days when you got the wire and then one person is telling the others what's going on.

Late in the game—maybe in extra innings—Pat Kelly, of all people, hit a remarkable two or three-run homer, and the Yankees won. The game went on forever, but just as a voice said, "Okay, everybody get on board," the Yankees got the third out and won the game.

We got back on the train and all of us repaired to the bar car. We had a pretty good time with the Red Sox fans the rest of the trip. Their team was winning the division that year anyway. They were ready to bury the Yankees that night, and I was the lone voice on the train platform, and Pat Kelly, God bless him, never did much after that, but the Yankee second baseman hit a huge homer that kept Yankee hopes alive that night and got Don Mattingly to the playoffs for the first time in his career.

Though disaster then struck at the Kingdome, that night had been such a classic. The only thing lacking was that the men weren't wearing fedoras or straw hats. The bartender in the car was a big baseball fan so even at the point when people were saying, "No more drinks for anybody," he made sure we all bought another case of beer.

The trip was really nostalgic for me. I was traveling from Boston, where I had lived for fifteen years, through Massachusetts. My father is from Worcester, my mother is from Adams in the Berkshires. Then the train proceeded through New York State, where I grew up and knew so well and where my father had been a school furniture salesman. The entire sixteen or seventeen hour trip that it took to get to Cleveland was a very sentimental journey. When we would reach a stop where someone had to get off, rather than say, "All right, I'm finally home," the person would say, "Well, sorry, I gotta go."

The common bond was baseball. There was nothing better to do on the train platform than to listen to this Yankee fan who everybody thought at first had some horrible disfiguration because of the way he leaned up against the window, and then later on became the entertainment for dozens of people. Everybody was chatting with one another, and I was passing along the details and talking too loud because I had headphones on and I couldn't modulate the volume. It was a precious moment of baseball fandom that I'll always remember. Even the friendly adversarial banter with the Red Sox fans added to it. It wasn't the kind of contentious, mean-spirited stuff that sometimes gets out of hand. It was a lot of fun.

A few years later, my girlfriend, Karen, and I really wanted a dog, but getting a puppy turned out not to be easy. A couple of really tragic things happened. We picked one out at the pound, but when we went back the next day with our little leash to pick it up, the head of the pound summoned us to his office and told us the dog had parvo and they had to kill it. Then we went to different pound and got a really great dog, a full-grown Lab. We had the dog over a weekend. But it turned out that the owners of the dog had been away on vacation for two weeks, and when the dog ran away the idiot who had been taking care of it didn't check the pound three-quarters of a mile from the house. We had the dog for three or four days and had really bonded with him. The people at the pound told us we could technically keep the dog because of the length of time it had been there, but we weren't gonna say, "We're keeping your dog," so we brought him back.

The worst was yet to come. We bought a third puppy, had him for several weeks, but then he got sick and he could have been saved if we hadn't been going to an incompetent vet. So it was a three-dog nightmare. We named the dog "Keed," because that's what **Babe Ruth** called everybody because he couldn't remember anybody's name.

> David Wells paid $35,000 for an authentic Babe Ruth cap and wore it during a Yankee game...On hot days, Ruth would wear a cabbage leaf under his cap....Wells and his grandmother use the same tattoo artist.

Keed died just as the 1998 regular season ended, right at the beginning of October. It was such a great season but this dog stuff was really tempering it because Karen and I were in constant remorse and mourning over dogs. Karen had never had a dog before and this was really sad. I went to a rescue league and got another dog, but it was too soon after Keed died, and Karen couldn't deal with it. She couldn't look at the dog without weeping. It was just terrible. I brought the dog back to the rescue league and made a big donation because I felt so bad.

A week after the Yankees had won the pennant, I drove to New York with my friend Steve. Steve is a great Yankee fan. We met on an Internet mailing list, and the first time we ever went to a game together, we were like the "Blue Angels" of the Yankees. We said the exact same thing. We stood up at the same time. He is like the long-lost Yankee fan I didn't grow up with. We go back over Yankee history and say things like, "You know what, I don't care what anybody says, I really loved Andy Kosco." "Oh, yeah, I love Andy Kosco, too." No matter what it is, we are always on the same page. He's had the Friday night package at Yankee Stadium since about 1980. He always gets playoff tickets, and fortunately, his wife doesn't care about baseball at all so I always go to one or another round of the playoffs with him and a World Series game if the Yankees get there, which they have for years.

Things were going great, but we had this dog nightmare. It's a long drive from Cleveland—across Pennsylvania, which is wider than it is interesting—but I think nothing of driving to a game at night, maybe staying overnight at Steve's house and then going back the next morning.

The Yankees beat Texas that week, and then they played the Indians. In Cleveland, the reaction was ridiculous. The front page of the *Cleveland Plain Dealer* had a cartoon with that Chief Wahoo, or Uncle Tomahawk, as I call him, the buck-toothed, bright red Indian who is smiling so happily. The paper said, "Official Yankee Haters Guide." Chief Wahoo was flying over Yankee Stadium, and dropping bats like bombs.

Everybody in Cleveland jumped on the bandwagon. I had a simple task for these recent bandwagon-hopping friends. I would ask them one question about their team. I would say, "Name any Indians manager prior to Mike Hargrove." Two-thirds of them were blank, had no idea. No Mel McGaha, no John McNamara, no Frank Robinson, the first black manager. Nothing. They did a test pattern, so I thought, "Okay, thanks, you're a great fan, talk to you later."

What really annoyed me was that it was so hard to get into Jacobs Field. I thought about the old days when I would pass through town and go to a ball game, and there would be three thousand people there. Those three thousand people probably couldn't get into Jacobs Field anymore. Those people were great to sit with. They loved their team. They knew everything. They weren't ridiculous. They were much more sporting about other teams because they really appreciated baseball. They'd be at the game because they wanted to see the Twins play and wanted to see Harmon Killebrew or whoever was playing. You could sit and talk and have a nice time with those people. Now you're sitting next to a grown person wearing a Chief Wahoo oversized T-shirt to their knees and feathers going down their back.

> **Those people were great to sit with. They loved their team.... You could sit and talk and have a nice time with those people.**

So the Yankees were playing Cleveland after beating Texas for the millionth time. I always get these last-minute calls from my friend, Steven Wright, the comedian. He said, "Hey, I'm playing Cleveland Saturday night. Do you want to open for me?" I said, "Sure." He played the Palace Theater on Saturday night, and I had to miss the game. The Yanks were down two games to one. There was a TV in the dressing room so everybody in the place was looming around my dressing room to watch the game, but I was rooting for the "wrong" team. As ever, this is why I like attending other games. I get a chance to be sporting and nice.

The next morning, I was in a good mood. The Yanks had won. But it was still two games to two. I was listening to the radio, and this idiot was literally provoking the Indians fans to come out and hassle David Wells by denigrating his recently-deceased mother. Classic Cleveland stuff. This is what I'm talking about. It's just ridiculous.

I wanted to find tickets to the game. I somehow know how to spot the people like me who dump their tickets at face value. I believe in ticket karma. I've never sold a ticket for more than it cost, and I've given plenty away. I just feel like I've got a few chits coming anytime I go to a game, and I usually get pretty lucky.

I went downtown early to scout things out, to see if something's at the hotel. I didn't see anything. Then I happened to see Tino Martinez hop in a cab to go over to the park. I waved to him. He waved at me and gave me the thumbs up. It was early in the afternoon, well before the game.

I went home and Karen and I were looking through the newspaper classifieds when Karen saw an ad for some puppies. Although we had wanted to get a dog from a pound, we'd had so much trouble with pounds, I said, "Okay. I can put that altruistic notion aside." We went and looked at the puppies. There was this great little guy with two much bigger sisters, and he was over in the corner looking like, "This is awful." He is half Shepherd, half Lab. He's chocolate brown and looks like a little bear cub. He is really beautiful, but Karen wasn't sure. We had just about driven home, when Karen said, "No, we should have gotten him." So we drove back and got him.

I immediately named him Lloyd, after Steven Wright. One time when Steven and I were on tour, we were eating dinner on the road, and we had some insane waiter named Lloyd, who told us his name about a thousand times. If Steven's in town somewhere playing a concert and we're in a big hotel, and I yell across the lobby, "Steven," everyone's gonna spot him, but if I yell "Lloyd," no one will pay any attention. He would call me Lloyd a lot, too. At this point, I decided I was not going to go to the game. I had a new puppy to take care of. I was gonna stay at home with the dog.

The Yanks beat Cleveland that night. Wells hates the Indians because of that night. He hates Cleveland. There have been many times since that he could have signed with Cleveland, but he's kept it from happening, because he'll never forget the fact that the fans were screaming at him about his mother that night.

The Yanks finished the job in Game 6. During those games, whenever Lloyd was with me, in my hands, sitting on my knee, whatever, something great happened. I actually have a little picture of him with a Yankee helmet on. So he's "Lucky Dog Lloyd, the Lucky Yankee Dog."

The following Saturday the World Series was to begin. The Yankees had dispatched Cleveland and turned it from the phony rock capital back into the polka town it is. I was back in the car early Saturday morning driving out to New York. It was a beautiful autumn day. I was driving through Pennsylvania when the leaves had really begun to turn and I was going to a World Series game. You know, there are worse feelings! But I felt a lot of anticipation, too, because it's a heck of a long drive if the Yankees lose, and I would have to drive back and get home in time to not miss Game 2 on TV. When Game 2 was done, I'd have a pretty good haul driving from Cleveland to New York and back.

I got out there in plenty of time. Steve and I always get there for batting practice. I said to him, "You know, Lloyd's the lucky Yankee dog. Maybe I should have stayed home with him. He's never been to a World Series game before at Yankee Stadium. I'm sure it's okay, but, Steve, I know it sounds weird, but can I use your cell phone to call Karen and get Lloyd into the room if we need him?" Steve said, "Of course." He didn't question that at all. He said, "It's the weekend and I get a thousand free minutes anyway."

The Yanks were down 5-2 against the Padres in the seventh inning, with two men on. There were two outs. They'd driven Kevin Brown from the game. **Tony Gwynn**, in his first World Series game, hit a laser home run right off one of the signs in Yankee Stadium. Steve and I both got up and gave him a round of applause like you're supposed to. Tony Gwynn had never been in a Series before so people were looking at us like, "What's that all about?" No big deal.

They got a couple of men on and Donnie Wall was about to come up when I said to Steve, "I gotta call Karen now. I've got to get Lloyd in

Tony Gwynn still holds the San Diego State University basketball record for single season and career assists. He credits the longevity of the record to "poor recruiting." He was drafted in the 10th round of the NBA draft by the San Diego Clippers on the very same day he was drafted by the San Diego Padres.

the room." He said, "Okay, get Karen on the phone." There are people behind us, and I hear them scoff, like "Who could get on a cell phone at a time like this?" I would have thought the same thing.

I got Karen on the phone and told her to get Lloyd in the room. As soon as Lloyd was in the room—and she's holding him aimed at the TV—Chuck Knoblauch hit a ball that just skimmed over the fence, just past the reach of horrible-fielding Greg Vaughn, and a three-run homer tied the game. The fear that the whole of Yankee Stadium felt was transformed from, "Oh no, our team's won 114 games, got to the World Series, and now these Padres are gonna win. What happened?" and the place just exploded.

> **Steve said, "But he's calling his lucky dog in Ohio. He's got to get that dog on the phone in Ohio.**

I had been on the phone yelling, "Lucky Dog Lloyd." As that ball went out, Steve started yelling, "Lucky Dog Lloyd. Lucky Dog Lloyd." When the person behind us said something about me being on the phone, Steve said, "But he's calling his lucky dog in Ohio. He's got to get that dog on the phone in Ohio. It's very important for this inning." The people behind us were looking at us like, "What an idiot!"

When sure enough Knoblauch hit the homer, a couple of people said, "Wow! That dog—keep him on the phone." Then the next Yankee got on and people were starting to say, "Lucky Dog Lloyd." Other people around us began picking up the cheer. "That guy's got a lucky dog on the phone." The bases were loaded.

Tino Martinez came up and Karen said, "He sat up on my knee, and now he's staring right at the TV." I said, "Oh yeah, Tino's his favorite." The count went to 2-2 and now Mark Langston was in and threw a pretty darn close pitch, but I was sitting just about right on third base and didn't have an angle to see. Rich Garcia, the umpire, called it ball three. Whew, that was close because it would have been a strikeout with the bases loaded. Martinez has had a lot of post-season trouble since then, except for when he helped beat the Yankees with the Mariners. Boy, that was close. Langston came in with the next pitch, and Martinez hit a shot to right, a grand slam World Series home run. Seven runs, seventh inning.

Everybody was screaming, "Lucky Dog Lloyd. Lucky Dog Lloyd." I said to Karen, "Okay Karen, that's good. I'll talk to you later. It's 9-5 now. It was 5-2 when we called you, so that's a pretty good call."

In the eighth inning, the Yanks got in a minor jam, and people behind us said, "Hey, get that Lucky Dog Lloyd on the phone." We called him up, and the rally was immediately extinguished, and the Yanks won 9-6.

We didn't want to overuse our luck with Lloyd, but in 2000 we were at Game 1 of the Subway Series, when we had to make another call to him from Yankee Stadium. You know the difference between the Yankees and the Mets? The Yankees are the team with twenty-six championships in two uniforms. The Mets are the team with twenty-six uniforms and two championships.

Game 1 of that series was when Timo Perez created that new axiom in baseball: Never break into another guy's home run trot, particularly if he hasn't hit a home run. Derek Jeter made the great relay throw and they threw Timo out at the plate. Well, in the ninth inning of that game, we needed to tie it up. We called Lloyd, and the Yankees tied up the game. When the Yankees won the game a couple of innings later, we had Lloyd on the phone again. So he's 2 and 0 in the World Series, and that second win was Game 1 against the Mets, which looked like it was gone, but the Mets kicked it away.

In 2001 when Tino Martinez hit the homer to win the World Series game, Lloyd was again in the room. Lloyd also had something to do with the last good thing that happened for the Yankees that season. Lloyd and I had turned the radio on for Alfonso Soriano in the eighth inning of Game 7 of the World Series against the Arizona Diamond-backs, and he hit a homer to put the Yankees ahead. Then I foolishly gave Lloyd the night off. I don't have to tell you what happened.

Lloyd is very cool about it all. He doesn't care much about other sports, but when baseball season comes around, he literally will sit down. If he comes in and just naturally starts watching the game, the Yanks are gonna win. He sees the ball moving around, and it gets his attention.

Lloyd's well taken care of. He's the only meat eater in our house. He's well provided for.

# OUTSIDE OF A DOG, A BOOK IS MAN'S BEST FRIEND. INSIDE OF A DOG, IT'S TOO DARK TO READ

Jim Bouton

*Former Yankee pitching ace, Jim Bouton wrote* Ball Four, *the best-selling book in the history of baseball. Scorned by the baseball establishment—many of whom had not read it—it brought great joy and insight to fans nationwide.*

*Now living in a beautiful, hill-top retreat several hours north of Yankee Stadium, Bouton, 64, looks young enough and fit enough to take the mound again.*

The first time I walked into Yankee Stadium as a player was awesome. I had never been there before. I had grown up in Rochelle Park, New Jersey, where you were either a Giants fan or a Dodgers fan. You were never a Yankee fan. I was a Giants fan. The only time I rooted for the Yankees was if they were playing the Dodgers in the World Series. I didn't want to see the Dodgers win because they had beaten the Giants so many times to get to the World Series.

When my brother and I used to sit up in the Polo Grounds, we'd look at the scorecard and players' numbers and then look to the outfield. We'd ask each other, "Who's got Number 42? Who's that?" "It's Clint Hartung." We'd call out, "Hey, Clint." If the player turned around and waved to us, we thought that was great because he had acknowledged our presence. As a player, I always turned and waved to the kids and went over and talked to them and signed autographs. I loved signing autographs for kids. They would come right up to me and say, "Are you anybody?" "Are you any good?" It was great.

I was a cocky kid and was excited to be with the Yankees. I knew I had good stuff, and thought I could pitch in the big leagues. I think I pitched a couple of innings of relief on the road and then got my first start at Yankee Stadium in the second game of a doubleheader against the Washington Senators. I had gotten a bunch of tickets, and my family was there, my parents and brother, my cousins, aunts, and uncles. I pitched a shutout. It was the worst shutout in the history of baseball. I walked seven guys and gave up seven hits so I pitched the entire game from the stretch position. The bullpen was up and throwing the whole game. After the game, Ralph Houk said any more complete games like that, and we're going to need a new bullpen.

I left the Stadium with my mom, dad, and brothers. In those days, players had to walk from the Stadium across the street to the players' parking lot, which was a fenced-in area. Before we even got to the parking lot, kids approached me, asking for my autograph. I signed about ten and then I said, "Okay, I've got to go. I'm gonna have dinner with

**My mom said, "No, you don't. You stay right here and you sign every one of these autographs. We'll wait."**

my parents now. So long. I'll sign more tomorrow." My mom said, "No, you don't. You stay right here and you sign every one of these autographs. We'll wait." So I spent twenty minutes signing every single kid's autograph because my mom said I had to.

My first real relationship with fans was with my fan club. It was nice to have kids set up a fan club for me. This happened during my rookie year. I said to them, "You don't want me. I'm not anybody. I'm just a rookie." They said, "We like you, and we want to start a fan club for you." I said, "Okay."

Then the next year, I won twenty-one games. It was like the kids had bought me when I was a penny stock and now they were big shots. I enjoyed the fans very much. I always thought having fans holler your name was the most fun part of being a ballplayer.

Two boys are playing hockey on a pond on Boston Common when one is attacked by a rabid Rottweiler. Thinking quickly, the other boy takes his stick and wedges it down the dog's collar and twists, breaking the dog's neck. A reporter who is strolling by sees the incident and rushes over to interview the boy. "Young Bruins Fan Saves Friend From Vicious Animal," he starts writing in his notebook.

"But I'm not a Bruins fan," the little hero replied.

"Sorry, since we are in Boston, I just assumed you were," said the reporter, and he began writing again. "Red Sox Fan Rescues Friend From Horrific Attack," he continued writing in his notebook.

"I'm not a Red Sox fan either," the boy said.

"I assumed everyone in Boston was either for the Bruins or Red Sox. What team do you root for?" the reporter asked.

"I'm a Yankees fan," the child said.

The reporter started a new sheet in his notebook and wrote, "Little B——d from New York Kills Beloved Family Pet."

——Joke circulated on the Internet

# Chapter 2

# There's No Expiration Date On Dreams

## Growin' Up With The Yanks

# MY FAVORITE PLAYER IS EITHER MICKEY MANTLE OR CLIFF MAPES

### Al Stauffer

*Reared in upstate Binghamton and later Hell's Kitchen, Al Stauffer, 68, may have failed as a father by raising one son who became a Mets fan, but as a Yankee fan himself, he's a glittering success. Al now lives in Phoenix, Arizona.*

In 1946 I found out the Yankees had bought a pitcher named Allie Reynolds from the Cleveland Indians, and that's when I became interested in the Yankees. I was ten years old, my name is Al, and my mother's maiden name was Reynolds. I just drifted into becoming a Yankee fan, and that was the way it was. I followed Allie Reynolds' career.

I first began to go to Yankee games in the late 1940s. They would let a kid into the stadium if you had a baseball. During batting practice, the players used to deliberately hit balls over the wall in order to get more kids into the stands. The balls were your ticket into the grandstand. Of course, you were returning the baseballs to the players, and they would use them for batting practice. The right field wall in Yankee Stadium was real low at field level, and guys like Charlie Keller used to come over when they were changing pitchers and chat with the kids.

Autographs then were no big deal. Nobody thought about selling autographs, and nobody would dream of asking for an **autograph** on the field. The only place you got autographs was by standing outside the players' locker room and waiting for them to leave. It wasn't like

> NASCAR legend Richard Petty once had an autograph session that attracted 65,000 people.

it was something that was worth money or worth anything other than for the pleasure of having it.

I got the autograph of the only player who had the two numbers he wore retired. His name is Cliff Mapes. When he came up, he was a center fielder, kind of a utility outfielder and the relief for Joe DiMaggio. He wore Number 3 then. In 1948, the Yankees retired Number 3, Babe Ruth's number, while Mapes was wearing it. Then he took Number 7. Of course, that was Mantle's number, which was later retired. In the middle of all that, I was able to get Mapes' autograph. We caught him on his way out one day after he had a fairly decent game, and he was getting into a cab. This was back in the days when retiring numbers was no big deal. Nobody really thought much of it, although, of course, it is a tribute when a number is retired. It was just one of those things.

In 1949, I was coming out of church one Sunday, and there was an old guy standing there. The parish priest said to me, "You better get this guy's autograph. You'll treasure it someday." This man looked like he was a hundred years old. It was Connie Mack. The Athletics used to stay at the Hotel New Yorker, which was right down the street from St. Michael's Church on 34th street in New York. Cornelius McGillicuddy, which was the way Connie Mack actually signed his name, was a devout churchgoer. He was at Mass that Sunday morning, and I got his autograph. It's in my eighth-grade autograph book, which I happened to be carrying around with me that Sunday. It was spring, and we were graduating, so anytime we saw our friends we wanted them to sign our autograph books. I didn't really appreciate the significance of Mack's autograph until quite some time later.

My friends and I used to wander down on the field after a game. This was in the 1950s, when they let kids do it. One time, we had gone to a day game. After the game, we were looking at the monuments, taking pictures, and posing at various spots along the wall. All of a sudden, we realized we were the only ones in Yankee Stadium. We started to look around to find a way out. It turned out that they had locked just about everything. We ended up finding a groundskeeper who let us out.

# SO THERE I WAS, PLAYIN' RIGHT FIELD FOR THE YANKEES. PLAY ALONG, OKAY?

### Al DiDonato

*Al DiDonato, 64, lived and breathed baseball in the shadow of Yankee Stadium. Al drives a transit bus for the coastal New England city of Gloucester, Massachusetts.*

When my friends and I were junior high age, ten or so of us would go to Yankee Stadium to play in their parking lot. It was so large you could probably play four games at the same time. We were called the Stars, and booked games with other teams, though we didn't belong to a league. We played sandlot rules: no stealing, no sliding, no taking a lead off the base, no tagging up after a fly ball. If a baseball game was being played in Yankee Stadium, we'd wait until the seventh or eighth inning, and they'd let us sit in the bleachers, so we'd see Joe DiMaggio every single day. I loved baseball, and it was a free ball game.

Most of the teams we got in to see were the deplorable teams. When we got older, once in a while, we'd get up enough money to go see a full nine-inning game. No one would ever go to the Polo Grounds because it was on the other side of the river. One time when we had a game going, someone from one of the local men's clubs—they had a lot of men's softball leagues in our neighborhood—came around and said, "Hey, you want us to take you to the Polo Grounds?" All the kids said, "No." I said, "Yeah, I'll have it." It happened to be 1951, the banner year for the Giants. The team had won seventeen games in a row in August, so I said, "Yeah, I'll go." I went to the game, but the day before, the seventeen-game **winning streak** had been broken.

One day I was playing right field in the stadium parking lot, which is along the fence and across the street from the players' entrance. Someone hit a tremendous fly ball. I loved going after flies because there was no ball I couldn't catch. On this day, this kid hit a ball—did he ever hit it! I said, "How the heck did he ever hit that?" As soon as it left the bat, I started running. I wasn't wearing sneakers. I was wearing loafers made of cloth, which had a soft creosole sole on them like sponge. The ball was way over my head, and I ran as fast as I could and caught the ball and stopped short. My right sole split and went flying, and my knee hit the curb. I thought my knee was broken. I heard a voice call out, "Nice catch, kid." There was Whitey Ford with two other players. All the kids said, "Look at that. They saw you make that catch. Whitey Ford saw you make the catch." If you catch the ball, the play is dead so everything stops. You can't steal or run. So I just laid there, and the Yankees looked at me, did a couple of claps, and they disappeared inside the players' entrance.

In the summer of 1949, Billy Papa, one of my best friends, and I decided to sell newspapers. Everyone else was selling papers so we thought we'd try it. We weren't the type to go shoe shining. My dad was a custom tailor, and after the war he made a pretty good living. My family was first in the block to have new appliances, all the new gadgets. Billy and I tried selling papers, but we weren't as aggressive as the average newsboy, who would walk around with a stack of papers he could barely carry and sell them all. We'd manage to sell just a few.

The only paper route in our neighborhood was Van Cortland Avenue, so you made your money in the bars. We were selling the *News* and the *Mirror*, and sometimes customers would buy two papers, which I could never understand, and they'd give you a quarter and tell you to "keep the change." That's where we made our money because we only made two cents profit on each paper. We always depended on the tips, and in the bars, people always gave you a dime for a

In 1916, the Giants has a 26-game winning streak. When they started the streak, they were in fourth place and when they finally lost, they were still in fourth place.

newspaper, or a quarter. Very seldom would they give you a nickel. Some people would even give you a dollar for two papers.

One day we were passing a restaurant, which was right at the end of Van Cortland Avenue and 161st Street, not far from Yankee Stadium. We went by there, and Billy Papa said, "Look, there's Yankees." This was before we had a TV in our house so I didn't know what the players looked like except from newspaper pictures. Of course, everyone knew Phil Rizzuto and Yogi Berra and some of the others.

We looked in the door kind of sheepishly. The door was open, but they had one of those kid gates across the doorway, one of those accordion kid gates. As soon as we looked in, these two Doberman Pinschers came up and started barking at us. We figured we weren't allowed in. One of the workers or the owners, I'm not sure which, came by and said, "Beat it kids."

We started walking away and someone yelled out, "No, let's see the paper." That same man who told us to skedaddle took the dogs away and opened the gate and let us in. There they were. The Yankees were having their dinner after the ball game. They were wearing street clothes. We were afraid to walk all the way in so we just stood there. We didn't want to walk by their table. All of a sudden, Yogi Berra said, "Hey kid, let me see the paper." I showed him the paper. He looked at it. Ball players like to read what's written about them in the newspapers so he looked in the back to the sports page. He apparently liked what he saw, and he said, "Here kid." And he handed me a dime.

I turned around to walk away, and I could see in my peripheral vision that he still had his hand out. I was embarrassed, of course, and said, "Ooh, I'm sorry." I reached in my pocket, put the nickel in his hand, and turned around to walk out again when he said, "Where's my change?" I said, "I just gave it to you." I turned around and his hand was empty. I couldn't imagine. It was the most embarrassing situation. I thought, "What happened? I know I gave him the nickel." I reached in my pocket and there was no nickel, but when I looked at my hand, I saw that the nickel had stuck in my right thumbnail. I just said, "Oooh, sorry." It was unbelievable.

I put the nickel in his hand and said, "Sorry," and walked out.

# EVERY TIME YOGI SEES ROBERT REDFORD, HE THINKS HE'S LOOKIN' IN THE MIRROR

### Charlie Fuoco

*Charlie Fuoco's love of the Yankees reaches back to July 4, 1939, when Lou Gehrig made his momentous speech at Yankee Stadium. The Bronx-born Fuoco, 69, has amassed whole bleachers' full of great memories.*

That was the day in 1939 when I was five years old that I began rooting for the Yankees. My family lived in Pelham Bay, about half-hour away from Yankee Stadium by car, maybe twenty minutes by train. It was the very first Old Timers' Day and my first game ever. My father, who was a Yankee fan, brought me there knowing that Gehrig was going to make a speech, but I did not know anything. In fact, I didn't know until the movie, *The Pride of the Yankees*, came out in 1949. I don't remember Gehrig's words, but to this day I remember the crowd and the cheering.

The Bronx was a nice place to live in those days and I was going to games myself with friends from the age of ten. My father used to give me a dollar and the bleachers only cost fifty cents. My friends and I used to go to the World Series at four o'clock in the morning and wait outside the bleachers to get into the Stadium. The bleachers weren't reserved seating, so it was first-come, first-served. We used to bring sandwiches.

In 1947, a friend and I were on our way home from a game. We were getting on the 8th Avenue subway when we saw Yogi Berra, Charlie Keller, and Tommy Byrne, who was a very good left-handed pitcher for the Yankees at the time, getting on the same train. They were going get off at the 59th Street stop and go to their hotel. I told my friend, "Let's follow them and see what goes on."

Tommy Byrne was one of the biggest ball-breakers on the Yankees then, a kibitzer who tried to lighten everything up. Now, Yogi Berra is a very unattractive man. I saw him in person when he was young and saw him again later in life, and I have to say he's one of the ugliest men I've ever seen. There's no getting away from it. His ears stuck out like he was a taxicab with the doors wide open coming down Fifth Avenue. Charlie Keller was called "King Kong Keller" because he was a very dark guy from Maryland who had very, very hairy arms. My friend and I were much smaller than they were and we sat down between them.

The subway seats faced each other like a booth, and Tommy Byrne was sitting next to me. I was in the middle. My friend was on the left. Byrne said to me, "Listen, ask Yogi who he thinks is better looking—him or Charlie Keller." I said, "I will not." He said, "Oh, go ahead. Don't worry about it. They won't say nothing." I said, "I will not. I won't do it. You ask him." He said, "Nah, I don't want to ask him." I said, "You've really got some nerve to ask me to do a thing like that."

As they were getting off the train, I wanted to follow them. Yogi said, "Hey kid. What were you talking to Byrne about?" I said, "Well, I don't want to tell you." "Come on, tell me," he said, "Don't worry about it. I know he's a big horn buster." There were so many different ways of saying what Tommy Byrne asked me." Finally, I said, "Well, to be honest with you, he wanted me to ask you who you thought was better looking, you or Charlie." Yogi said to me, "Well, you know what? Me and Charlie are both better looking than Tommy Byrne." I don't know if he was kidding or serious, but in all honesty, Tommy Byrne was better looking than both of them.

My friends and I were always having arguments about who was the best center fielder. In our clique, we had guys who were Dodger fans, Giant fans and Yankee fans. We used to sit in the park right across the street from Yankee Stadium until four o'clock in the morning, arguing about baseball until the milkman came around. I learned an awful lot from these guys. We were about fifteen, sixteen years old, but our parents knew where we were. Even after I got married, I went there. I loved baseball.

# FREAKIN' FINELLI

### Jerry Finelli

*The realization that his heroes Mickey Mantle, Whitey Ford, Yogi Berra and Moose Skowron were actual mere mortals was a shock to young Jerry Finelli, who lived in Parkchester in the Bronx.*

We lived in Parkchester and in 1963, I attended school at Fordham Prep, a Jesuit school in the Bronx. We had to wear jackets and ties. During the World Series, I brought a small transistor radio to school. The earpiece ran from my inside jacket pocket, down my arm and into my left ear. I was in chemistry class, not paying any attention to what was going on, and I was called on for some ridiculous formula or something. The instructors were pretty sharp, so mine probably suspected what I was doing. I was trying to fake it, and looking over at friends and trying to get answers.

I ended up down in the Dean of Discipline's office and had to "walk jug" that afternoon, which meant I had to walk around the quadrangle as punishment for getting caught doing something I shouldn't have. When you got "jugged," you walked for half an hour. Generally, when I got "jug," I would get in trouble with my parents, too, but not this time because my father understood what I had done. When it came to the Yankees, he was very understanding.

My dad, being a doctor, had connections so we were able to get tickets to attend those "Yankee Welcome Home" dinners at the Concourse Plaza Hotel on the Grand Concourse, a few blocks from Yankee Stadium. We would be sitting in this large room, and the Yankees would all be sitting on the dais. In about 1958 or '59, Yogi, Mickey, Whitey Ford, Elston Howard, Moose Skowron, Gil

McDougald, Andy Carey, and Hank Bauer were all there. We would have dinner, and there was a master of ceremonies like Mel Allen, who would talk about the upcoming year and introduce the players.

After dinner, we would form a long line around the dais, and the Yankees would sign whatever you brought. I was star-struck. I remember being in awe that they actually ate and that they were really people, that they come off that ball field and do something other than play ball. It was incredible that I could be that close to people who were my heroes. I couldn't get over the fact that I was sitting maybe five feet from where Whitey Ford was eating his dinner, and that we would have the opportunity to get up and talk with them and actually have them sign something.

**We got along in many ways, but when it came to Yankee and Dodger rivalries, it was almost a blood sport.**

One of the things that made my life very interesting when I was growing up as an elementary student at St. Helena's in the Bronx was that my best friend, John, was a Dodger fan. Those intense Snider-Mantle rivalries are memories that still stand out in my mind today. We were very friendly. We walked to school every day together. We got along in many ways, but when it came to Yankee and Dodger rivalries, it was almost a blood sport. We'd go at each other left and right.

John gloated so much after the Yankees 1955 World Series loss, and I was the type of kid who kept trying to be reasonable saying, "It's the first time, and everybody's entitled…" We were walking home from school a couple of days after the loss, and we actually ended up in a fistfight. I just couldn't take it anymore. We had on our school uniforms and we were rolling in the street fighting each other over the fact that the Dodgers beat the Yankees in '55. To the best of my recollection, adults broke us up, and we both were a little worse for wear. I do remember I was bleeding. Johnny wasn't. Not only did his team win, but he beat me in the fight. I got into trouble for that. I was defending my Yankees, but still, fighting was not tolerated in my house.

# JOE DIMAGGIO WAS AL KALINE PLAYING IN NEW YORK

Ron Guidry (L), Mike Lobell (R)

### Mike Lobell

*When it comes to the Yankees, even a big shot Hollywood producer like sixty-year-old, Mike Lobell still has a bit of the hero-worshipping Yankee fan in him. Mike was a top high-school catcher who played in Brooklyn with and against future pros like Joe Pepitone, Joe Torre, and Tommy Davis.*

When I was six years old, my father took me to Yankee Stadium to see Joe DiMaggio play and from that day on, I was a Yankee fan. I grew up in Brooklyn, around the corner from Ebbets Field. I was one of the few kids in the neighborhood who did not like the Dodgers and loved the Yankees, although we used to go to Ebbets Field all the time. My friends and I knew the cops and we used to sneak in.

I played hooky a lot because both my parents worked. I watched every pitch of the Don Larsen perfect game against the Dodgers in the 1956 World Series, which is one of the most famous games in baseball history. I went out in the morning as if I was going to school, then when my parents left, I went back home and watched the entire game. That was a big moment for me.

In primary school, we had a class called "shop," which I hated. We were cruel to the teacher. His name was Israel Broder, and we used to call him "Izzy" and run away, and he hated that. I just hated the class, and to this day, I can't fix anything. Growing up in an apartment in New York, we didn't have tools. We had a Super, and when something went wrong, we called the Super and he came up and fixed it, so nobody had to learn anything.

At the time, I was very into Al Kaline, one of the greatest hitters—I believe the youngest guy to ever win a batting championship. He hit 399 home runs, yet never hit 30 in one season. I read a book that described how during the winter, he would swing a leaded bat to strengthen his swing. I said to myself, "I don't know where to get a leaded bat so I'm gonna make one." So I took a bat into shop and drilled a hole in the end of the big barrel, and got some lead. I melted the lead and poured it into the bat. I had a lead bat.

All winter long in my bedroom, I would swing my lead bat, and my father used to go berserk. I would try to do it when nobody was around, but then he would catch me and say, "You're gonna break something." Every night for about fifteen or twenty minutes, I would swing this bat.

**He was all the myths of baseball and the dreams of the kid from the cornfield coming to the big city and taking the city by storm.**

One night, about 6:30 or 7:00, the bell rang in our apartment. I answered the door. It was Israel Broder. He said, "Is your father home? I want to talk to him." I couldn't believe it. He came to our apartment to complain to my father about me. He said, "You know, your son doesn't do anything we do. We make ashtrays. We make…. He's made two things, a belt and a lead bat." Thick leather belts were very hot then, and I had spent weeks putting studs in the belt that spelled my name. These were my two accomplishments in shop that semester. It was awful. This stupid guy coming to the apartment and embarrassing me like that.

Mickey Mantle was my idol along with millions and millions of other people. When all that stuff came out about how he lived and drank and women and all that, nobody really felt that he was a bad guy. It was so great when he straightened himself out. The saddest thing was he spent several years getting sober and stopped all the crap he had done to himself, and when he got himself all straightened out was when he got sick and died. When Roy Firestone interviewed him—I cry every time I see it. It was just so sad. In that crazy guy was that great sort of American fiction character. He was like Frank Merriwell. He was the guy. He was *The Natural*. He was Robert Redford. He was Roy Hobbs. He was all the myths of baseball and the dreams of the kid from the cornfield coming to the big city and taking the city by storm. That was Mickey Mantle, and you never wanted anything bad to happen to Mickey. Guys like Mickey Mantle should never die. Joe DiMaggio, who was a jerk all his life, lived to be eighty-something. Mickey wasn't that. He was just a little naughty boy.

In my teens, I played baseball at the Parade Grounds, which is a very famous place in Brooklyn and is still there. A lot of great ball players came from there: **Joe Torre**, Joe Pepitone, Tommy Davis, who was an amazing ballplayer who played with the Dodgers. We played all our summer and sandlot baseball there when school was out. I played against Pepitone and Torre. Joe Pepitone was phenomenal. He hit home runs all the time. He played for Manual Trades High School in Red Hook, Brooklyn, which was the school where the bad guys went.

There were thirteen baseball diamonds at the Parade Grounds, but only two of them were fenced in and had stands, and you always wanted to play on those two because people came and watched and scouts came. One time, **Tommy Davis** and I were on the same team—I was a catcher—playing on one of the fields that did not have any fences. Davis hit a ball and arrived at home plate before the out-fielders even got to the ball. That's how far he hit it and how fast he was. He later played for the Dodgers and won batting titles.

Joe Torre and I played against each other from the time we were kids. I was about nineteen and was playing for a team called the Senecas, which was like semi-pro. It was a very high level team in the sandlots. Joe Torre was playing for Nathan's of Coney Island. We

Joe Torre was player/manager of the Mets for 18 days in 1977. Since 1962, there have been four player/managers with Pete Rose (1984-1986) being the last....In 1935, there were nine player/managers.

In 1962, Tommy Davis had 153 RBIs for the Dodgers. No one drove in 150 runs in the majors for the next 35 years.

were playing on one of the fenced-in diamonds. With the bases loaded, Torre hit a ball as far as you could hit it. I was playing left field that day, and our center fielder and I were running for the ball at full speed. He was running so fast he fell over the fence. The ball went over the fence, and it was a grand slam home run.

Several years ago, a very good friend of mine, Norman Steinberg, was running *The Cosby Show* and when the Yankees won the World Series, he had David Cone and Joe Torre on the show. So I said to Norman, "Ask Torre if he remembers the grand slam he hit on diamond thirteen against us." Not only did Joe remember it, he signed the script to me, which I thought was nice. I never kept up my relationship with him. I don't know why. I was silly.

I played baseball for Michigan State from 1958 to '62, and eight or ten of us guys used to go into Detroit whenever the Yankees were in town. Everybody in other ballparks outside of New York hates the Yankees. They really hated them back then because the Yankees were always winning. In Detroit, it was really scary because I was probably the only guy in Briggs Stadium rooting for the Yankees. People would get really drunk. I'd be screaming for the Yankees. I was surrounded by my pals, but they were all Tiger fans. I never kept silent. I was being a full-blown Yankee fan, but I wasn't any more obnoxious than the Tiger fans who were screaming at the Yankees.

I didn't really meet any Yankees until I was older. In the early 1990s, I was making a movie in New Orleans. Whenever you make a movie outside the big cities, the locals always do nice things for you. In this particular case, they called me when I was in New Orleans and said the city wanted to throw a party for us in Lafayette. I told them we would do that, but I couldn't guarantee we would get everybody there because they really wanted Kathleen Turner and Dennis Quaid, the stars of the movie. In any case, they threw this party. It was outdoors. They had two Zydeco bands and all the great chefs in the area did the cooking. It was really a great time, great music, and amazing food. They introduced me to this guy who was cooking who weighed around three hundred pounds, named Bubba Guidry.

I said, "**Bubba Guidry**? Are you any relation to Ron?" He said, "Yeah, he's my nephew." I said, "God, I'd love to meet him." I told him I wanted to throw my own party just for my cast and my crew the next week. I asked him if he would cook for my party and invite Ron. "Tell Ron I want to see him. I'm a huge Yankee fan."

So Guidry came with his wife. He didn't leave me alone. We were together the entire night, just talking about the Yankees, the game, Steinbrenner. It was fantastic. My wife took a great picture of us, which I have hanging in my office. He said, "You were a catcher. Why don't you come over to my house. I'm building a new house. I'll pitch to you." So I slapped my face, and said, "Is this guy kidding?" I said, "Ron, I haven't caught in a long time."

He was building this house that had big wrought iron custom gates. In the circle were the letters "LL" with a lightning bolt, for "Louisiana Lightning," which was his nickname. It was a lot of fun. I caught a few balls, and then I had to leave. It was great. He didn't throw smoke like he used to, of course, but it was pretty good. Pretty good.

When the George Brett "Pine Tar" game was concluded, Ron Guidry was the center fielder and Don Mattingly was the second baseman.

# SHORT STORIES FROM LONG MEMORIES:

## GROWIN' UP WITH THE YANKS

When I was a kid, I had a cousin or cousin in-law who dated someone who was related to Whitey Ford. The second I heard this, I became convinced that Whitey Ford was my cousin. I told the kids at school. I told everybody that Whitey Ford was my cousin. I did this forever, and then one day my father heard me tell someone. He said, "What? You're not related to Whitey Ford. Are you crazy?"

I have no idea how long they dated because I only heard about it that once. It wasn't somebody I even knew.

———DAN MCCOURT, 54, Port Chester, NY

When ninth grade came, I wrote book reports on baseball. The first one I did was on John Tunis' *High Pockets*, a fiction book. When the Yankees lost the pennant that year, I read the book, *The Year the Yankees Lost the Pennant*, on which the play *Damn Yankees* was based. After the second report, my English teacher said in front of the whole class, "Can you do a book report on something other than baseball?" My third report was on *PT-109*.

———VINNY NATALE, 52, Cranston, RI

Growing up, I was a little tomboy. I played ball in the streets. One time, the ball I was playing with rolled over by this teenage guy, who was with his girlfriend. I said, "Give it to me." He said, "No. I'm not going to give you the ball. I want my girlfriend to hear this—you need to tell me the Yankees infield." I named the infield, the catcher, and the outfield. He said to his girlfriend, "See, I told you she knows all about the Yankees." "Here," he said to me. "You can have your ball back."

I was able to take that open stance like Joe DiMaggio. I wouldn't do that at the plate but just when I was being silly. When I was about thirteen, I played on a girls' PAL softball team as an outfielder. We also played basketball. We played out of the Harlem House community center on 116th Street and First Avenue.

———THERESA ARO, 67, raised in East Harlem, NY

Nineteen sixty. October. The World Series. If you've ever seen Robert DeNiro's movie, *A Bronx Tale*, that's my life. In the opening monologue, Chazz Palmentieri, the lead actor, says, "I was born in the Belmont section of the Bronx. It was 1960. I was eight years old. And the Yankees lost the World Series to the Pirates. That was the worst day of my life." This guy is my age. He has the same problem with the Yankees in 1960: Game 7.

In those days, you'd run home from school at about 3:00, 3:30—it would be fifth, sixth, seventh inning by then. You'd be lucky to see the last few innings of a World Series game or any away game. So for the seventh game, we rushed home, and I got there and see Ralph Terry on the mound. I cannot look at that film of Bill Mazeroski hitting that home run over the ivy wall in left field. I can see the clock. It says about 3:40. Yogi Berra's back looking at the ball. I can see Number 8 right at the wall. That's it. I cried for hours. And that's before I'd even gone to a game at Yankee Stadium. I was running home to my little black and white TV. My mother said, "What are you so upset about? It's only a game." "Ma, you don't understand." I was depressed.

——JOE SANTOIEMMA, 50, the Bronx

We didn't have ball fields when I was a kid so we played in the paved parking lot of St. Frances de Chantal Church. We used to play with rubber-coated baseballs. We'd tape the balls up, but the worst thing was if you lost the ball in the sewer. We tried to remember to put something across the top to prevent the balls from going into it. We'd put a couple of neighbor's garbage cans or we might make one of the younger kids who wasn't playing sit on the receptacle. If the ball came by, the kid had to kick it away.

I went to All Hallows High School, an Irish Christian Brothers school, which is on the Grand Concourse about six or seven blocks from Yankee Stadium. I used to have to get off the train right in the shadow of Yankee Stadium. We saw Yankee players all the time. We could watch them over the edge of the platform, because you could look into the stadium from there. Guys like Whitey Ford, Moose Skowron, Mickey Mantle, Roger Maris we'd see all the time between games, after practice, getting out of their cars.

Regardless of what people say about Mickey Mantle, I remember times that he stopped for kids that would mob him. People weren't hounds the way they are today. But if you were a local kid in school there or you lived nearby and you hung around, you'd see Yankees.

They were as familiar as the ace of spades. They were that recognizable. If you were a young kid and were a baseball card collector or used to flip cards with other kids to win more cards, you had your Mickey Mantle or your Moose Skowron card or their rookie card.

Still, when you see them in the flesh, you were in awe of them. They were bigger than life. A lot of these guys would sign cards and sometimes they would even bring stuff out to the kids, like a ball. I saw a kid get a bat one time from Moose Skowron. I saw Mickey Mantle give somebody a ball. Now you can't get a guy to sign for a kid unless he gets twenty-five bucks.

——**KEVIN BRADY**, 54, the Bronx

When I was at St. Denis School in Yonkers, the World Series always started on a Wednesday afternoon. On Wednesday afternoons, the public school children who were Catholic came over to my school to take what they called "religious instruction." So we'd be let out early, at noontime.

In those days, the World Series was always on the Yankee station because the Yankees won the pennant every year since I'd started watching. So in 1959, when the White Sox won, I asked my brother, "Why aren't the Yankees playing? What's going on?" He said, "Well, Chicago won the pennant." I said, "No, the Yankees are always in the World Series." They had been up until that point.

Growing up, I just thought the World Series was part of the Yankees' season. You were spoiled then. You didn't understand the way things really were.

——**MARK ROLLINSON**, 50, Yonkers, NY

*Jerry Faden*

When the Dodgers won the 1955, World Series, I couldn't leave my house for two days. All the kids who were Dodger fans were running around trying to find all the Yankee fans. They weren't mean spirited. They would harass us, because we had harassed them. This was their one chance. Of course, I had to go to school, but after school and on weekends, I wouldn't come out and play.

I remember getting into very, very heavy arguments with them, not only over Duke Snider and Mickey Mantle, which was the common disagreement, but even over who was the better announcer—Mel Allen for the Yankees or Red Barber for the Dodgers. I was a fanatic about Mel Allen. When my friends and I found out his real name was Israel and that he was Jewish like we were, we went crazy.

——JERRY FADEN, 57, Brooklyn

I was raised tough, so I wasn't supposed to cry, but the Yankees broke my heart many times. The loss to the Pirates in 1960 really broke my heart because they were winning in the ninth inning. Of course, I never wanted them to lose to the Dodgers. After a bad loss, I would sulk and be miserable and then try to do things to make myself happy. When I was a kid, I would go and stay with my grandmother and my aunts because they made me happy. Later, and to this day, I'll go shopping and buy myself clothes or shoes. When I worked in Manhattan, sometimes I would go to the stores on Fifth Avenue that opened before nine a.m., so I could buy something even before I went to work.

——THERESA ARO, 67, Deltona, FL

I once wrote a fan letter to Roger Maris, but I never got an answer. I didn't care because I knew he was a busy guy, but my mother never forgave him. After that, she always bad-mouthed him because she said Roger Maris didn't answer his fan mail.

My mother and father had weekly business meetings in the Concourse Plaza Hotel, where a lot of the Yankee players stayed. My mother thought Dale Long was the most gorgeous guy. She went on for years about Dale Long. She would bring home an autograph of Dale or of Ralph Terry. She knew somebody whose husband was a Stadium groundskeeper, and she brought home an autographed team picture of the 1964 Yankees with Mantle, Maris, and Ford. Of all the things I've lost over the years, that's one of the ones I regret most.

——PHIL PANASCI, 47, the Bronx

At St. Aidan's grade school where I went to school on Long Island, there were some nuns who, when the Yankees were in the World Series, would put the radio on so we could listen. But when I was in the first grade, I had a pretty tough nun named Sister Mary Leoni. This woman was legendary because not only was she tough, but she was also an older lady. Sister was trying to introduce to the students the idea of growing up with the desire to have a religious vocation, to become a nun or a priest. She wrote the word "vocation" on the board, and she would have little discussions, and the priest would come in and talk about life as a priest. This was a form of indoctrination for kids who were only seven years old.

One kid, Joseph Fitterer, was a good student and very pleasing to Sister Leoni because he said that he wanted to become a priest. This was the right answer to any question. I didn't want to become a priest. Sister said that was quite all right, but I would have to defend myself, defend the choice, and describe what else I would want to be.

I actually engaged in the first debate of my life. Sister Leoni stood Joseph up on one side of the room, and he argued about why he wanted to become a priest. I stood on the other side of the room, and described how I wanted to be center fielder for the New York Yankees, which I learned later was another kind of priesthood. This was not the answer Sister Leoni wanted to hear.

———ROY PETER CLARK, 54, Nassau County, Long Island

Nineteen sixty-nine, which, of course, was the first year the Mets won a World Series, was the year I became a Yankee fan. To me, rooting for the Yankees was like rooting for the underdog, because that year they were horrible, and all you heard about was the Mets. They were really bad, and I guess I'm a sucker for underdogs. But when they become "dogs" or even "overdogs," you still root for them. You don't stop rooting for the underdog just because he wins. If you suffer for years and years and finally the underdog gets somewhere, then you've got a little happiness coming.

So whenever people talk about how the Yankees are a dynasty and how it's like rooting for General Motors, I tell them "No, you didn't start when I started. You didn't start in the days of Jerry Kenney and Celerino Sanchez, Horace Clarke, Jake Gibbs, and Jim Mason"—nice guys but not a winning team by any stretch.

———VICTOR LEVIN, 41, New City, NY

In the early 1960s, my friends were either Yankee fans like I was or Giants fans. There were a few Dodger fans mixed in. There were no Mets until 1962 so no one was a Mets fan. In sixth grade, we were a little bit progressive in our PS 32, the Belmont school, in the Bronx. We'd have entire class debates. One of the debates was: Who was better—the 1962 Giants or the 1962 Yankees? They had played against each other in the World Series and it was Mantle versus Mays, McCovey versus Skowron, Richardson versus Chuck Hiller, Whitey Ford versus Juan Marichal. I remember it like it was yesterday. We were at the front of the auditorium. Guys were pointing at each other, making accusations. It was pretty much a stalemate. I made the argument player-by-player, position-by-position, and compared them. I got to Mantle and Mays, and I looked at the audience and said, "All right, that one's even."

The teacher of my class, Mr. Riley, was the overseer. He was a big, tall male teacher that no one had had at that point. The debates were a real macho thing. The teams were all boys, and we were obviously showing off for the girls.

Recently, our class had our 30th reunion. We remembered the debate. There were so many different conversations going on at one time, you can imagine after thirty years or so. But we did talk baseball. Of course, the Yankee fans had their chests out. They had won four out of six or whatever championships. The Giant fans really had to be quiet. Every now and then I mail my little Giant fan buddy who lives on Long Island, Nelson Yumptov, a Willie Mays card just to keep him happy.

——JOE SANTOIEMMA, 50, the Bronx

I loved Thurman Munson. When he died, I was taking the bus from the Bronx to Yonkers with a friend of mine named Charlie Hage. Charlie and I were very, very close. We liked the Yankees. We liked the same TV shows. We went to school together. We got the paper and I was reading about Thurman Munson and the crash and he said, "So, he's dead. What are we gonna do now? So what?" I said, "What are you talking about? This is Thurman Munson who just died. What's the matter with you?"

We stopped speaking then over Thurman Munson, and I haven't spoken to him since that day. And we were very close at school and growing up. It's really strange.

——TOM LEMME, 43, the Bronx

I became a Yankee fan by mistake. I was born in Brooklyn, moved to Queens when I was five, then to Spring Valley in Rockland County, New York when I was twelve. My first recollection of baseball was the 1955 World Series. The Yankees were the losers to Brooklyn.

People were celebrating in the street, and I felt sorry for the Yankees and decided that I was going to root for the underdog.

So I became a Yankee fan, totally ignorant of the history of the club. Somewhere in my mind, it must have made me feel better about myself to be identified with winners, like a better person, or at least, better than people who rooted for the "losers." I would wear my Yankee jacket or my Yankee cap with such pride. I did go to watch the Mets in their first season at the Polo Grounds in 1962, but I never considered becoming a Mets fan. I couldn't switch no matter what. It's like changing religion. You just can't do it.

I played second base when I was a kid because Bobby Richardson was a hero of mine. I was short in stature so it seemed like the right position for me. I still play softball and to this day, I'm more comfortable at second base. I knew all the moves from watching Bobby Richardson—how you open and close your mouth to signal to the shortstop who's covering, how you hold up your fingers to show two outs so the outfielders see and are reminded. You hold up your index finger and your pinkie because two fingers side-by-side would be hard to distinguish. If you make an error on a ground ball, you sort of smooth out the dirt in front of you as though you're blaming it on a pebble. The coolest thing, of course, was catching the last out of an inning, and then just arrogantly tossing it onto the pitcher's mound as you ran in. I had all those things down perfectly.

———MARTY APPEL, 53, Spring Valley, NY

I first started to really follow baseball in the early 1950s when the Yankees were always in the World Series and generally won all the time. I was so used to the Yankees winning that when they lost the seventh game of the World Series in 1957 to the Braves, I remember my whole family sitting in a restaurant in Greenwich Village, and I was absolutely devastated. It was without a doubt the lowest point in my young life. I really couldn't believe it, and my father said, "There's nothing you can do about it. It's over." But to this day, I can remember how I felt. It was as though I'd been betrayed in some manner, way, shape or form because the Yankees never lost.

———JERRY FINELLI, Parkchester

# Chapter 3

# Fathers' Day

# The Old Man and the Wee

# MEMORIES, LIKE HEROES, NEVER GROW OLD:

## DAD

My parents had a very unusual and interesting marriage, which, for all intents and purposes was over shortly after I came into this world, although they didn't get divorced until I was eleven or twelve. My mother's boyfriend, Mark, owned a kids' toys and clothing store on the Upper East Side where my mother and a lot of bored, frustrated, young Jewish mothers on the Upper East Side used to congregate and occasionally work part time. The staff would play with the kids, and the mothers would go downstairs to the basement and get high with Mark. It was sort of an interesting time.

Mark was everything my father wasn't. My father is an opera queen. He would dress us up in ties and jackets on Saturday morning and take us to down to Avery Fischer Hall and make us watch opera, which was about the last place in the world I wanted to be at age seven. My father was not averse to going to a Yankees game, but he certainly wasn't much fun to go with. In the world I came from, when your mother's bouncing in and out of rehab and your father is a total closet case, I don't know where baseball fit in for either one of them. But it was my primary escape and my brother's, too. We were passionate Yankees fans and went to as many games as we could.

Mark was a big-time Yankees fan and a sort of impetuous person, and I remember nights when we'd be hanging around, closing up the store at six o'clock, and as he'd lock the door, a stretch limousine would pull up. He'd say, "Okay, get in." The limousine would take us out to the Bronx for the Yankee game. This was in the 1980s. When his business was going badly, he'd get rid of his apartment and sleep in the store, but when things were going well, he spent a lot of money and hung around with a lot of unseemly people. All in all, Mark, who died a few years ago, remains the true guiding spirit of my passion for the Yankees.

I went to Billy's Bat Day, a huge promotion, after George Steinbrenner hired Billy Martin back the first time. It was just part of a circus. I was supposed to go to that game with my mother's boy-friend, but he was too drunk to go. I wound up going with my mother and my godmother, which was really odd. I went to maybe three Yankee games with my mother. She sat there the whole time reading *People* magazine. My dad saves everything, and I think he still has a T-shirt from that day.

———**VAUGHN SANDMAN**, 27, raised in Manhattan

My father wasn't really a baseball fan. He would watch the World Series, but that was it. But my father had a great influence in supporting my baseball habit in that he knew I was a big reader and would bring home for me every *Sports Illustrated* and other sports magazines that his co-workers would discard after reading them. I started my subscriptions soon after, so I was reading sports magazines from about the age of ten. I saved all those magazines and still have them.

The only time I ever remember my father listening to a baseball game was in 1961, when I was ten years old. We were visiting my godparents one Friday night in September. I don't know which team my godfather, Abraham Silverman, was a fan of, but he hated the Yankees. He was a typical Yankee-hater. The Yankees and the Tigers were close. First place was up for grabs during this series. The game was on the radio, so the three of us were outside listening to the game. I had my Yankee cards in my hand. It was a tight game. Proba-bly in the seventh or eighth inning, late in the game, something went the Yankees way and they took the lead. Somehow my godfather grabbed my baseball cards out of my hand and he threw them down. He was quite angry and upset. He said, "That always happens with the Yankees." I was only ten years old and I had never seen him behave that way. You could really see the intensity with which he hated the Yankees.

———**VINNY NATALE**, 52, now living in Montague, MA

My dad worked at a place called Metropolitan Tobacco in the South Bronx that sold tobacco and other sundries. They sold baseball cards, so every once in a while my dad would bring me home a box of baseball cards, with 36 packs in it. I'd spend an eter-nity just opening them and saving them and collecting them. That experience never left me. I kept all my cards. I have my Mickey

Mantle cards from the late 1950s and early 1960s. My oldest son has worked in a baseball card shop since he was fifteen so this stuff really gets passed on. I have a ten-year old who's just starting Little League so we just got him interested. He's collecting cards, and he goes to games.

When I was young, my father was too busy to be a baseball fan, too busy to be with his children, one of those nine-to-five, serve-my-dinner guys. He recently passed away after a long illness, but a funny thing, in my father's later years, one of his great pleasures was sitting down and watching the Yankee games. Sick as he was and despite all the tough times he'd been through, we'd sit down every now and then and watch a Yankee game and talk about it. It seemed to be like an escape, and it was really good to see the family together for something like that.

My wife and I have two kids in college, a ten-year old who's in Little League, and a five-year old son, John, who has autism. John has not been to a Yankee game. He's actually in a baseball league for the physically and mentally disabled. New Rochelle is one of the few towns that have a "challenger" league. It started about six or seven years ago. Anybody can play. They don't charge. They give the kids a uniform, they bring the snacks and the drinks, and a very disorganized game is played that doesn't mean a thing. The kids are just out there. I think it's more for the families than it is the kids. My son can identify the NY logo as meaning the Yankees. He has very little language, but he can say, "Baseball game. Yankees." We're always pointing to the insignia on my chest, and asking, "Johnny, what's this? What's this?" "Yankees. Yankees. Yankees." That thrills us to no end. John was a late-arriving baby and a surprise, but he's the joy of our life.

——JOE SANTOIEMMA, 50, New Rochelle, NY

My father is the one who took me to games when I was a girl, though I can't even remember the first time I went to Yankee Stadium because I was little, maybe five or six. My father worked for the city, first as a bus driver, then later as a dispatcher. He taught me how to keep score. We would get to the Stadium early and find seats in the grandstand behind home plate. We got there early because you didn't want to sit where you'd have a pole blocking the view of the entire field. One time, we sat in the bleachers, and I remember hating it because it was so far away.

By the time I was eleven, I was going to games on my own. When you come from an Italian family, you're pretty sheltered, so when I think about it now, it's amazing to me that I was allowed to go. People today would probably accuse my mother and father of abusing me, but I wanted to go to the games, and nobody on my block wanted to go with me. My father would give me a dollar, and I would go on Ladies' Day. He would tell me the one condition of my going was that I had to keep score. He would say, "Remember, when you get off at 125th Street, make sure you take the train which has the green light, the Jerome Avenue train." I knew anyway. I would take it up to 161st Street, get out, go into the Stadium, find myself a seat, and yell and scream the whole game. The trip would take me about an hour, including the walking. When I got home, I would give my father the scorecard and we'd talk about the game. Boy, did I think I was a big shot.

———THERESA ARO, 67, raised in Manhattan

In 1967, when I was ten years old, I took two of my brothers, who were eight and seven, to a two o'clock game at Yankee Stadium. The game went eighteen innings. My father had dropped us off, and when we didn't come home, he came to the Stadium and found us. At that time, it was okay to walk to the Stadium and sit by yourself. It was about seven o'clock when he showed up. He was livid, absolutely livid. I'll never forget it—he showed up in the right center field bleachers. I could see him coming out of the walkway. He was looking around, and I saw him and caught his eye. How he found us, I don't know. There were no assigned seats in the bleachers.

I waved to him, and he waved back, motioning for me to come down. I brought my brothers down. He laid into me. "What is wrong with you? You have the two younger ones with you. You're at the ball game. You know better. After the ninth inning, you should have just come home. Come on, we're going now." I said, "Dad, the game's not over." He piled us into the car and drove home.

The Yankees won the ball game in the five minutes it took us to get from the stadium to my house. Joe Pepitone hit a ground-rule double. I was so disappointed.

My brothers and I would go to Ball Day and Bat Day every year. My father would make sure that we went with him or my uncles. I even went to some games with my grandmother, who was a bigger baseball fan than my father was. She was a Giants fan. I remember sitting with her on Saturday afternoons and watching the Game of the Week program. After 1962, she became a big Mets fan. She was a pretty bright baseball lady. She knew her stuff. I never would get into anything with her about being a Mets fan. I was afraid of her! She packed a good wallop so I didn't mess with her. No, she respected the fact that I was a big Yankee fan.

——**MIKE SPELMAN**, 45, raised in the Bronx

My dad contracted polio in 1910 at the age of two, and he used crutches his whole life. When my brother and I were young, he took us to a lot of games. We would drag him up to the upper deck and never think anything of it. I don't think it ever occurred to us growing up that our father had a handicap. It was fun to go to baseball games with him because he would always be telling us, "I was here when **Lou Gehrig** did this or Dickey did that." He saw Ruth play in 1927.

My grandfather became stone deaf at about the age of sixty. In those days, a hearing aid was about the size of a small portable transistor radio. It was quite a large gadget with the earphone piece that went up to the ear, and he would wear it in a shirt pocket. My grandfather was an absolutely wonderful man who did everything for his family that he ever could, but you couldn't bother him during a Yankee game. He would tune you out. He would take the hearing aid off, put it on the shelf right in front of the TV and turn it down low while he watched to the game. My grandmother would come in. He'd pick it up, turn it off, put his hand up in the air and say, "I just tuned you out." She'd walk back into the kitchen, and he'd turn the thing back on and listen to his Yankee game.

——**MARK ROLLINSON**, 50, Yonkers, NY

My first actual knowledge of baseball came in 1958 when I was eight. My father, who wasn't a big baseball fan—I had to beg him to take me to a couple of games—was watching the World Series

> Jacob Javits, Charles Mingus, David Niven and Catfish Hunter have all died of ALS—Lou Gehrig's disease.

on television with my mother in the den. I was being punished for something and wasn't allowed to watch TV. I wanted to know what my father was watching so I sneaked outside the house and peered through the window. I figured out that he was watching this great game of baseball.

The first Yankee game I ever went to was in 1961 when I was eleven. My dad took me. The baseball I had seen up to that point had been on black-and-white television. I remember walking into Yankee Stadium and seeing see that magnificent green field. My eyes popped out of my head, and they haven't returned to their sockets since. It just blew me away. Things just came to life. Then to see all my favorite stars in person: Mickey Mantle, Roger Maris, Tony Kubek, Yogi Berra, Elston Howard just blew me away.

"The Mick" was my guy. He's still my guy. He could do no wrong. Though I found out later that he was basically a drunk and wasn't a good father to his family, we forgive him for all these things. He was just that good. Nobody could touch the Mick. The Mick is up there on his own level.

That first game my father and I ever went to, Whitey Ford was pitching for the Yankees. They were playing the Washington Senators, an old baseball team that has since moved and became the Minnesota Twins. Whitey Ford pitched a one-nothing shutout. The one run was an inside-the-park homer by Mickey Mantle. That will draw any kid in for life. All these years later, I still vividly remember it like it was yesterday.

I try to bring that memory back every time I walk into Yankee Stadium, but it's not the same. First of all, the Stadium was rebuilt. The lighting is different. I think they're using different grass. The coloring of the grass is just not the same as it was back then. Again, it may be the lighting, but I don't think so. They put the new halogen lights in when they rebuilt the stadium so it just doesn't look the same. Every time I walk into Yankee Stadium, I think about the old memories, and I cherish every moment. I just do. It's almost like a religious place. It's hard to explain. It's hallowed ground. Baseball is the one constant in my life with all else that's change. It's the one thing that has not changed.

——STEVE KOHLREITER, 53, raised in Fort Lee, NJ

*Lori Schwab*

I grew up in Forest Hills, New York. Queens. It's Mets' territory, but who cares?

Each of my parents grew up as Yankee fans. Both my father and my mother were born in Germany. When they emigrated to America in 1936 and 1938, respectively, they each landed in the Bronx. In their families, it was very important to their parents that they become "American." I suppose they thought baseball was one of the ways they could do that. My father as a youngster was more the baseball enthusiast growing up, whereas my mother came to it a little later. To them, baseball was just so very American. I think that's how they became Yankee fans. It was just mandatory in the family. When I was growing up, our whole extended family—uncles, cousins, etc., would all go to Yankee games.

I do have this other set of cousins, though, who used to live in Brooklyn and are Mets fans. I really do remember asking them, "Why? I don't understand." I was young then, and it was so inconceivable to me how anyone could be part of my family and be anything but a Yankee fan? I was serious.

To this day, my family still carries on a tradition of going to Yankee Stadium on Fathers' Day and on my dad's birthday in August, although as he's gotten older, he says he prefers to watch the game on TV. We had planned to take him a couple of years ago but his sister died. We had arranged for birthday greetings to be flashed on the scoreboard. Although he didn't go, we do have pictures of it: "Yankee Stadium. Happy Birthday Herbert!" He loved it.

——LORI SCHWAB, 44, now living in Manhattan

My early Yankee fandom came straight from my dad. My father's from the Philippines. He came to the United States in the 1960s when there was a shortage of doctors. He and all of his friends went to medical school together, shipped over here and started residencies and internships. He met my mother, who was a patient in a hospital in New York City.

My father wanted to be American, to eat apple pie, speak English, and do all sorts of other "American" things. He tried football first. He did some kind of a residency in Buffalo, and some people took him to a football game up there. It was freezing cold, and he didn't have a coat. This is what a greenhorn my dad was: He thought that when they were in the huddle, they were praying because the game is so dangerous. He didn't understand football at all, and it seemed kind of ridiculous to go outside in the freezing cold to see an outdoor sport.

When my father moved to New York City he got very into the Yankees and learned about baseball. You can't get more American than the Yankees. They're America's team. They've got the star spangled top hat as their logo. By the time I was five or six years old, we were living in Englewood, New Jersey, practically on the other side of the George Washington Bridge from the Stadium. So my dad started to take the family to games.

I think the happiest day of my entire childhood was July 4, 1983. I was a young teenager by then. My mother, brother, dad, and I went to the game and we were sitting in the upper deck. It was already a perfect day—sunny, beautiful. I was not one of those teenagers who did not want to spend time with my family. I was occasionally the surly youth, but for the most part I really enjoyed, and still enjoy, being with my parents and my brother.

We all loved Chuck Mangioni at the time. That day, Chuck Mangioni played the National Anthem. Life couldn't get better than this. Then Dave Righetti pitched a no-hitter! By the sixth inning, nobody in the stadium had any fingernails left.

If you look at a scorecard, you can see the way a no-hitter looks. There are only little numbers. There are no little flashes or lines because nobody's been on base with a hit. A couple of guys had walked, but there were no hits and by the fifth inning we were saying, "My God, he's pitching a no-hitter." Fans at Yankee Stadium are very astute so by the fifth-sixth inning everyone in the entire stadium knew what was going on, and we were all on the edges of our seats.

My dad's the one who taught me to keep a scorecard. What I didn't know at the time was that he didn't know how to keep a scorecard. He was just following the little directions that come with it. He wanted us to grow up as American kids so he didn't teach us any of his native languages or customs. We were a totally American family that grew up loving the Yankees and baseball. My dad is a very astute watcher of baseball, but we didn't know that he was learning as he went along teaching us.

We hardly ever stayed to the end of a game. Usually my parents were the, "We'll leave a little bit early and beat the traffic" type. On this day, we got to stay all the way to the end of the game, and then we went down to the press gate to wait for Righetti to come out, and we stood there for about two hours in this group of two or three hundred cheering fans. We thought our parents were the coolest ever for letting us do that.

*Jonathan Coburn, Cecilia Tan, and Julian Tan at Monument Park.*

Afterward, we went to Chinatown, had a great dinner, and watched fireworks over the East River. That was quite a day. I wrote about it in my diary as one of the greatest days ever, all because my parents were willing to let us experience something like that. When my dad turned fifty, neither I nor my brother could be there for his birthday party. My mom said it would be cool if we faxed something for her to read to him. My brother and I each faxed something separately, and apparently we both talked about the July 4, 1983 game. I wrote, "Thanks dad, for bringing us to all those games."

——CECILIA TAN, 35, Science Fiction Writer, raised in Englewood, NJ

*I'm the only one to play for one team—*
*the Cubs—*
*under one owner—*
*Philip K. Wrigley—*
*in the city of one mayor—*
*Richard J. Daley—*
*under one light—*
*God's—*
*in one park—*
*Wrigley Field.*

——*Ernie Banks*

# Chapter 4

# I Saw It on the Radio

## I Never Met Mel Allen
## But I Knew Him All My Life

# IT WASN'T SCHOOL HE DIDN'T LIKE, IT WAS THE PRINCIPAL OF THE THING

Roger Fischer

*Roger Fischer, 55, a longtime editor at the* St. Petersburg Times *newspaper, moved from New Jersey south to Florida years ago, but even during the lean years of the 1960s and early 1970s he continued to keep hallowed his Yankee memories.*

My Yankee obsession as a kid was my needing to have my hand on the pulse of every Yankee game. When I was nine, ten, and eleven, I kept my radio with me all spring, summer, and fall listening to the ball games. If I could, I would more or less divorce myself from any family gathering or activity to stay home and watch the games. When I was growing up, all the Yankee home games were on TV. I would memorize every roster of every player in the American League. My father was a Yankee fan, but he didn't follow the details the way I did, so he used me to keep up with his team.

All this may have been a reaction to my brother, who was two years older and was an anti-Yankee fan. I don't know why Dodger and Giant fans felt this way. There's a cultural explanation, but I don't know what it is. When the Dodgers and Giants left town, their fans were so angry and they became anti-Yankees fans. Now tell me why they would hate the team that stayed and actually loved the teams that left, continue to follow them, and remain anti-Yankee fans. It made no sense to me whatsoever. I guess they felt stripped of their own teams. They always hated the Yankees so the only thing left for them to do was to actively hate the Yankees. Not just when they played the Dodgers and the Giants in the World Series, but all the time.

My brother and I would constantly argue. Now he's a Yankee fan and almost acts as if he always was. I don't really know what happened. I think he had kids who liked the Yankees and he felt he had to become politically correct. But when we were kids, he was Willie Mays and I was Mickey Mantle. No one was Snider. We didn't have any Dodger fans in the family. Dodger fans were looked down on. They were always called "the Bums," so we figured there must be some reason for people not to be Dodger fans.

When the Yankees lost, I was depressed. During my early years, the Yankees were in the World Series just about every year except 1959. I took every loss personally. I had to justify that loss to my brother and to any other family friends who vehemently hated the Yankees. They would say, "Well, what do you think of your Yankees now?" I would have to live with that as if it were a mark against my character. What am I supposed to say? I still think Whitey Ford was the best pitcher, even though it was said later that he cheated. They said he used to clip the baseball with his wedding ring.

**I would have to live with that as if it were a mark against my character. What am I supposed to say?**

My friends and I would play stickball in our large back yard in northern New Jersey. We would pretend to be all the teams but one of them would always be the Yankees. It would be one-on-one stickball so we memorized all the pitchers' motions and all the batters' swings and announced the games as though they were being played. Whoever was at bat got to announce the games. We emulated the three Yankee broadcasters at the time: Red Barber, Mel Allen, and Phil Rizzuto.

I can remember so many enjoyable afternoons listening to those voices while I was delivering the papers, or mowing the lawn. Back then, you didn't have headsets. You had to carry the radio along with you. I would be sitting on the tractor mowing the lawn and holding this beat-up radio in my hand.

The World Series was played in the daytime then, and some teachers would actually bring a TV into the classroom, and we would watch the games. Others would have a monitor in the hallway and one person would be allowed to post the inning-by-inning scores on a board out in the hallway, so you can imagine what the grab was for hall passes to get to the boys' room. Everybody needed to get to the rest room to check out the score. The humorless teachers wouldn't even let you pass on the score if you found it out on the way back from the restroom.

During the 1961 World Series, when I was in eighth grade, I had an afternoon paper route. I was sitting in the front row of the classroom, and a Yankee fan friend of mine was sitting in the back row with a transistor radio, monitoring the game. Somebody passed word up to me, "The Yankees are ahead 3-0." The boy just whispered the score to me, and I quickly turned my head around to face front. Our teacher was not a baseball fan, even during the World Series. She blasted out, "Where did you get that score?" I could never get in trouble at school because then I wouldn't be allowed to deliver my newspapers. I was the one well-behaved kid. My friend with the radio had a newspaper route, too, and he had to stay after school. I didn't say anything and I didn't get in trouble.

---

I know a great joke. This guy goes up to his rabbi and says, "Listen, I don't know what to do. I've got these season tickets, and I have tickets for the World Series, and the game is on the evening of *kol nidrei*—the night before the start of Yom Kippur when you begin fasting. I don't know what to do. Should I go to the game? Is that important to me? Or should I come to the services? What would you suggest, rabbi?" And the rabbi says to him, "Well, what do you think a VCR is for?" So the guys says, "Oh, you mean, I can tape your sermon?"

——JONATHAN MILLER, 41, Tel Aviv, Israel

---

# THE INTERNET?
# YOU MEAN THAT'S STILL AROUND?

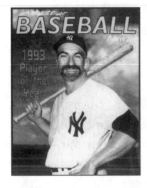

Vinny Natale

*Could Robert Heinlein have been thinking of Yankee fans growing up New England when he entitled his novel,* Stranger in a Strange Land? *Lifelong Yankee fans like fifty-two-year-old accountant Vinny Natale, of Rhode Island, know firsthand the cost of belonging to a scorned society.*

I grew up in Rhode Island—Red Sox country. In the third grade, I was constantly being asked if I was a Yankee fan or a Red Sox fan. I didn't know. I had no context to even make a decision. Finally, I got tired of being asked, and I just blurted out, "Yankee." I had nothing to base a loyalty on, but I just stayed a Yankee fan.

In 1960, when I was nine years old, my friend, David Izo, and I were at his house watching the World Series. The Yankees were playing the Pittsburgh Pirates. His grandmother was at home doing jewelry work at a table and she was watching the game with us. I still remember Tony Kubek being hit in the throat with the ball. Someone hit a ground ball, a double-play ground ball, and all of a sudden, it hit a pebble and went off his throat. He had to come out of the game, and actually he suffered a severe injury that really shortened his career. Years later, I bought the game on audio tape, and even though the Yankees lost, I've listened to it about three times because it was an extremely exciting game.

David's grandmother was really into the game, and we were so excited, making so much noise, that she couldn't hear the game and threw us outside. At that time, children obeyed adults without question. We went outside and played, and then we came back upstairs and we asked her who won. She said, "The Yankees." We were jumping up and down, hugging one another, but she was only teasing us.

She said, "No, the Pirates won." We were very upset. We went downstairs and I noticed—that year on the baseball cards they used to include decals with the cards—that David had a Pirates decal on his bicycle. I said to him angrily, "Get that thing off there."

> **That was my introduction to baseball. I just thought every year was going to be like that.**

It was very difficult to follow the Yankees in Rhode Island in the early 1960s. I lived two hundred miles away from the Bronx. I could never see them on TV, so I had to try to hear them on the radio. My father had one of the new transistor radios, and he would lend it to me. I would be able to listen to the Yankee game at night if the reception was clear, or if I put it next to a telephone or under the antenna wires that ran up outside the house. If the Yankees were playing the Red Sox, I would have the Red Sox broadcast on TV, and then on my left side, I would have the Yankee's broadcast on the radio, and on my right side, I would have the Red Sox broadcast on the radio. So I'd be getting three inputs of the game.

In the summer of 1961, my family stayed at the beach for about ten days. It was a long way away but we were on the water right opposite New York City so there was nothing to impede the radio signal. I could hear the games clearly at night, plus it was the 1961 season when the Yankees won the most games they'd ever won up until 1998. They had Mickey Mantle and Roger Maris hitting home runs like anything. That was my introduction to baseball. I just thought every year was going to be like that.

The announcers were Mel Allen, Red Barber, Jerry Coleman, and Phil Rizzuto. I liked Phil Rizzuto's story telling. It was always interesting. I thought Red Barber and Mel Allen were deadly dull. Rizzuto was definitely enthusiastic about the game whereas the other two were not. Back then, unlike now when they have national announcers do all the games, they had the announcers from the teams do the actual announcing for the World Series. I remember for the 1964 World Series, listening to Phil Rizzuto for the Yankees and Joe Garagiola for the Cardinals. They were totally entertaining. The next year, when I

*Joe Garagiola, Harry Caray, and Jack Buck, spring training, 1957*

was fourteen, **Joe Garagiola** became a Yankee announcer on the radio with Phil Rizzuto. At that point, I'd been a Yankee fan about four years. Those announcers really taught me a lot about baseball. They discussed things that no one else ever discussed.

I guess the radio's always been a constant for me and the Yankees. When Mantle retired, I listened to the entire ceremonies on the radio. But the year before, in May of '68, my friends and I were playing a pickup game on a Little League field. It was Memorial Day. I had my radio with me, which I always did. Mickey Mantle went five for five that day, and I remember being very excited. When I played softball in high school, I would have my radio on the field with me. Even now when I play softball, I have the radio on the field, a Walkman in my pocket, and I'm out in the outfield with the earplug. In 1990, the year the Yankees came in last place, I had the game on. One of my softball

In the 1970s, the Joe Garagiola Tucson Open was the only PGA Tour Event named after a major league player....Garagiola's wife, Audrey, once was the organist at Sportsman's Park in St. Louis....His son Joe Jr., former legal counsel for the Yankees, is the only General Manager in the history of the Arizona Diamondbacks.

teammates said, "Oh, I can tell you're a real fan, listening to the games while they're in last place." I heard David Cone's perfect game in 1997 while I was playing in the outfield.

I'm a self-employed accountant, and I sort of make it known now that I do not work any time the Yankees are playing in the post-season. If they're on TV, I am not working. I remember in the fall of 1976, I had a meeting scheduled with a client and a bank at what turned out to be the same time as a World Series game. I had to call my client and say that the meeting had to be rescheduled. One of the owners, who obviously wasn't any kind of a sports fan, said, "Oh, he can't make it because of some ball game!" But in the end, they rescheduled it. There was no way I was going to miss the game.

The Internet has been wonderful for me. My Yankee experience is no longer solitary, just listening to games by myself. Here I am with other Yankee fans listening on the radio or watching it on TV, and we're all excited, especially during the whole post-season. One time I was in a Yankee chat room with sixteen other fans from all over the world, including two fans in Italy. It was about five in the morning their time, and they couldn't get the games, so we would be telling them what was going on.

With the Internet, too, I'm now able to get all these Yankee articles from the New York papers that I never was able to get. Living where I do in western Massachusetts, you can get the New York papers, but only the early edition, and so you never get the stories of the games. That's why I get a ton of Yankee information from the Internet. In 2000, I got DirecTV, so now I get to see almost all the Yankee games. During the post-season, I get every single Yankee article. It sometimes takes me two hours to receive them all. Then I have to spend many, many more hours reading them. I start watching and listening to the pre-game half an hour before the game. The games are three and a half, four hours almost. Then there's the post-game. All told, during the post-season, that takes eight to nine hours a day of my time. I was not even disappointed that the Yankees lost the World Series last year because I was exhausted from the whole month of going to get these articles, reading the articles, just spending all this time with the Yankees. I was just exhausted.

# TURN YOUR RADIO ON

Theresa Aro

*Theresa Aro, 67, has migrated from New York, to Texas, and in recent years to Florida. Theresa is a retired credit operations employee.*

I never, ever remember not being a Yankee fan. The game was always on the radio. When we'd be at my grandmother's house listening to the game, the announcer would say, "Two and two," and my grandmother, who was from Italy, would say, "Four." Then the announcer would say, "Three and two," and she'd say, "Five." I'd say, "That's not what you're supposed to do," but she would do it anyway, just to tease me because I was so serious.

I grew up in East Harlem, and people always had radios blaring from the candy stores. I remember the time Allie Reynolds pitched two no-hitters in 1951. All the guys in the candy store were yelling and screaming. Of course, I couldn't get in the middle because I was not supposed to be around grown-up men. I remember how the guys in the neighborhood went wild and made speeches. It was funny. One guy, Johnny White, a blind man who was my friend's father, got up on a crate and started singing songs about the Yankees and about former Mayor LaGuardia.

To this day, it warms my heart to listen to a Sunday ball game on the radio, hearing the announcers, especially in the summertime, say, "There's a lazy fly ball." There's nothing like it in the world. I love baseball so much, especially when it was on radio because that's when your imagination began to run. I loved Mel Allen. I loved the "...going, going, going, gone," and "...for a box of White Owls," the cigars they were selling, and the ads for Ballantine beer.

My mother, Grace, became a huge Yankee fan after we bought a television sometime between 1951 and '52. We lived on 117th Street in Manhattan between Second and Third Avenues, and we had the first TV in our building. It was a Dumont, and then later we had a Muntz. The World Series was on TV so everybody from the building came to our apartment to watch it. Everybody would be yelling in the living room, and I guess it made her interested.

Before this, my mother did not understand what my excitement was about. Looking back, I remember that she had never understood why I loved the Yankees so much. "How could you listen to that radio?" she would yell. She would let me listen to the game, but she always talked about it annoying her. Then she became interested and she drove me nuts. She wanted me to explain everything to her. I began to take her to games. My mother was the firstborn of nine children of Italian immigrants, and didn't get to do anything or go anywhere when she was young. She was so funny because in later years, I'd call her up and she'd be home alone watching a Yankee game. One time I called her and said, "What are you doing?" She said, "I'm watching the Yankee game, and they stink. They're losing." Here was this woman in her seventies watching the Yankee game, getting upset because they were losing, and saying things like "they stink."

One time when my friends and I were about fourteen, we were at a game and somebody said that Vic Damone, the singer, was in the Stadium. Suddenly, we saw him and we all started running up the stairs. Some guy said to me, "Why don't you sit down?" I said, "Why don't you mind your own business?" We got to where Vic Damone was and he smiled and put his arm around me. I was on one side and my friend was on the other, and we walked with his arms around us, and I thought I had died and gone to heaven. He was so cute.

When I was sixteen years old in 1952, I quit school. I later went back and got my GED, went to college for a while, and had a pretty good career. But when I quit school, I was supposed to be out looking for a job. The problem was, it was World Series time. My friends were always older than me by a couple of years, and one of them said, "Let's not look for a job. Let's go to the World Series."

So we went to Brooklyn to Ebbets Field. When we arrived, the Yankees were behind, I think, 3-2. It was standing room only. We yelled and screamed and carried on. The Yankees won the game, and came from behind and won the Series, too. I couldn't go home and tell anybody that I went to the game because I was supposed to be out looking for a job. Years after, I did confess. When you're a kid like that, growing up in New York, there were many things you didn't tell your parents. Once you were out of the house, you were so independent.

> **When you're a kid like that, growing up in New York, there were many things you didn't tell your parents.**

At the time, Rocky Colavito was with the Tigers. I just got on Colavito, who was playing left field, because he struck out with men on base. In fact, I think he struck out four times that day. I just kept on him. Finally, he just turned and looked up at us with his hands on his hips. Well, that made that whole section get on his case. My sister wanted to drop dead she was so embarrassed. But it didn't make any difference, I just carried on so. Afterward, I was so ashamed. The funny part is that Colavito became a Yankee in 1968. It was the very end of his career and the Yankees were so bad then that he was brought in to pitch one time and was the winning pitcher.

Even during that period when the Yankees were terrible, I would go to games. I was a Yankee fan, and I didn't go because they were winning, but because I loved them so. I have always felt it's a privilege, an honor, to sit in the Stadium and watch the Yankees. I'll never forget the very first time I went to a night game. I never in my life saw anything so beautiful. The sight took my breath away.

I moved from New York to Denton, Texas in 1975. The company I worked for moved out of state and I didn't want to go. I had a friend in Texas and went for a visit, and I ended up moving there. I don't know what I was thinking.

I remained a Yankee fan. I went to the Ranger games when the Yankees were in town, and whenever the Yankees were on TV, I watched them, but it wasn't the same. It was difficult to go to the old Rangers stadium. I was there once in August and at ten o'clock at night it was still ninety-something degrees so it was miserable.

I don't know why I get so mad when the Yankees lose. I'm a darn fool. I kick and curse. I feel a dig in the pit of my stomach. I was raised in East Harlem and have been known to use every word known to man. I have the YES network—Yankees Entertainment System—on my DirecTV, and I will not watch the game replay if the Yankees lose. If they lose, I don't even want to read the newspaper the next day.

I've been here in Florida since 1999. I never got over leaving New York back in '75. Even now, I pine for New York City. I've always felt that there's nothing like a New Yorker. I guess that's my arrogance. I've wondered all these years why I left New York and my family. I am just dying to go back, but my sister is here in **Florida**, I have two dogs and a cat, and I own my house. Where would I go? Still, for a long time I went around carrying a Yankee schedule in my purse. That's how nuts I am.

> In the 1980s movie, *Back to the Future Part II*, Biff Tanner scans a sports almanac brought back from the future. Biff reads aloud, "Florida's going to win the World Series in 1997. Yeah, right." The Marlins were not a team at that time, but they did win the World Series in 1997.

# QUICK HITS AND INTERESTING BITS

## YANKEE RADIO

My grandfather was a power broker in the Bronx. He was friendly with the mayor of New York and all the borough presidents. One time, he brought me home a case full of Japanese transistor radios, which were a pretty new item back then. I can't tell you how many years that lasted me, listening to Yankee baseball with the radio under my pillow at night, letting my imagination run wild. My mom would yell at me to go to sleep all the time. She was a half-Irish, half-Jewish girl, but she was a Jewish mother in every respect, right down to the guilt.

———STEPHEN MASCIANGELO, 53, raised in the Bronx

My whole family was Yankee fans. We got a television set in 1955, but we used to listen to games on a big Motorola radio. I think if you have good announcers, listening to a ball game on radio can be more exciting than watching it on TV. We used to hinge on ever word, and if there was a pause, and you heard the crack of a bat, the next thing you knew, you were wondering if it was going over the fence. Everybody would be leaning toward the radio. You were waiting for the next thing and there were no visuals to distract you from that excitement. My father was a bridge and dock worker and he was in and out of work so I never, ever went to a game. That was a luxury we couldn't afford so radio was vital.

———KEVIN BRADY, 54, the Bronx

During my high school years, I went to a seminary up in Lake Saranac, New York, right near Lake Placid. Back then, the idea was that the earlier the Church convinced kids they really wanted to be priests, the better. As it turned out, my class had sixty kids and none of us became priests. There were kids from Boston, from Philly, from Canada, so there were a lot of the kinds of battles fans have in terms of which city is better, which team is better. But most of the arguments actually revolved around basketball because we all went home for the summer.

When we'd return to the seminary in September, it was very tough for a baseball fan. We tried all kinds of things to catch a game. We'd smuggle radios, but the priests had time on their side and would always find out. There was a TV and radio room, but it was always locked. A couple of times a week they'd let us watch select shows which they considered to be uplifting. A few friends and I had a master key of the entire building. We would open the door and then leave it that way, but the priests continuously checked the room, figuring, I guess, that sooner or later they would catch us, which they did at some point. We would sneak in there, not so much for live games because you couldn't spend that much time away without anybody finding out, but you could get reports on what had happened.

I was the kind of kid who always got caught. There was a kid who was really smart and really good at this kind of stuff. He had the master key. I had a copy. Throughout the time we were there, nobody ever suspected he had a key. Everybody sort of knew that I had a key. I've always been a bad liar. I've always been a bad sneak. When I was a kid my parents used to drink Pepsi. It was kept in the pantry. I would go and sneak a little sip, and every time I walked into the living room, the whole family would be watching TV or sitting around, and as soon as I walked in, they'd all turn around and say, "Oh, man, you've had the Pepsi again." Maybe I was like a "bandit priest," but I didn't feel guilty about having the key and sneaking in. I knew there was nothing wrong with me finding out how the Yankees were doing or what was going on in the world.

———DAN MCCOURT, 54, Central NJ

One time I was listening to Mel Allen broadcasting the game. He was going along his merry way, when all of a sudden there was another voice on the air, and it was using foul language. The voice was saying, "What the ____ is going on? What's Mel Allen doing on my telephone conversation?" Mel Allen couldn't hear any of this. What had happened was that the telephone lines had gotten crossed. It was funny because you could listen to Mel Allen describing the game in a normal way, going along very nicely, and this other guy is saying, "Mel Allen, get the ____ off my phone." Suddenly, Mel Allen got cut off, and he had no idea this was happening. This went on for a while. They cut him off, and they put him back on, and this guy was still on the air saying, "Mel Allen, get the _____ off my telephone."

—AL STAUFFER, 66, Phoenix, AZ

In 1956, the year the Yankees won the World Series and Don Larsen pitched the no-hitter, I was in basic training in the army. The sergeant came into our barracks at Fort Knox, Kentucky. He said, "This barracks is full of New Yorkers. How many of you are Yankee fans?" A lot of hands went up. He said, "Okay, come outside because the Yankees' pitcher is pitching a no-hitter, and we're going to let you listen to the game." That was great.

He hooked up the radio to the top of the barracks and all us Yankee fans, and even some who weren't who figured, "What the heck? It's better than staying inside," went out to listen. There were about eighteen or twenty of us. He made us stand at attention and look straight ahead and listen to the last three innings of that no-hitter. I guess the reason we had to stand at attention was that we were in basic training, and he just did it to be mean. We couldn't cheer. It was weird. That's the way they tried to break you down in the military—get you mentally tough. He watched us the whole time. But at least I got to listen to the no-hitter, standing at attention, in a military base at Ft. Knox, Kentucky in October of 1956.

After it was over, the sergeant thought he had done a wonderful thing. He had said, "I let you guys listen to the ball game," like he wanted everybody to be real pleased with him, but everybody was not pleased. At one point, the guys who weren't Yankee fans wanted to come out and listen, but weren't allowed. Instead, they were given work to do.

—JOE FOSINA, 65, New Rochelle, NY

In the Jewish religion, you're not allowed to turn off the lights on the Sabbath, so the synagogue employs a non-Jewish person who is allowed to break the laws of the Sabbath. This is an old Jewish tradition that there was always a helper who was not Jewish. There are some famous stories about certain baseball players who were Jewish who would refuse to play on Rosh Hashana or other Jewish holidays. Ron Blomberg was one. Sandy Koufax was another.

My father was a rabbi, and the caretaker of his synagogue was named Henry. He was an African-American. Henry was a really nice

*Jon Miller*

guy. He always had a little transistor radio in the back of the women's coat closet, and he would listen to the games. Since services were all day long, sometimes when people would go outside, I would go into the women's coat closet with Henry and we'd listen to the game. I never got in trouble for this. A few of the senior members of the committee of the board of trustees would sometimes come in, too. I don't think we had a minion in the closet but now that I think about it, it's pretty funny.

I was so crazy about the Yankees that I even went one day and donated blood for a blood drive just to get tickets. I got four box-seat tickets, but we didn't make it back to the game that day. We had a rehearsal with the band, and I was trying to bribe them all to come to the game with me. But no one could make it.

——JON MILLER, 41, Dumont, NJ

My father never took me to a Yankee game although he promised me he would. He never did. He was a big Yankee fan, too. It was really odd because he used to listen to the Yankee games—he was a strange bird—on a radio that got TV reception. He would put on the TV channel and then listen to the game at the kitchen table. I said, "Why don't you put it on the radio channel?" "No, no, no, I like to follow Phil Rizzuto," he'd say. In the old days, the announcers switched off play-by-play between the radio and the TV, and then they did color commentary. The Yankees had three announcers so wherever Phil Rizzuto was doing the play-by-play, my father would listen. I guess I got to like Phil Rizzuto from my father. It was funny because around the third inning they would switch who was doing what, and my father would switch, too.

——TOM LEMME, 43, raised in the Bronx

During the Vietnam War, I was in Phu Bai, near the imperial capital, about four hundred miles south of Hanoi. It was the air base for the imperial Hue. I wasn't in combat. I was in communications there, and twice a month we had guard duty up in this guard tower over an ammunition depot. This was 1972. It was a very dangerous place to be, especially if you really didn't know what you were doing with a gun.

I was sitting up in this watchtower and it was very, very lonely. Nothing really happened that night. I had a little radio with me. I could have been on the other side of the moon as far as I was concerned. This seemed as far away from reality as I could imagine.

The furthest thing from my mind was baseball, Yankees or otherwise. I turned the radio on. There is a twelve-hour time difference between New York and the other side of the world. It was two o'clock in the afternoon in New York, and on Armed Forces Radio, Phil Rizzuto was calling the Yankee game.

I can't explain how happy that made me. I would like to tell that to Phil Rizzuto one of these days. It brought me home for a couple of hours. I don't even know who won the game. I couldn't care less at the time. It was totally surreal. This was unbelievable, and it kept me up all night, which, of course, I was supposed to do anyway. It totally took my mind off the fear. I became immersed in the game, and even though I don't remember who won, the mere wonder of hearing Rizzuto's voice and the sound of the crowd was incredible. I was trying to capture the smell of the ballpark. It took me home for a couple of hours. It made me feel safe. It made me feel like the world was okay.

————STEVE KOHLREITER, 53, raised in Fort Lee, NJ

*I can imagine a world without baseball but I can't imagine wanting to live in one."*

—Leonard Koppett

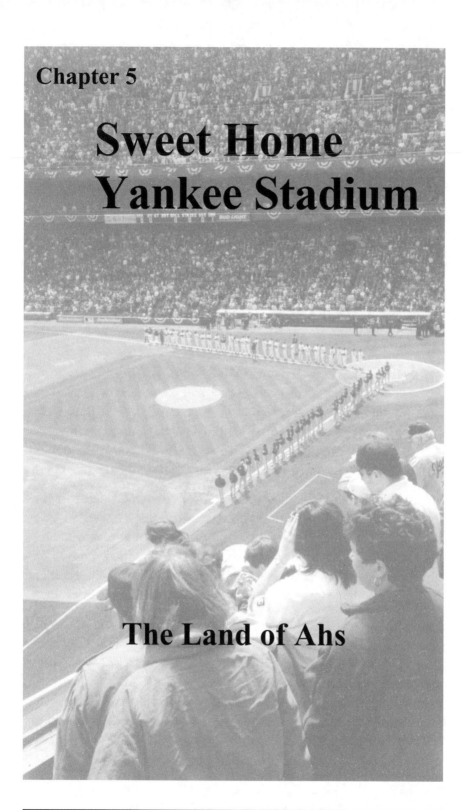

# Chapter 5

# Sweet Home Yankee Stadium

# The Land of Ahs

# HEY, BUDDY, CAN YOU LOAN ME A DIME...OR 4 TICKETS TO THE WORLD SERIES?

### Stan Starman

*Seventy-two-year-old Stan Starman grew up in Brooklyn as a Yankee fan amidst a sea of Dodger fans. Stan is retired and living in Tamarac, Florida.*

I lived in the Coney Island part of Brooklyn with my sister and brother-in-law because my mother had passed away in 1944 and my father in 1946. We lived in a four-family house, and in our building lived a fellow named Milton Guttenplan. We called him Mendy, and he was a Yankee fan. His father, Henry, was a rabid Yankee fan. I became a Yankee fan because of Mendy and his father.

Mendy would take the radio out in the back yard in the summer time and we would listen to the radio because we couldn't afford a TV yet. Twelve of us together couldn't have scraped up enough money to buy a TV. The radio had a very long extension cord because there were no portable radios then either. We learned the game highlights, the good and the bad about the teams, and what we hated about this player or that.

Henry Guttenplan, my friend's dad, would compare the players he grew up with to the players we were growing up with. He would always say, "Joe DiMaggio is great, but when I was a kid, we had Bob Meusel in center field." Although he wouldn't admit it, he knew DiMaggio was the greatest, but he just wouldn't let go. He said, "Bob Meusel was great in a clutch." We all know Joe DiMaggio was the better player.

When Mendy, my friend Donald and I went to Yankee Stadium, just being there, we were awestruck. In those days, when the game was over, all the fans went on the field. You can't do that today. There were two exits near the bleachers, and we would walk out that way because that's where the train station was at 161st Street and River Avenue. The bullpens were in front of the bleachers. You didn't have to but you could walk out through the exits just behind the bleachers. It was very homey.

> **It was very homey. The players didn't try to hide from the fans.**

The players didn't try to hide from the fans. There were no cops. We were able to talk to the players, and we spoke to all of them.

Except for Mendy and Donald, the rest of the world in Coney Island was made up of Dodger fans. We would make fun of each other during the season. It just so happened that the Yankees played the Dodgers in the 1947 World Series. I was sixteen years old. There was not much money around.

In those days, a candy store was like a luncheonette. The gentleman who owned the candy store, Buddy Schwartz, had just gotten out of the Coast Guard two years earlier when the war ended. He was a rabid Dodger fan so every time we would walk into the store, we would razz him and he would razz us. It was all friendly. We'd say things like, "The Dodgers, those bums," and "They can't wipe the shoes of DiMaggio," and he would say, "We've got Jackie Robinson." We'd say, "You can keep him. We've got Joe Gordon on second base who was the Most Valuable Player."

The '47 World Series was incredible. Bill Bevens almost pitched a no-hitter. Al Gionfriddo made the famous catch on Joe D. It went seven games and the last game was to be played in Yankee Stadium. Four of us were in the candy store, and we said what we wouldn't do to see tomorrow's game. The owner, Buddy, said, "Well, how about I send you four kids. I'll pay your way into the bleachers." Bleacher tickets for the World Series were a dollar, up from sixty cents. Buddy gave us four bucks. He gave us train fare, which was a nickel in those days. He gave us each another half a buck. So he gave us six dollars, plus train fare.

It was wonderful, but the problem was that we had to go early. We left around twelve thirty, one o'clock in the morning to get there because we knew there was going to be a line. When we got there, we were right—there were about a thousand people already waiting in line, and the box office didn't open for a long time. Luckily, it wasn't cold or damp. There was such great camaraderie among the people on the line. We were so excited to be going to a World Series game. Around four thirty, five o'clock in the morning, the milk company, Sheffield Farms, came around to everybody who was waiting in line and gave out pints of milk. The time went like nothing.

Inside the Stadium, the Dodger fans and the Yankees fans were razzing each other, but in a nice way. It wasn't cutthroat. It was a wonderful atmosphere. I had a seat adjacent to the Yankee bullpen, and I was talking to Joe Page, who was my favorite player. I said, "What's new?" And he said, "Everything is gonna be fine. We just had a little detour, but we'll take care of these guys today." It was wonderful. Frank Shea was the Yankees starting pitcher, but the Dodgers began to knock him around a little, and the manager brought in Joe Page. Page winked at me and jumped over the fence. That's why they called him the "Gay Caballero." He was a good-looking guy. I was talking to the bullpen coach and he said, "He'll do okay. If he comes back out, I'll break a bat over his head."

Page walked in and they couldn't touch him. That was the end of the game and the World Series, and it was just pandemonium. We ran out onto the field. Everybody was hugging each other. It was a wonderful day, and my best game ever. I didn't get his autograph that day. I didn't have anything to sign. I never thought I would have the opportunity to be that close.

When my friends and I got home, we went to see Buddy to thank him. I wanted to give him the program I had gotten. He said, "You keep it. Your team won." He was really a great guy. Growing up with no money was not easy. It's still not. But when you had people like that, it made life a lot easier.

# IT'S HARD TO CHEER
# WITH A BROKEN HEART

Peter Marino Jr.

*Peter Marino Jr., 45, hails from Manhattan, where he catches baseballs and Opening Days.*

I was an altar boy when I was eleven or twelve years old. One day, a couple of priests, a few nuns, and some chaperones took us to a Yankees-Red Sox game at Yankee Stadium. Of course, in those group trips, you always had the worst seats. They were always in the upper deck. The Church wasn't going to buy box seats. I remember a big fight broke out. Here we are, all altar boys, and we're yelling, "—— 'em up. Beat the —— out of them. Get that ——. Kick him in his butt." And all the nuns were saying, "Quiet, quiet boys, please. You're a church group."

Mantle was on his way down when I was growing up. He was in his last four years. The Yankees were bad. At the ages of eight, nine, ten, and eleven, my father would take me to games, and I would hope that the Yankees would win while I was there and that Mickey Mantle would hit a home run. In the fifteen or so games my father took me to, I never saw Mickey Mantle hit a home run. Then on Memorial Day, I asked my father if I could go to the game with friends. He said, "How old are these people?" I said, "Oh, they're older guys." Actually, they were twelve-year-olds and I was eleven.

It was 1968, Mantle's final season, and what happened that day was Mickey Mantle went five for five, hit two home runs, a double, two singles, five RBIs, and the Yankees beat the Washington Senators 13-5. Now, Mantle sat out the second game, but with two outs and a man on base—the Yankees were losing either 2-1 or 3-2—Gene Michael was the batter. All of a sudden, who comes out to pinch hit for whoever was up next? Mickey Mantle. All we hoped for was for Gene Michael to get on base somehow, and if Mantle hit a home run, he would complete a doubleheader sweep. Of course, Gene Michael looked at strike three. The twelve-year-old who I made friends with that day, the leader of that crew, was a kid named Jimmy DeBlasé.

> **I must have gone to three hundred Yankee games in all those years after 1964, and I never caught a baseball.**

I must have gone to three hundred Yankee games in all those years after 1964, and I never caught a baseball. Opening Day, 1999. I'm late. I arrive in the bottom of the first. I had missed the 1998 championship flag being raised because a friend of mine made me late. So here it is, bottom of the first, Chuck Knoblauch fouled off a ball really nowhere near me, but the ball squirted out from under the box seats. There was nobody near me, and I dove on the floor, dove on the ball like a hockey goalie. I dropped it. I fumbled it. I swatted it away. I skinned my knee. I ripped my pants. I cracked somebody in the chest going for the ball. It was either an eight-year-old boy or an eighty-year-old man. To this day, I don't know. I finally picked it up.

I heard this voice yell out, "You big doofus, that's the first ball you've caught since Little League." Who was it? Jimmy DeBlasé. Very funny. He was sitting in the box seats and he was a very boisterous guy, a real leader. I hadn't seen him in a few years, and I was trying to get down to him. The guard said, "No, you don't have a ticket. You can't go down there." Jimmy yelled, "That's my friend, Peter. You let him down. Come on."

Jimmy came up himself and just opened the chain and the usher didn't say anything. I went down. Jimmy told his friends, "This is my friend Peter. This is the first ball he caught since Little League, and the first ball he ever caught at Yankee Stadium."

Now, Jimmy DeBlasé was with a bunch of stockbrokers, led by a good friend of mine, Ralph Figliuolo. Ralph asked me, "Why don't you come out with all of us stockbrokers? It's on the company." Fine.

Before I left the Stadium, though, I found Joe Torre's sister, the nun, Sister Marguerite, and asked her if she would bless my **foul ball**. She carries holy water with her and she sprinkled some on it. To this day, you can still see the water stain it made.

So the bunch of us guys went out to a nice restaurant, and we made it a tradition where every Opening Day, I would pay my way in and then meet up with Jimmy DeBlasé and Ralph Figliuolo.

It wasn't a long tradition. We went in 1999, 2000, 2001, then, lo and behold, my friend Jimmy DeBlasé was killed in the World Trade Center. He worked for Cantor Fitzgerald. It was a friendship that began in 1968 at that Memorial Day doubleheader.

At the memorial service, I saw Ralph, and he said, "The tradition continues, and Jimmy will be there in our hearts. From now on you have Jimmy's ticket."

A major league game uses 80 balls…Each one lasts an average of five pitches…Major League Baseball uses 29 tons of balls each year.

# IT WAS A FOOLPROOF PLAN AND WE WERE THE FOOLS WHO PROVED IT

Vaughn Sandman

*Twenty-seven year-old Vaughn Sandman has had more life experiences than most men twice his age. Now a television writer in Los Angeles, the Manhattan-raised Sandman's love of the Yankees proves that team loyalty and family dynamics can make for interesting bedfellows.*

My Yankee fandom started with Thurman Munson's death. It's the first thing I really remember. I was three years old and I remember the headline in the New York Post that day. My brother, who is twenty months older than I, was a huge Thurman Munson fan. I was a big Reggie fan. When I heard that Thurman had died, I was in the lobby of my apartment building on the Upper East Side, and the doorman had the paper in front of him and the radio on.

I was taken to my first Yankee game the year before by the woman who was my mother's helper. She had grown up a Brooklyn Dodgers fan from a large Polish Catholic family in Brooklyn. I guess more than a few people switched allegiances from the Dodgers to the Yankees as opposed to the Mets. So between this woman and my mother's boyfriend, and also occasionally my father, I was going to Yankee Stadium ten to fifteen times a year from the time I was three or four years old. I loved riding the subway. Yankee Stadium was always pretty much my favorite place to be even though as a seven-year-old kid, I took for granted that I was going to get burned by somebody's cigarette every single time I went to a game.

Interestingly, the Yankees are the only New York sports team that I ever cared about. Both sets of grandparents lived in the Philadelphia area, my parents both went to the University of Pennsylvania, and I was always a Flyers and Sixers fan. When I was nine or ten, my grandparents took me to a baseball game in Veterans' Stadium in Philadelphia. They asked me if I had a good time. I said, "Yes, but there was something that puzzled me." They asked me what it was. I asked them, "How come there were no moments, let alone three or four moments, when everybody stood up on their seats to watch a fight in the stands?"

I absolutely thought that fights in the stands were as much a part of baseball games as da-da-da dat-de-do–CHARGE. Without fail, there were three or four times in every single Yankees game of my childhood when two people would start swinging, everyone would stand up and security would rush in and start dragging people away. Also, two or three times a game someone would jump out on the field. Of course, I became a tremendous Yankee fan in the late 1970s, early 1980s, at a time that coincided with the only real downtime of the franchise.

> **I absolutely thought that fights in the stands were as much a part of baseball games as da-da-da dat-de-do–CHARGE.**

This period in New York exists for me in a very surreal time capsule-like space because the New York that I grew up in was an uncivilized place where the police pretty much let you do whatever you wanted. My mother remarried and I moved out of New York in 1989, right around the time New York really started changing. Thereafter in Mayor Giuliani's New York, you didn't fight in the stands at Yankee Stadium. The whole texture of the crowd became different. I got a citation for drinking a Budweiser outside of Madison Square Garden. I said to the policeman, "What do you mean? It's in a bag." I was just incredulous.

The day the Yankees clinched the Eastern Division championship in 1980 in Yankee Stadium, we were sitting at the top of the left-field bleachers in an area that's now fenced in, above the Con Ed sign and below the scoreboard. There was a little ledge that had about four or five feet of space. It's now fenced off, but at the time I remember being up there with my brother and a few other kids who were small enough to fit in there, just dancing when they won the first game of a double header and clinched the pennant. Then in Game 2, Graig Nettles made his triumphant return from his battle with hepatitis. The Yanks lost the playoffs that year, signed Winfield, lost the World Series the next year, and that was it.

Somehow I got tickets to Opening Day in 1996, the day the game was played during a driving snowstorm. It was the oddest thing. I'd never seen a baseball game in a **snowstorm**, and a lot of people stayed home. It was a rather odd affair. Someone would hit a popup in the infield, and against the backdrop of the white sky, the players couldn't see the ball, so they were dropping pop-ups. The snow accumulated a little bit, but, of course, it didn't look like one of those crazy football games you see. The field was still more green than white. It wasn't like a heavy winter snowstorm, though it became more significant later in the game. I recall they actually played the whole game.

The cool part of this story is that they flashed on the scoreboard the message that in appreciation of the fans who had come out and stayed to support the Yankees in this weather we could turn in our tickets for free tickets to one of a series of games they posted. I'd only seen that once, and it had been during a doubleheader in 1982 when the Yankees got beaten in both ends by about twenty-eight runs. It was about six or seven hours long, with the Yankees getting shellacked something like 14-2 and 10-0. They flashed a message on the scoreboard, literally, that Mr. Steinbrenner was so embarrassed with the play of his team that he would exchange these tickets for tickets to another game. We thought it was pretty cool and kept the stubs as an opportunity to go again in the future.

The 1996 season was very special for the Yankees because they won their first World Series since 1978. I was in my junior year of college at Brown University. I used to sit in my dorm room and listen to John Sterling and Michael Kay on the radio. I had found an AM radio

In the late 1950s, the Washington State Cougars had a home game during a blizzard. The paid attendance was 1. The Athletic Department gave that paying fan a lifetime pass to Washington State football games.

affiliate in Rhode Island that broadcast Yankee games, and I would listen to the games as I wrote my papers.

To knock out my political science requirements, I wound up taking a course on Mexican labor relations. It wasn't boring, but it was very technical and the reading wasn't by any means fun. The professor was a visiting professor from the University of Connecticut, a younger associate professor type and not particularly uptight. I remember calling him and saying, "Okay, what's the absolute last conceivable moment you will accept a paper from me?" He said, "Well, Tuesday at 5:00 p.m. I'm leaving my office, and I'm going back to my home in Connecticut, and that's it."

I was doing the math in my head, and I thought, "There's no way I'm going to have a good paper by then." I said, "What if I gave it to you the next day, but I dropped it off at your house in Connecticut?" He was surprised and stunned, but logically he wasn't going to finish reading all the papers before then, so he said, "If you really want to, fine."

I had these ticket stubs from the day of the snowstorm, and I called my brother who was at Harvard at the time, and I said, "Okay here's the deal. I have to be in Connecticut tomorrow to turn in a paper by three or four p.m. so we're cashing in our "snow" tickets and making this an excuse to celebrate the end of my semester and going to the Yankee game." I stayed up all day and all night writing this paper and finished it maybe around one or two in the afternoon. My brother was waiting in Providence for me to finish, anxiously wanting to get to the game. I printed it out, hopped in my truck, and started driving. I had to find the professor's mailbox somewhere in Storrs, Connecticut and haul butt to the stadium.

We made it and wound up in some seat in the right field upper deck for a Yankee game against the **Mariners**. I remember Bernie Williams wasn't playing that night for whatever reason, which was really disappointing to me. Gerald Williams was playing in his place in

> During the Seattle Mariners first year in 1977, they measured the distance to the fences in fathoms. A fathom is 6 feet. For instance, where a park may have a sign that denotes 360 feet, the Kingdome would have the number 60.

center field. The second batter of the game was Alex Rodriguez of the Mariners who was a rookie at the time. He hit about the hardest screaming line drive to dead center field that one could imagine. Gerald Williams turned and went back on it, and I and everybody in the stadium said to ourselves, "Okay, that's a triple. There's no way." Williams ran like some kind of demon and at the absolute last second jumped straight up and back toward the center field wall behind him and lunged up his glove and made one of the top three or four catches I've ever seen. I was thinking, "Wow! That's got to be significant."

**For some reason, it just felt like that was going to be the night he did it. We weren't saying anything, but the whole place was on its feet for maybe the last three or four innings.**

By the third or fourth inning, Dwight Gooden, who was pitching, had settled down, and after giving up a couple of walks, actually started to strike people out. Lo and behold, he kept going, and that was the night Dwight Gooden threw his no-hitter, which is the only one I have ever seen. It was just one of those nights. I don't think I'd ever been anywhere where a pitcher got past the fourth or fifth inning with a no-hitter intact. For some reason, it just felt like that was going to be the night he did it. We weren't saying anything, but the whole place was on its feet for maybe the last three or four innings. One of the things that made that game so special was the Yankees only had a 1-0 lead as Gooden tried to work the top of the ninth. I think he walked somebody and he hit somebody and there was a stolen base.

With the no-hitter intact, the Mariners had runners on first and third with one out. He was clearly gassed. He had thrown a hundred and twenty five or a hundred and thirty pitches, more than he had probably thrown since he had joined the Yankees. Even though he still had his no-hitter going, he was clearly losing it, and clearly there was the concern that not only might he not get this no-hitter because with one base hit, they could lose this game, and that it might be a better scenario to go to John Wetteland. This was an added intrigue.

I had often wondered whether I would see a no-hitter or catch a foul ball first. I've still never caught a foul ball. I'm an agnostic, but I do believe that there are certain odd rhythms that we fall into in this world. The fact that I was at Yankee Stadium for Gooden's no-hitter on freebie tickets from the day we had sat through Opening Day in the snow and the fact that I had had no concrete intention of when I might use those tickets is really amazing to me. I had just needed an excuse to rationalize driving to Connecticut to be able to get an extra day on this paper.

I've heard rooting for the Yankees compared to rooting for General Motors, that it's not really fun. I have to admit that I'm not particularly excited about this baseball season just because of the way the team is stacked, it takes all the fun out of it. I feel that there are a lot of things wrong with baseball that have led to this circumstance. In 1995, I would have said, "I don't give a —— about this inequity. I want the Yankees to win," but now that I've been to five World Series games and seen some pretty incredible things, I still want them to win, but it would be more fun if I felt like it weren't a situation where either they win and everybody says, "Well of course," or they lose and everybody complains.

*Baseball gets in your blood and stays with you far longer than any other sport.*

*—Jack Buck*

# GOING TO OPENING DAY IS LIKE PLAYING HOOKY FROM LIFE

Steven Kohlreiter

*Steve Kohlreiter, 53, was raised in Fort Lee, New Jersey. He owns a business telephone system company and lives in Washington Township, New Jersey.*

Growing up in New Jersey, I was friends with these kids whose uncle was the head of the Vito Genovese crime family. I'm literally talking about the top guy. These guys, of course, had primo seats behind the Yankee dugout. So I'd go to at least a dozen games a year courtesy of them and sit in the best seats in the house. They had some kind of phony corporation because in those days the names of the corporations were actually attached to the box itself. One of the guys who used to go to the games assassinated somebody, and it was all over the front page of the newspapers. My friends and I joked about it because this guy was going in for an indictment or something like that. All of a sudden, he collapsed in the courtroom with a phony heart attack, because as they were wheeling him out to the ambulance, he was smiling for the cameraman. He hadn't wanted to testify in court.

I would ask my friends what their dad did for a living. They would say, "Well, he owns every vending machine in New Jersey." That was their father's answer. When we were sitting in those boxes, we knew enough not to talk about anything. I certainly knew enough not to talk. But it didn't matter to me. I just wanted to go to the games.

My family lived in Fort Lee, which was within walking distance to the George Washington Bridge. If you made the connections right, you could take a bus across the bridge, hop on the subway and literally be at Yankee Stadium in fifteen minutes. I wouldn't dream of letting my thirteen year-old daughter go anywhere by herself, but in those days, it was different. I used to go to the games myself or with a friend. It was very cheap to get across the bridge, and the subway was fifteen or twenty cents. A dollar thirty-five to a dollar-fifty got you unreserved seats behind the plate, the same seats today they call box seats. I'd get a doubleheader out of the deal on Sundays.

My parents didn't give me my money. I had to work for it. I had a paper route and a dog-walking route specifically to have money to go to Yankee games. I couldn't care less about anything else.

I delivered *The Bergen Record* newspaper in high-rise apartments. In those days, it was strictly an afternoon paper, Monday through Saturday. I had a little laundry cart and I could deliver the papers in fifteen minutes. I would tie up the elevator, run up and down the hall, and fling the papers in front of the doors.

> **I still play hooky whenever possible if I can get away from work and make Opening Day.**

I had this little lady who had a French poodle I was supposed to walk. I would take the poodle down to the basketball court, tie up the dog, and play basketball for thirty minutes. She finally came down and caught me, and that was the end of that.

I probably made about twenty-five bucks a week. I was rolling in dough. I could go to games every week. I spent the rest of the money eating French fries or hot dogs at Hiram's or go to the movies, but mostly, I went to the Yankee games.

Every Opening Day I would cut school to go to the game. My mother would first make me lie. She would say, "Steve, how was school today?" knowing full well I didn't go to school. "Fine," I'd say. But my mother was onto me. She'd say, "Who won the game?" Going to Opening Day was a religious thing for me. I still play hooky whenever possible if I can get away from work and make Opening Day.

About a year ago, I took my wife's parish priest to a game. During the game, this really drunk guy fell out of the upper deck and landed on the screen above home plate, motionless and sprawled out. He looked exactly like Jesus Christ on the cross. I was so uncomfortable. This was about the most uncomfortable sight I've ever seen in my life. I tried not to turn my eyes to the priest.

The players all stopped. Everything stopped. Everybody was looking at the guy. Finally, I built up the nerve to turn to the right to face the priest. He said to me, with a big smile on his face, "This guy is drunk, and there's nothing wrong with him." Then, sure as heck, a couple of minutes later, the guy started crawling up the screen. He was okay. He had just fallen out of the seats. He was nuts. I just didn't know how to react with the priest there. If anyone else had been sitting with me, I probably would have said some colorful things, but I felt that I had to be on my best behavior.

The beauty of baseball and of the Yankees is that no matter who you are, what you are, what kind of background you are, how much education you have, how much money you have or don't have, the common thread of loving them is there. It's the one element that unifies. There is no race when you walk into a baseball game. Everybody's the same. I really mean that. It's unbelievable. People who would normally never talk to anybody anywhere else will talk to each other at baseball games.

# KEEP YOUR EYE ON THE BALL...
# NOT YOUR EYE ON THE BALL

Stephen Masciangelo

*Fifty-three-year-old Steve Masciangelo grew up near Fordham Road and the Grand Concourse in the Bronx. Steve, now living in Aquebogue, on Long Island, recently retired after thirty-two years of teaching.*

In 1986, six suburban boys in our thirties—three Italian boys and three Jewish boys—from Sussex County went to Yankee Stadium for a nice evening. In the tenth inning of an extra-inning game against the Detroit Tigers, Dale Berra, Yogi's son, hit one into the left field stands in our direction. My good friend Mark Flaum, stood on the seat, screamed, "I got it," and the ball hit him right in the eye. He started pouring blood. A woman two rows behind us jumped over the seat, jumped in Mark's lap, said, "I'm a nurse," and put something up to his head to stop the bleeding.

They took him by wheelchair to the Yankee training room. The remaining five of us waited outside the trainer's room. A doctor came out and said, "Is there a Steve here?" I said, "That's me." The doctor said, "Well, your friend is badly injured, and he refuses to leave unless he gets the ball he was hit with signed by Dale Berra." They temporarily patched him up, and told him he needed plastic surgery. The closest place was Harlem Hospital

Now, it was after midnight, and the six of us drove to Harlem looking for Harlem Hospital. We got him there, and they were about to treat him when a guy came in with a bullet in his eye. Mark couldn't get treated, so by 3:00 a.m. we were out in West Islip, Long Island, at Good Samaritan Hospital.

Mark didn't have permanent eye damage. As a matter of fact, we saw the incident on the next day's evening news. The ball had bounced on

*Mark Flaum*

a fly directly off his eye into the bullpen. This is how hard he was hit. It happened to be Dale Berra's last major league home run. He retired two weeks later. It was quite an evening. Mark had also been hit on the head during batting practice.

Mark subsequently did get the ball, signed by Berra. He wrote a letter to stadium management, and they sent him a couple of **free tickets** for another game.

The prized item in our neighborhood in those days was a Spaldeen rubber ball. My father worked for the city, and in emptying garbage cans, he would find some. At the end of the week, he would bring home maybe thirty or forty. My mom would take the Spaldeens to the kitchen sink and scrub them before I was allowed to play with them.

My mother's brother was mentally retarded and disabled in many ways. I really am loathe to use the term idiot savant, but the only two things he knew in life were every line of dialogue from *The Honeymooners* and every Yankee statistic.

He did attend some games, but to be honest, it was rather embarrassing to go with him. He would pick a person out of the crowd, find some characteristic, and heckle the person throughout the game. One time, a guy had an extremely long beard. My uncle had some intelligence, and he said the guy looked like a cross between Mitch Miller and some rube that just came off the farm. He kept screaming "Mitch Rube" at the guy.

Former Pirates and Rockies manager Jim Leyland was a second-string catcher in high school in Perrysburg, Ohio. The starting catcher was Jerry Glanville. When Glanville, a huge Elvis Presley fan, became an NFL Head Coach, he would leave four free tickets at "Will Call" every game for Elvis. When he stopped leaving tickets in the mid-1990s, he said "I think Elvis is dead. When he heard his daughter married Michael Jackson, it probably killed him."

The only thing he was really cogent talking about was baseball. Whenever you'd start talking about Yankees, he would just come out with something like, "Roger Maris had thirty-four doubles in 1962." Very much like the Dustin Hoffman character in the movie *Rain Man*. My uncle knew his baseball. He loved the game.

He was sixty-four when he died, and he had more disabilities than I can begin to tell you. It was amazing that he could function in some ways. He held a job for forty-one years. He took me to my only game at the Polo Grounds. For his funeral, my mother had him laid out in his Yankee jacket with his Yankee pin. Some people sent big flower arrangements decorated with the New York Yankees logo.

As soon as our son, Jeff, was old enough, I began to take him to games, sometimes with my father. Well, Jeff went into the army and was sent to the war in Bosnia. While he was in Bosnia, my dad passed away, so Jeff felt that when he returned, on his first night, that in honor of his grandpa, he'd like to go to Yankee Stadium.

It was an interleague game against the Atlanta Braves. Jeff was emotionally winding down from Bosnia because he had been through some horrible stuff. He had cleared mine fields, and he was among the first hundred U.S. troops into the country, so unfortunately he had been exposed to these factories that were filled with massacred bodies, and he was trying to make an emotional transition. I think he knew that Yankee Stadium was the place to do that. It was sort of the core of the male chain in our family. I have photographs of both myself and my dad out in Monument Park, and I have pictures of my son right near the Yankee dugout on the night he came back from Bosnia.

We went early and had a burger and a beer at The Yankee Tavern, and then we just sat back and enjoyed the heck out of the game. As the evening wore on, he became more himself. I really think being at Yankee Stadium, watching a game, was cathartic for him. It was a really good choice of what to do on his first night home.

# BLEACHER CREATURES!! WE HAVEN'T SEEN ANYTHING THIS CRAZY SINCE THE MICHAEL JACKSON INTERVIEW

Keith de Candido

*Keith de Candido, 33, has lived all his life in New York City, where he is a novelist. At Yankee Stadium, he sits in the boisterous Section 39 with the rest of the notorious rooters known as "The Bleacher Creatures."*

The tradition of the hard-core fans in Section 39 of the bleachers goes back a ways. Section 39 encompasses everybody who sits in the right-field bleachers. There is a certain group of regulars who go to every home game, who hang out together, who lead the roll call, for example.

The roll call is a big deal. At the top of the first inning of every Yankee home game, the Bleacher Creatures, as they're known, call out the name of each player, starting with Bernie Williams in center field. One fan starts and then everybody follows. They call out the name of each player and keep calling it out until the player acknowledges us with just a quick wave or wave of the glove. It goes like this: "Ber-nie." Clap-clap. "Ber-nie." Clap-clap. Once the player acknowledges, then depending on the mood of the fans, we either move to left or right field players. How the cheer sounds depends on the rhythm and cadence of the player's name. Like the call for Alfonso Soriano goes, "Sor-e-an-o" clap-clap. Clap-clap-clap. Derek Jeter's goes the same way. Robin Ventura's is more basic: "Ven-tur-ah, Ven-tur-ah." The players always respond. The only ones whose names we don't call are the pitcher and catcher because they're busy. Of course, if there's a pitch being thrown, players won't acknowledge until the

*The "Bleacher Creatures" of Section 39*

pitch is completed. The only exception is David Wells. David Wells always gets a roll call when he pitches.

I chose to sit in Section 39 for a variety of reasons. One is financial; the seats are only about eight dollars per game. The view is not the best in the Stadium—for that you have to go to the upper deck behind home plate, but the only part of the field we can't see is right up against the wall in right or center field. Other than that, we have a clear view.

It's great to sit among this group. At any baseball game, there are going to be people who are just there for fun, or because it's a nice thing to do, or the kids insisted, or it's a good way to kill a few hours on a Sunday. In the bleachers, you get the hard-core fans. These are the serious Yankee fans who are there all the time, who are paying attention to the game. No matter what little else they might have in common, a whole bunch of people are united by their love the Yankees. You don't see people in the bleachers sitting around talking about what they're having for dinner that night, or chatting about what a pain in the butt the boss has been at work this week. I've noticed that everybody in that section is focused much more on the game than people sitting in the seats that have backs.

Most of the hard-core bleacher fans are male, although there are some women. One woman, whose real name I don't know, is referred to as "Da Queen Bee." She has been going to Yankee games for twenty-five years and has been sitting in the bleachers in Section 39 for nineteen of them. She's sort of the den mother of us all.

> **The fans in the bleachers will sometimes be rowdy because people who are having a lot of fun tend to get rowdy.**

Da Queen Bee usually wears the Section 39, Bleacher Creature T-shirt like everybody else. It says, "Bleacher Creatures" on the front, and on the back there's a number 39 with the word "Section" above it. Da Queen Bee has an American flag that she holds up during the singing of the national anthem and "God Bless America" during the seventh inning stretch. She's just a good fan and has taken it upon herself to maintain order among us. She's friends with all the police who are stationed in the bleachers. She'll point out if somebody is getting out of control. She'll make sure everyone sits in the right place. She's tough, but she has a good sense of humor and doesn't back down if somebody tries to give somebody else a hard time. The fans in the bleachers will sometimes be rowdy because people who are having a lot of fun tend to get rowdy.

Some Yankee fans probably think we're all jerks, but the way we act is part of the passion that we all have for the team. Actually, a small number of fans, maybe half a dozen, do most of the shouting, but everyone gets swept up in the fun. I remember one time some people there were complaining about the heckling, saying we weren't paying attention to the game. They were completely missing the point that everybody was paying close attention, in fact, more attention than they were. They threw a pall over our sense of fun.

There is a seat in Section 39, second one over from the right-field side as you face the right-field bleachers, where a guy named Mr. Ramirez used to bring a cowbell and lead fans in chants and cheers.

When he died about ten years ago, the Yankees actually put a little gold plaque on his seat.

We have certain codes of behavior. For instance, it's fine if someone wants to talk on a cell phone before or after the game or even between innings, but if a person is on a cell phone while actual baseball is happening on the field, then everyone around the person will yell, "Get off the phone." They make a lot of noise and make it really difficult for the person to talk.

We also make fun of the people who sit in box seats. We'll say something simple and direct like, "Box Seats Suck." The people in the box seats will attempt to retaliate by pointing out that they can buy beer, which management banished from the bleacher section several years ago. The bleacher fans still get rambunctious but they're not a danger to anyone. I think management felt that so long as they stay sober, they will stick to heckling and yelling but nothing worse. I remember one Opening Day, we started the "Box Seats Sucks," chant, and the people in the boxes all held up their beer. We responded by accusing them of being alcoholics.

My favorite is the ritual heckling of the opposing team's right fielder. My absolute favorite heckling happens when the Mariners are in town. Ichiro Suzuki speaks very little English, so most of the heckling is lost on him. One time, somebody went to the trouble of finding a **Japanese** heckle. It was very simple: "Bak ah Ichiro." I asked a friend of mine who speaks Japanese what it meant, and he told me that it basically means, "Ichiro is stupid." It's a double pun because the way Japanese is pronounced, "Bak–ah–ito" means "stupid person," which is very close to how you would say "Bak–ah–Ichiro" in Japanese. The heckler showed incredible resourcefulness.

Anytime somebody shows at Yankee Stadium up wearing the paraphernalia of another team, particularly Mets or Red Sox, they're in

> The Yomiuri Giants are sometimes called "The New York Yankees of Japan." They have won the most pennants and have the deepest fan base in Yakyu (Japanese Baseball)....The Nippon Ham Fighters give free tickets to foreigners on "Yankees Day."

for a world of heckling. Most of them are smart enough to just sit, smile and take it. Usually we'll yell, "Boston sucks!" or "Mets sucks!" I admit, a lot of the heckling doesn't rise above the third-grade level, and that's part of the charm. People mostly shout things like, "Hey, whoever's in right field, I got a message from your mother. She says, 'Moo.'"

One day I came home and there was a package from the Yankees with a nice little postcard from George Steinbrenner, though it was probably written by one of his secretaries. It was sent to all bleacher season-ticket holders, thanking us for being "true Yankee fans." It was a home-plate shaped pen with the Yankee logo that read, "Yankee Stadium Bleacher Creatures," with a rendition of three fans holding a sign saying, "Go Yankees!"

I was really impressed. The Yankees make the least amount of money off the bleacher season tickets and they make less money from us on concessions because the expensive concession beer isn't sold there. Despite this, they understand these are arguably their most dedicated fans.

# AURELIO RODRIGUEZ' CARDS ARE SELLING LIKE HOTCAKES— $2 A STACK

### Leo Egan

*Leo Egan, 43, was raised on Long Island. He now lives in Forest Hills, NY, where he and his wife own a lighting and furniture business.*

One of my earliest Yankee memories was driving to Yankee Stadium in 1967 when I was seven to see a doubleheader between the Yankees and the Detroit Tigers. We were crossing the Triborough Bridge and it was about ninety-eight degrees with no air conditioning in stop-and-go traffic. The song playing on the radio was "Hot Town, Summer in the City." The Tigers had just about the best team then. They had Dick McAuliffe and Norm Cash and Mickey Lolich—a great squad. They pounded the Yankees twice. Every time I hear that song, I remember exactly where I was and how hot I was. That day never, ever seemed to end.

One of my biggest memories of seeing baseball in person, though, is of how green the field at the stadium looked when you first came out of the portal. It was always greener than any grass you'd ever seen. Also, it was amazing just being in the place you watched on TV so much. It was an experience that took my breath away. I used to look forward for weeks before I would go to a ball game, whether to watch the Mets or the Yankees, but when I was at **Shea Stadium**, I didn't root as much. I more just took in the atmosphere. When it came to the Yankees, I lived and died by every play.

> During a 1979 Jets game against the Patriots at Shea Stadium, a remote controlled model airplane crashed into the stands at half-time, hit a Patriots fan and killed him.

I used to listen to the games on the radio because only about fifty or sixty games were broadcast on television each season. Also, my parents used to send me to bed at eight-thirty or nine o'clock at night. I would turn on the radio and listen to the game and try to picture what was actually going on.

I bought the game called Strat-O-Matic baseball. I used to pit the Yankees against other teams. I would give myself the American League and I would get a few of the National League teams that happened to be good from the year before, and I would just play games, but the American League team was always the Yankees. I would never play the Oakland Athletics against the **Kansas City Royals**. I couldn't care less about that. When you're playing by yourself, of course you're not going to make the right move for the Cincinnati Reds to beat the Yankees. You're not going to bring in their ace relief pitcher to shut the Yankees down in the last inning. So it wasn't exactly realistic, but it was a lot of fun.

When I was home from college in the summers, almost every night when the Yankees were home, my friends and I would call around to each other and say, "Hey do you feel like going to the Stadium?" We'd jump in the car and for under ten dollars, you could have a couple of beers, your dollar-fifty bleacher ticket, and you'd get to see a Yankee game. That was the Reggie Jackson, Oscar Gamble, Thurman Munson, then post-Thurman era. We were in college, it was summertime, I was totally relaxed, so I have fabulous memories of those games. We sort of soaked in the whole Yankee experience. There weren't many women around, at least not in the bleachers back then. Once we got out of college and began working for financial institutions, which offered free tickets, then we started to see more women down in the box seats.

I remember going to Shea Stadium in 1974 and '75 when the Yankees played there while the new stadium was being built, and really just hating it. I felt disoriented being at Shea Stadium and rooting for the Yankees as the home team. It was very, very strange. Yankee

In the 1979 baseball draft, the Kansas City Royals drafted high school baseball standouts Dan Marino and John Elway.

Stadium used to be so much more casual about everything. We'd bring beers in our pockets and there was a guy in the men's room in the bleachers that used to sell joints. Literally, he would sit on the bathroom sink and say, "Yankee joints." The cops must have known that fans were smoking dope.

Once, my friends and I were there for a Sunday afternoon game—I think it might have been a doubleheader—and one of our friends, a guy named Kevin, got bombed. I remember Kevin saying, "I think there's more pot being smoked out here in the bleachers than in the whole state of Rhode Island." From that point on, for about two years, we called him "Rhode Island Kevin," just because of that comment.

You could overhear some incredible conversation when you were sitting out in the bleachers. One time, the Yankees had made a trade for a third baseman that very afternoon, and we hadn't heard about it. We were sitting behind two guys as they bantered back and forth. They wore some kind of uniforms, and we assumed they were building superintendents or something like that. One guy said, "Yeah, yeah, he's a great third baseman. In fact, I think his name sounds just like George Brett." We found out the Yankees got **Aurelio Rodriguez**. So for a period after that, anytime someone would say something really stupid, we'd say, "Sounds like Brett." We'd fool around saying idiotic stuff like that.

There was another guy who always brought a cowbell. He was there for a long time, from the 1970s to about 1994. If you sat in the bleachers you could always bank on him being there. He used to get the crowd really riled up with that cowbell. The Yankees would rally, and he had this beat that I can still do. It's like dun, dun, dun—tadun, dun tadun….You could hear the bell throughout the stadium because it would echo. All the Hispanic guys would start rocking.

In 1979, I was absolutely devastated when Thurman Munson was killed. I was at home when I heard. At the time, I worked for the public schools in the summers. I would start very early, like 6:30 in the

Aurelio Rodriguez was the only Major League player to have every vowel in his name….The NBA Washington Bullets were the only major professional team to have every vowel but never two of any of them.

morning and I would be done by 3:30 in the afternoon. Typically, my routine was to get home and take a nap. Then, if the Yankees were home, my friends and I would go to the game. If not, we'd go to a movie or we'd go to a bar because back then the drinking age was eighteen.

> **He epitomized the resurgence of the Yankees, going from Rookie of the Year in 1970 to being regular-season MVP in 1976 to being the World Series MVP in 1977.**

I remember I had just woken up from my nap and the front door opened. My mother came in the house and yelled up to the top of the stairs, "Leo, Thurman Munson died." My first thought was, "What the heck are you talking about?" Thurman Munson died? I said, "What happened?" My mother said, "Turn on the radio. He was killed in a plane crash." Of course, I turned on the radio and heard the news. Thurman Munson was the Yankee captain. At the time, he was my favorite Yankee. He epitomized the resurgence of the Yankees, going from Rookie of the Year in 1970 to being regular-season MVP in 1976 to being the World Series MVP in 1977. He was a great guy and all of a sudden he's dead.

My father had gotten tickets months early for a September game, and it turned out to be the game after Munson's funeral, which had taken place that afternoon in Akron, Ohio. The whole team had flown out to Akron and then had flown back for the game against the Orioles. It was a packed house for a mid-season night game. I remember they had a tribute to Thurman before the game where the Yankee catcher did not take the field. There was no umpire there. All the other players had taken the field, but they left home plate empty. The team wore black armbands. All the Orioles wore black armbands. The Oriole players stood at the top of the dugout steps with their hats over their hearts. There wasn't a dry eye in the place.

It was incredible. I'd love to have the box score of that game. The Orioles were ahead the whole game, but then the Yankees rallied in the ninth inning with key base hits. I believe **Willie Randolph** started it off, and then Lou Piniella got on base, and then I believe Bobby Murcer hit a double down the line to drive in Lou Piniella with the winning run. These guys jumped up into each other's arms as if they had won the World Series. It was really a relatively meaningless, mid-week game, but the place went nuts. Of all the Yankee games I've been to, that one's probably the most emotional in terms of feeling part of the Yankee tradition, the Yankee history and also seeing how the players were like little kids. Baseball goes on, life goes on. It was a great, great experience. It's definitely something I'll remember the rest of my life, no question about that.

To this day, the Yankees periodically play a short tribute to Thurman Munson between innings, and it still gets a standing ovation. A friend of mine had a '72 Skylark that he had put a Thurman Munson bumper sticker on. After Thurman died, that bumper sticker was never gonna come off the back of his car. In fact, the car became known as "Thurm."

> Willie Randolph's brother was drafted by the Green Bay Packers and played for the New York Jets.

# GOD ALWAYS ANSWERED HIS PRAYERS BUT USUALLY SAID "NO"!

Dan McCourt

*Reared in central New Jersey, Dan McCourt, 55, is the production editor for Motor Boating magazine. He now lives in Port Chester, New York.*

Growing up in the 1950s, we had a big old Philco TV. It would be the ninth inning and the Yankees would be losing by two runs, and I would kneel, and say, "Okay, God, if You're so great, let's see the Yankees come from behind." And they never did it. They had some big wins but they never came from behind in the ninth inning, not in the World Series, not in the playoffs, not ever. So, to live until I was fifty-three and to see them do it in back-to-back nights in 2001 against the Diamondbacks was the most incredible thing.

In 1995, the Yankees were in the playoffs, and we were determined to get World Series tickets. The Yankees won the first two games in Seattle in a best of five, and we went to Yankee Stadium all three nights they played Seattle. My brother and I brought chairs and a TV, and we sat outside the ticket office. We were not alone. There were about twenty people there, all figuring that the morning after we won the third game they would put tickets on sale. We sat there for all three games and we lost all three games. We had to go home.

So in 1996 my brother and I did the same thing, both for the ALCS and for the World Series. We spent the night in line. During the second game of the World Series, we brought my wonderful Irish Terrier named Finnegan, but we told people his name was Scooter because we thought standing outside Yankee Stadium that that was cute. There was nothing particularly special about us, but when the news people went by, they saw him, and his picture ran in the newspaper. Everybody on line was talking about how they were going to try to sleep, but nobody slept. We all sat and talked, except Finnegan. He had a great time with everybody petting him. We actually brought a little dog bed for him and when he got disgusted with us, he rolled up in a ball and went to sleep. When I got to the front of the line, I did ask if I could buy three tickets—two for us and one for him, but the person at the window said, "No."

While we were standing in line for those tickets, people tried to cut in. They would appear in the morning and try to be very clever. The stuff they would come up with…One man said, "I'm a minister, and I had to minister to my flock, and I couldn't be here, but just because I have a love of God is no reason why I shouldn't have a chance to be able to see the team I love, too." There were people behind us who had brought their dog, too, and their dog didn't get along with Finnegan. They took their dog away, which I felt was sweet because we didn't have that option. We were there on line, and we had no way to get out of there.

Sometimes people had good excuses, and so we let them cut in. When we stood in line for tickets to the ALCS, Yankees versus the Orioles, there was a group of people who had been at the game down in Camden Yards earlier that night and then drove up after the game ended. They had an excuse we could understand.

That night was fun, but it was disgusting, too. Standing in a line like that is like camping out, but every once in a while the police would make us move to tighten up the line. There was a McDonald's down the street, and people were buying chicken, burgers and fries. You could be very careful in your area, make it very clean, but it didn't matter, because in a couple of minutes when the police moved you along, you would be in somebody else's area where they hadn't been so clean.

Bathrooms were a problem, too. There is a bowling alley bar across the street from Yankee Stadium, and that closed at one a.m. There really was no place to go to the bathroom after that. I honestly don't know how my girlfriend made it. The line started at the Big Bat, then ran past the sidewalk café all the way out to River Road, and then continued down that way. By the time the tickets actually went on sale, we were in line thirty-six hours, and when we showed up there were already four or five hundred people there, so there must have been thousands of people on line. They were all walking around carrying about a thousand dollars in cash because you couldn't buy tickets with a credit card. How many times are people walking around with all this cash in the Bronx? So that was very neat.

> **It was like a baseball Woodstock. But it's no more.**

We had a lot of fun, even though it was disgusting and tiring. It was like a baseball Woodstock. But it's no more. In 1997, they instituted the bracelets so that the whole process of getting division and World Series games would be fairer. They distribute sequentially numbered bracelets and then have random drawings and the winners are given the option of buying tickets. When all the winning numbers are used up, they begin the process again. When they began that system, sleeping in line for days no longer guaranteed you a chance to buy playoff tickets.

Over the years, as I've rooted for the Yankees, I have developed an ability I didn't at first realize was anything special: I can hold a note really long. Most people, when they're cheering, have to stop to breathe, but I can yell something and just keep yelling it. It started out with Roberto Kelly. Every time Roberto Kelly would get up, we would stand up and yell "Roberto – o – o – o – o – o – o," on and on and on until the pitcher finally threw the ball and he hit it or whatever. I have a ticket plan for Box 622, and I realized that the people around us who were also yelling with me were dropping out while I was still holding. One of the other regulars who sits two rows in front of us said he was literally thrilled with my cheers and said that we could make an awesome Yankee fan website, so about a year ago, I started *TakeHimDowntown.com*. We give game highlights, spring training notes, that kind of thing. One guy now lives in Bermuda and says he gets all his Yankee news from it. Fans send me e-mails from places like Boston and Seattle.

There's one place on the site that says, "The View from Box 622" and there's a button you can push to get sound bites of me doing my "Charge." People are always surprised because I'm a rather softspoken guy, but I cheer pretty loud.

# SHORT STORIES FROM LONG MEMORIES:

## YANKEE STADIUM

I was at the last game in the old Yankee Stadium. It was understood that people were taking home souvenirs during that game. A friend of mine wanted to take home the seat he was sitting in. He had come with the implements of destruction to do exactly that. He had a little toolbox with pliers and a screw bar and a little crow bar because you had to actually break the end of the seat to get it out. The problem with that was it was part of a group of four seats, all joined together.

So after helping him take the four seats out of the floor, we thought the hardest part would be getting them out of the Yankee Stadium past the security guards. But we just walked out of the stadium. The security guard seemed to turn the other way. Maybe he was supposed to yell at us, but he didn't. Everybody was taking stuff. It was ludicrous to watch people walking out with stanchions and with seats and pieces of Formica. It was insane. We were home free, or so we thought.

We were out on 161st Street and River Avenue where Yankee Stadium is. We had to walk through the Grand Concourse near the courthouse to take the Number 1 bus to get home to the East Bronx where I lived. We couldn't fit the seats in the bus. The bus driver thought we were out of our minds trying to squeeze these four seats into the front of the bus. That was humorous enough, and people on the bus were laughing at us. The bus driver said, "Yankee fans?" "Of course, we're Yankee fans." As I turned around, we weren't the only ones in line waiting for the Number 1 bus carrying gigantic pieces of Yankee Stadium.

My friend called his father and asked, "Can you come pick us up?" "Why?" he said. "Because we have seats." His father said, "No, absolutely not. Throw the seats away." We ended up walking home, about three or four miles, carrying four seats from Yankee Stadium down Fordham Road.

I was merely an accomplice in this. They were his seats. As luck would have it, his father wanted no part of the seats so I had to keep them in my bedroom in my parents' house until he cleared it with his parents. When we took them into my parents' house, they said, "Are you out of your mind?" but that was the end of it. For about four weeks, I had Yankee seats in my bedroom. I was about seventeen or eighteen at the time, a crazy, jerky kid.

——TOM LEMME, 43, raised in the Bronx

When I was nine years old, my mother and I went to a baseball game. It turned out to be Don Larsen's perfect game. My mother had seen games on TV, but this was the first time she had ever gone to a game. I was a huge fan, and even though I was a kid, I knew a lot about baseball. My mother had no idea what was going on, and couldn't understand why people were so excited.

The people sitting around us were very knowledgeable, and we explained to her that nobody had gotten a hit, but she had no idea what a perfect game was. She didn't have a clue what was going on, nor was she really interested. My dad was a real baseball nut, and the fact that he wasn't there was just a killer for him. He was a physician and he had an appointment that afternoon that he just could not break. That turned out to be the last time I ever went to a game with my mother—the first and the last.

——JERRY FINELLI, 54, the Bronx

Yankee doubleheaders I went to in the late 1960s were absolutely the best bargain you could find for a day's entertainment. They took the whole day. The first game started at one o'clock in the afternoon, and sometimes you didn't get back in the car till nine or ten o'clock at night. I remember one game where a guy in a Pirates hat was very drunk and was cheering for Catfish Hunter, which was interesting because it was still six or eight years before Catfish came to the Yankees. Catfish was not even in the park, but this guy was just screaming for Catfish Hunter.

——VICTOR LEVIN, 41, Television Writer

My mother had gotten tickets for a game against the Red Sox in May of 1967. I was ten years old. The night before there had been a big donnybrook, a big fight at Yankee Stadium between the Red Sox and the Yankees. So, of course, I wasn't going to turn down a chance to go.

It was the first and only time until I was about fourteen or fifteen years old that I ever sat in box seats. Back then, box seats were four dollars and fifty cents a ticket, which was big money. The only problem was that it was the night of the last episode of the old television show, *The Fugitive*, the night they were finally going to catch the one-armed man. It was my mother's favorite show. The game ended around 9:45 p.m. It was a quick game. The Yankees lost. We lived in the Highbridge section of the Bronx, right by Yankee Stadium. My mother was hightailing it, yelling at me, "Come on. Come on."

———MIKE SPELMAN, 45, Phoenix, AZ

My two friends, Jim Panko and Louie Pappas and I used to go down to Yankee games on our own starting about 1965. In those days, a general admission ticket was $1.50. We would actually walk from our houses in Yonkers, which was just under seven miles away from the Stadium, to save a total of sixty cents on train fare. We'd go to a Saturday game, leave at nine o'clock, get down there around 11:50 a.m., just about the time they were opening the gates. You could actually let a child walk to Yankee Stadium through University Heights in those days. It was a beautiful neighborhood. My father gave us plenty of money to take the bus, but we weren't going to waste money on transportation. We'd come away with another twenty cents each. You know what you could buy with twenty cents in the early 1960s?

When we arrived at Yankee Stadium, we would buy one ticket for a buck fifty. Fifty cents for each of us. We would go up to the upper deck, where there were louvers covering the windows. In fact, you can still see them on the outside structure where they've been covered over, where they have the Moorish-type dome tops. In those days, they were regular Venetian blind louvers, and you could slip something out through the louvers, and it would float right down to the ground. We'd take the one ticket we'd bought, slip it down to Louie, and then we'd go watch him, and Louie would go up to the usher and say, "I've got to come in." The usher would say, "You can't come back in." Louie would say, "Oh, but my father and brother are in there, and I went to the car, and now I can't go back in. Oh, God, he's going to kill me." They'd let him right in. No problem.

Then Louie would come up, take the ticket, drop it down, and Panko would pick it up and do the same thing at another gate. There are basically four gates at Yankee Stadium. There's the one down the right field line. There's one where that outdoor little café they have is now. There's one directly behind home plate, and there's one all the way down the third-base line. We did that every Saturday. We never bought more than one ticket. We went to different gates every time. These ushers were making two dollars an hour. They were cops, policemen, firemen—they didn't care. They got paid the same thing. They weren't going to bust anybody.

We never saw any other kids doing this. It was our exclusive. We feel as though we should have patented that. My brother, in addition to being a really smart guy, was also a very religious kid. He would never get involved in any of our trickery. He thought, I'm sure, that he would end up in jail for the rest of his life. That never occurred to me. All I knew is I had an extra twenty cents not spent on cab-fare, and now I had an extra buck because I only spent fifty cents on the ticket.

——MARK ROLLINSON, 50, Yonkers, NY

This past season I was very lucky. I went to fifteen games, which is a lot for me. I always go to Yankee Stadium early. I like to look around, and I like to meet people and talk to them. Once, I noticed a guy who had a tattoo on his arm that was a replica of Yankee Stadium. He was a big guy and he had these massive arms, and his entire right bicep was just this incredible image of Yankee Stadium. I thought to myself, "You know, I'm not that crazy."

——STEVE LOMBARDI, 40, Middletown, NJ

I went to the last game of 1973 at Yankee Stadium, before they remodeled, which took about two years. I was about fourteen years old and I couldn't find anybody to go with so I went by myself. It was late September. Just knowing this was the last game at the Stadium made it very moving. Now, when I look back at it with more significance, it's like saying, "I was at the Ali-Frasier fight."

One of the things I took as souvenirs—because people were taking things and I didn't know it was illegal—was a four-inch or so piece of metal from the side of a seat. I have no idea how I got it. There were guys around me who came with screwdrivers, wrenches, saws, and hammers, but I didn't bring any tools. Today we laugh, because you'd never get them through security, but that was 1973. I don't know what happened to the piece. I went away to college, and I remember putting it in the garage and storing it. Maybe it's somewhere in a box, I don't know.

That day, I also took a square piece of grass, maybe four inches by four inches, of the actual turf from the Stadium. We lived in an apartment so I didn't have any place to put it. The next day I took it to my grandmother's house. She had a lawn in the back yard. I remember planting that piece of grass in the backyard of her house. It was taken care of and grew but she has since died and the house has been sold.

As we were all leaving the Stadium after the game, there were huge piles of things like chairs because the ushers or security guards told people, "You're not taking that out. Leave it right here." I can remember telling my brother and father the story. The amazing thing is these people spent the whole game taking these chairs and other things apart only to be told, "You have to leave that over there."

During the two-year renovation, I would take the subway and stand on the platform of the Number 4 train with my little Instamatic camera and take pictures, which I still have somewhere, of the renovation in progress. I did that probably two or three times. I was a Yankee fan, and I thought it was pretty cool that the Stadium was being redone and that someday I would look back at these pictures and say, "Wow, I was there when they were doing it."

In those days, I thought the new stadium was just an expression of modernism. Out with the old, in with the new. As young as I was, I guess I didn't have the nostalgic, ingrained feelings of someone who was a lot older, who'd been going to the old Yankee Stadium for years.

——PAT CANTWELL, 43, Bronx native

When I was in fifth grade, about 1972, my friend, Robin Pisarek, was a huge Red Sox fan and his dad took me to a Yankees-Red Sox game. It was early in the season. This would have still been the old Yankee Stadium. There was one of those pillars right in front of our seats. The Yankees had the bases loaded in the bottom of the first with two outs. Graig Nettles came up, and he hit a long fly ball to the wall in right field, and it was caught for the third out, and the Yankees didn't score. I made a fist with my right hand, and I hit the railing in front of the seats as hard as I could. It hurt a lot. I said to Mr. Pisarek that I thought that I had broken my hand. He said, "That's ridiculous. No one would do that. No sane child would do that." But it turned out that I had, in fact, broken a finger, which remained in a cast for about six weeks. I had to explain hundreds of times to people over the course of that month and a half. People didn't understand. You learn very early that passion is for the few. I hated Graig Nettles for flying out.

——VICTOR LEVIN, 41, raised in New York

I remember all the sunburns I used to get sitting in the bleachers at Yankee Stadium when I was young. The seats in the old stadium were metal, and I remember dying on those seats, but not caring. It was such fun staring at these incredible men in their uniforms, always hoping that a ball would fly up to me. Until I was an adult, I never sat anywhere but the bleachers. We lived within walking distance from the Stadium, but my father wasn't into baseball so I would go with friends, and over the summer, I would go two or three times with my Y Camp.

There is just something about being at peace when I'm in Yankee Stadium. I feel like I'm home. There's nothing to me like sitting there on a warm June or July day with a cold beer in my hand and watching these men play. And it's not each one individually that I feel special about, but who they are as a team. It's captured in the fact that they don't wear their names on their uniforms. They're a team. Each one of them is spectacular, but together they're amazing.

———ARIANNA PATTERSON, 46, West Orange, NJ

In 1961, when I was eight, my cousins, Theresa and Mary Ann, drove me in a car to Yankee Stadium for the first time. At the time, Theresa was in her twenties; Mary Ann was around seventeen.

It didn't matter to me that I was the only boy going with a bunch of women because I'd never gone to a game before. Anyway, they were just as crazy Yankee fans as I was so being with them was just like being with the guys.

In those days, a ticket to the grandstand cost fifty cents. The Yankees used to have Ladies' Day. Well, Theresa and Mary Ann didn't want to pay, so they dressed me up like a girl so we could all go free on Ladies' Day. I was eight, so of course I had no beard. I was an Italian kid with blond hair, so I was this cute, curly-haired, blue-eyed, blond-headed kid in a little, God-knows-what I was wearing. My mother used to dress me like a girl for Halloween for some reason— I'll have to talk to her about that—and they borrowed a dress from my sister and put me in dark-colored leotards and sneakers. They wet my hair and styled it a little different. I couldn't pass for a sixteen-year old girl, but an eight or nine-year old I could pass for. They just got me in. It was hysterical. They were thrilled. It was really more of a joke than to save a dollar. Theresa and Mary Ann just wanted to see if they could get away with it. As I said, they were really fun people.

*Joe "Josie" Santoiemma in his Ladies' Day pose.*

Since I'd only seen games on black and white television, I had no idea what being at Yankee Stadium was going to be like. I can just see us driving down the Grand Concourse. You reach a certain point where you can see the height of the Stadium with the lights. It was a night game, which made the Stadium even more impressive. I remember those lights, the height of the Stadium, and that old green color it was painted—that school-green that's used in New York City.

I know my mouth was open—and that was just standing outside the Stadium. On Ladies' Day, you still had to pay tax on the seats, so of course, we got the cheapest seats, which at the time, were not in the bleachers, but in the upper deck of the grandstand. We call it the nosebleed section. There was no such thing as an escalator. You walked up the concrete ramp that's still there today. You climbed up and up and up, and you really can't see the actual field at that point.

It took an eternity just to get up to that point. Then I started to see the crowd and the Stadium, hear the noise and the smells—the beer, the hot dogs, the pretzels. I can remember almost losing my breath. First, I gasped because the height in the upper deck is amazing for a kid that's never been so high. But more amazing was the difference between watching the game on my little eleven-inch TV in black and white and looking down at the field and seeing that green grass, that dirt. It was unbelievable. I think the seats at that time were all green. The background, the white façade in the upper decks that Mickey Mantle hit once every year, was too much to take in. It was almost like I was going to pass out.

I can still see it all. Elston Howard was at the plate. The Yankees were playing the Washington Senators. We were late getting to the game, and I was walking to my seat when Howard grounded out into a double play. I was very disappointed because he was my first, real-life batter. This was 1961, so here it was my first season really following the Yankees, and Mickey Mantle and Roger Maris were having their home run race. Every day I had been looking at the newspapers, watching the statistics, and collecting the baseball cards, so to be at Yankee Stadium was just a great feeling.

——JOE SANTOIEMMA, 50, New Rochelle, NY

The Yankees had a left fielder in the 1940s named Charlie Keller. He was built like a tank. They called him "King Kong Keller." In 1947, after a game, we were all walking out of the Stadium. Someone wasn't looking and accidentally bumped into Keller, who was trotting in from left field, and knocked him down. When Keller got up, everybody thought he was going to kill this guy, but he went over to the guy, a young guy, and said, "Don't worry about it. It's not the first time." He patted him on the head and shoulder and that was that. He just walked away.

I was at another game that year when somebody hit a fly ball to Joe DiMaggio. The ball seemed like it was up in the air for hours. It must have been hit about seven hundred feet—at least, that's what it seemed like. By the time the ball came down, one of my friends, Armand Abbott, had fallen fast asleep. I know that's hard to believe, but he just nodded off to sleep as we were all watching the ball. Joe D. caught it, and the roar of the crowd woke Armand up.

———STAN STARMAN, 71, Tamarac, FL

In the early 1980s, the Yankees had what they used to call a "midweek mini-season ticket plan." You got sixteen midweek games. In the early Showalter years when the team was just dreadful, Juan Espino was the starting shortstop, and, besides Don Mattingly, nobody could hit. I still loved them, though. A friend and I had seats together and we would stay and watch the games.

By August, and certainly by September, they would be twenty games out of first place. But we would stay 'til the end because we looked forward to it. Sometimes by the ninth inning of a game, in the middle of September there would be maybe two thousand people left in the park. You could hear epithets being yelled by the fanatics from the upper deck on the other side of the field. Nowadays you have to be more careful before you call people a name, but in the 1980s, it was just more free-tongued. In a certain way you could understand their behavior by the fact that they were freezing, it was the middle of the night, and their team was terrible. They had paid money and they were just depressed.

At one of those games in the early 1980s, the Yankees were playing the White Sox, and Carlton Fisk hit a ball into the third deck down the left-field line. You don't see anybody hit the ball into the upper deck in left field. It almost never happens, certainly not eight, ten, twelve rows up. It was just one of those moments where you realized how bad your team was. The ball just kept going, and you thought "What a bad pitch that must have been." Granted, Fisk was a great hitter, but that trajectory is almost physically impossible. And they were losing. I can't remember who was pitching. I think everybody pitched that night.

——VICTOR LEVIN, 41, Former New Yorker

The greatest thing I remember as a twelve or thirteen-year old kid was going to Yankee Stadium. It was the biggest event in my life. We would send away for tickets. We had box seats, which were a big deal, and cost $3.50 in those days. We always went to a doubleheader on a Sunday, and even though my father wasn't a baseball fan, he would be interested in it because I was. We would take six or seven guys, take the subway from Brooklyn and spend the whole day in the Bronx.

We lived in Brooklyn, among the sidewalks and the cement. Going to the Bronx, being in the subway, walking in the Bronx, going to the Stadium, then walking into this big building and first seeing this beautiful green thing in front of you is the most magnificent thing I've ever seen in my life. You see this green field and all these guys playing—all your heroes out there. They're running around catching balls. Before you get to your seat, you stare at this thing. You can't believe it. Right in the middle of the Bronx, you have this unbelievable oasis. It's incredible. That's when I fell in love with the whole thing. We just sat there on a Sunday and enjoyed the whole thing. Just seeing something that beautiful would last me for weeks.

My parents wanted to make sure I had something to eat all day, so my father, who was a curtain cutter in the garment center in Manhattan, would go out on a Sunday morning and get a pound of kosher salami and two hero breads. My mother made me two sandwiches, which my father called "the three-seven deal." I was allowed to have half a hero in the third inning of the first game, half in the seventh inning and then in the second game, half in the third inning, and the other half in the seventh. Before I left home he would cut the sandwiches and label one of them "three" and "seven," and label the other one "three" and "seven." This way I knew what I was doing. I was allowed to buy a soda which each half, too.

——JERRY FADEN, 57, Tamarac, FL

I never stopped going to the Yankee games. I went there through the Bobby Murcer years. They were horrible. We'd even laugh at ourselves when somebody named Dooley Womack came in to pitch.

You have to laugh. The Dooley Womacks, the Thaddeus Tillotsons—where did we get these guys? Steve Whitaker, Bill Robinson—how can Bill Robinson, who hit .199 for the Yankees become a batting coach for the Pittsburgh Pirates? That doesn't make any sense. We picked up Bill Monbouquette and Bob Tillman from the Red Sox. The Charley Smith trade—that was a great deal, getting rid of Roger Maris! Oh my God. Horace Clarke still hasn't turned a double play. The Yankees loaned him money to buy a hotel or something in the Virgin Islands. Gene Michael, another great .200 hitter. God, those were tough years. But we went.

In those years, you knew you didn't have a great team, but you were just going to have fun at the game. You got your peanuts and your beer and you sat in the sun. I remember sitting through Al Downing, the guy who gave up Aaron's 715th home run. I was a teenager, so this was in the late 1960s. In the ninth inning, the game was tied. The game went eighteen innings—eighteen innings—and my mother was wondering where the heck I was. Al Downing pitched the last nine innings of that game. In those days, $3.50 bought the best seat in the house. We probably each had five dollars and we decided to buy the best seats and spend all our money on whatever we wanted. We sat there for eighteen innings and watched the game and did not have a thought like "Oh, your mother's worried," or "We ought to make a phone call." We were starving because after eighteen innings, we were out of money. We ate our hot dogs in the first five minutes, a bag of peanuts, drank a soda, and then just sat there and starved. But you're a kid, so you don't think anything of it.

———JOE SANTOIEMMA, 50, New Rochelle, NY

I really miss general admission seating. It used to be you could go to the Stadium and tell someone, "I'll meet you in Section Two." One person would bring some chicken. Another person would bring the pie. I can remember guys walking up and down in the bleachers saying, "Get your Yankee joints here." I have real fond memories of those years. Now, you have to buy tickets months ahead of time.

———PHIL PANASCI, 47, Bronx native

There are a lot of people, including my friends and I, who if you were to wake us out of a sound sleep, would say in our best Bob Sheppard impression, "Number 19, Ri-ghetti, Number 19." There's a whole secret society of people who work on their **Bob Sheppard** impression. I actually had occasion to meet him and shook hands with him, and it was so funny because even when he's just talking to you as a person, he sounds just like that. He's still Bob Sheppard, even though his voice doesn't have the echo. It's a riot. I loved Rizzuto and Frank Messer and Bill White. Messer, who recently passed away, was such a blissfully straightforward guy, and Rizzuto was a riot. He and White's play-by-play was always great. I remember once, I thought I heard the following when they came back from a commercial: Rizzuto said, "Moving on to the fourth hole...." And White just cracked up.

——VICTOR LEVIN, 41, Los Angeles

I went to the last game at the old Yankee Stadium in 1973 and the first game at the new Yankee Stadium in 1976. That last game was pretty cool. It was one of those years when the Yankees were awful by the end of the year. They still had a big crowd for that last game. Around the seventh inning, all of a sudden you started hearing from all around the Stadium, crunch, crunch, crunch. People were breaking chairs off and carrying them home. I managed to get a seat, but I lost it somewhere in my college years moving from place to place.

One of my all-time "almost" Yankee moments was when I was in college in Binghamton, New York. I heard on the radio that Whitey Ford was going to appear at this local card dealer doing a promotion. I was going to bring my Yankee Stadium seat over and have him autograph it. So I called up the place and said, "Is Whitey Ford there?" The man said, "Yeah, come over. Come over and have a beer with Whitey." By the time I got there, Whitey was gone.

——PHIL PANASCI, 47, Cape Cod, MA

The public address announcer for the Astros (Colt '45s) in 1962 was Dan Rather. John Forsythe, the actor, was the public address announcer for the Brooklyn Dodgers in 1937 and 1938.

The only major league game without a public address announcer took place on August 12, 1997 at Camden Yards in Baltimore...the day their Rex Barney died.

I went to the very first game at Yankee Stadium after 9/11. My friends and I made the decision to go because we knew it was going to be very emotional. We have season tickets and we were actually supposed to go to the game that was canceled because of the terrorist attack. The season was postponed for a week. The first game back was really emotional.

All the players took the field, which they very rarely do. There was almost an hour of delay bringing out singers, and Mayor Giuliani was there and spoke. He went out and hugged the players and it was amazing. They handed out American flags to everyone. I don't think there was a dry eye in the house while they were playing the National Anthem. I think every fireman and cop in New York knows how to sing the National Anthem, and they were all out there. Everyone was crying. I don't even remember who they played that night. I don't remember if they won or not.

We were in the upper deck in the tier box. We are all waving our flags. It was really, really something. People brought American flags from home and sheets with flags painted on them. We were at the first game of the World Series, and they brought in the flag that had been at the World Trade Center that had the two big rips in it, the one they dug out of the rubble that had been buried for three days. That really, really made everybody cry, too. It was very emotional. I went to all the games the rest of the season.

——KEVIN FITZPATRICK, 36, Manhattan

When it comes to baseball, we are where we start out. If you start out sitting in the upper deck, then essentially you sit in the upper deck your entire life. It doesn't matter where you sit, you're an upper-deck person. Because in the passion of the moment, whatever polish you may have acquired disappears. Whatever you've learned disappears. And, a second later, all that self-editing kicks back in, and a little voice says, "What's the matter with you?" But it's too late. You already said it.

My dad was a dentist with a small-time suburban practice. We had a modest, middle class existence, and we didn't have much money. When we would go to games, we would typically sit in the upper deck, and it was the greatest. The first time I ever sat in really good seats was six or seven years ago in Yankee Stadium on a not very crowded day, and my seats were just a couple of rows off of the field. They were right at the level of the Yankees' on-deck circle.

In the top of the inning, Tim Raines missed the cut-off man on a single to left, and an extra run scored. The Yankees got out of the inning, Raines came in, and of course, he was going to lead off the inning. So, he was in the on-deck circle seven and a half feet from me. It was a quiet day, the second game of a doubleheader, a lazy summer afternoon, nothing's going on. I stood up, and at the top of my lungs—the top of my lungs—I screamed, "Hey Timmy, how about hitting the cut-off man next time?" He turned around and looked at me with this expression on his face like, "I'm right here. I'm seven and a half feet away from you. Why are you screaming?" And also, "Why must I listen to things like that from a person like you?" Still, he didn't say anything. I was really embarrassed because I had no idea that he could actually hear me. You think you have complete immunity because they'll never hear you. But the one time the guy actually heard, I was appalled at myself.

——**VICTOR LEVIN**, 41, raised in New York

Although an NFL game has not been played at Wrigley Field since 1971, the Cubs ballpark has hosted more NFL games than any other stadium.

**Chapter 6**

# The Mick

## If Youth Knew,
## If Age Could Do

# WATCHIN' THE MICK DRILL ANOTHER

Larry Lieberman

*While millions of American men lay claim to being The Mick's biggest fan, forty-seven-year-old Larry Lieberman, originally from Long Island, might really be the one. Just walk into Larry's dental office in Palm Harbor, Florida and you'll see why.*

When I was about eight years old, we had front-row box seats. A ball came caroming off the side wall and hit me right in the head. It bounced off my head, and Elston Howard was in the first-base coaches' box. He got the ball and didn't give it back to me. Everybody started booing Howard, "Give the kid the ball." He never gave the ball to me, and I didn't like him as much after that. I was pretty dazed. Years after, when I was thirty-three, I ended up having a little benign tumor in my head right where I got hit. The only thing I could trace it to was when I got hit in the head that day at Yankee Stadium. It was the kind of tumor that can be caused by a blow to the head.

I felt like Mickey probably should have retired sooner than he did. To see how hurt he was and how he really didn't have it anymore was sad. But when I met him fourteen years ago, he looked like he was in incredibly good shape. I was really impressed with how big his fore-arms were. They were huge. He definitely had an air about him that was magical.

I met him at the University of South Florida, where he was doing a card show with Whitey Ford. I showed him pictures of my "Mickey Mantle Dental Treatment" room. It's my shrine to Mickey Mantle, as well as my little Cooperstown. I started it when I opened my practice down here in Palm Harbor, Florida, about seventeen years ago.

> **When I showed Mickey the pictures of my room, he yelled to Whitey, "Hey, Whitey, get a load of this. This guy's got a dental room for me."**

When I showed Mickey the pictures of my room, he yelled to Whitey, "Hey, Whitey, get a load of this. This guy's got a dental room for me." He was really nice. He was so excited. I was nervous because here I was, thirty-three years old, the first time I'd ever met Mickey Mantle, and a lot of people had told me to not be surprised if he's really a jerk. But he was as nice as could be. He said to me, "Anything you ever need..." He signed *Quality of Courage*, the book about him that I'd had next to my bed my whole childhood. He signed it, "To Doc. Thanks a lot. Mickey Mantle." He thought it was kinda neat that I had grown up with his picture and this book next to my bed. It was special for me. I had my son with me, and he was six years old, so I have pic-tures of him and Whitey and Mickey and me.

I only met him that one time, but I have lots of his things, lots of pic-tures and cards signed by "The Mick." I have a signed Mickey Mantle rookie card. That's a very valuable piece. I also have his base-ball bat from the last time he ever signed baseball bats in Dallas when they thought he'd had a heart attack. That was a couple of years before he died.

My baseball room just gradually grew and grew and grew. My patients loved it so much. By now I probably have at least fifty items in it. In the room in my house, I have an authenticated Babe Ruth-signed baseball. Actually that was a trade. I made a three-unit bridge for a lawyer, who had been given the Babe Ruth baseball as payment from a guy he defended. The lawyer paid for his three-unit bridge with the Ruth baseball. I had the ball authenticated by officials because I wanted to make sure it was the real thing.

One of the most valuable things I have is a six-foot baseball bat, which my wife gave me for a Father's Day gift. It was signed by twenty-five Hall of Famers back at an Old Timer's Legends Game in 1990 in St. Petersburg, Florida. The game was held at Al Lang Field, where the Yankees used to play spring training. I was on the field with a lot of other fans, only I had this big bat, and everybody was coming up to me and signing it. Ted Williams is right on the barrel of the bat. Stan Musial, Bob Feller, Harmon Killebrew—these guys are just giants. They were all coming up to me and signing it because they loved it. There were newspaper photographers from all over the country taking their pictures standing with the bat. They would say, "Man, that would have been a good bat for Frank Howard."

Most people who come to my office loved the old Yankees. Many of them are transplanted New Yorkers now living in Florida. But **Red Sox** fans hate the Yankees, so sometimes, one of them will come in and say, "Get me out of this room! I can't stand it!" Then I show them the Ted Williams signature on the barrel of the big bat, and they get all excited. They say, "Oh, I can stay now." Ted Williams signed the bat bigger than everybody. The only reason he signed it was that all the other guys kept saying, "Come on Ted, sign the guy's bat."

When Mickey was dying, the local newspaper ran an article about my room. The TV stations got wind of it, and they all came out and interviewed me, which was pretty cool. It was sad that he was dying then, but I thought it was great that he had become such an incredible person. He had taken his disease and the suffering and family strife he went through, and he made it into something people could really respect. He was apologetic. I thought he treated all this suffering at

> The Sam Malone character in *Cheers* was patterned after former Red Sox pitcher, Bill Lee. Bill Lee once demanded number 337 from the Boston Red Sox because 337, upside down, spells Lee's last name.

the end with total class. The things he did in his life were nothing to emulate—the alcoholism, the womanizing. He did a lot of things that were not to be envied, but he created awareness for organ transplants. He really tried to make something good out of his disease because he knew he'd screwed up. He lived a very selfish life. I always believe you try to make a positive out of things, and nobody should die in vain. My mom died of lung cancer, and so as a dentist I do whatever I can to get people to stop smoking as a kind of tribute to my mom. With Mickey Mantle, it was the same thing. He had lived his life the way he wanted, on his terms, and I can't judge him ill for that. I named my third son after him.

My first son was born in April, and as soon as he was born, when they handed him to me, I just laid him on my shoulder, and we watched a Yankee game right there in the hospital room. I had bought him a little baseball glove with a little, soft and furry lion face on it, and a little foam ball. Now he's eighteen and bigger than I am.

*I write about politics, mostly to support my baseball habit.*

*—George Will*

# MICKEY MANTLE WAS A REGULAR GUY WHO SOMETIMES WORE A CAPE

### Marty Appel

*Mamaronek-based public relations ace Marty Appel, 53, was just a fresh-faced college kid from suburban New York when he started working for the Yankee front office in 1968. Though he had not anticipated a career with the Yankees, he stayed until 1977.*

How I got a summer job with the Yankees was after my freshman year of college, I wrote a letter to Bob Fishel, the Yankees public relations director, and asked for a summer job. I told him what a great fan I was and that I had been sports editor in high school and now in college.

I was studying political science in school and never thought I would ever work for a baseball team. It was like a fantasy—writing the letter was something I never even expected to get an answer to. It seemed like it would be a cool thing to have a summer job with the Yankees. Everybody was looking for summer jobs so I had said, "Well, I'll write to the Yankees."

I got a letter from Bob Fishel saying to come on in for an interview. I told him I had won one of his scorecard contests, which he really liked to hear, but I still didn't think I'd get hired. Then they called me to say I had a job answering **Mickey Mantle**'s fan mail. My parents were flabbergasted and remained so throughout my career with the

> Pat Summerall played minor league baseball against Mickey Mantle. Summerall's first name is George. He is called Pat because when he was a kicker for the New York Giants, the papers would print "P.A.T.— Summerall." P.A.T. stood for **Point After Touchdown.**

Yankees. They watched every game on TV. They became total converts to the team.

Everyday I would drive from Spring Valley to Yankee Stadium and park in the players' parking lot and go answer the fan mail. I always saved some mail so I could go over it personally with Mickey Mantle. It was an unbelievable thrill. He made it a

> **There was nothing aloof or superstar about him in the confines of the clubhouse.**

pleasure. He was just so easy to talk to. There was nothing aloof or superstar about him in the confines of the clubhouse. I always felt a generation removed from him, but he made it so easy. Whenever he would do a radio interview, and they would give him a gift certificate, he'd always give it to me. So if I got a pair of shoes at Thom McAn, they were always my "Mickey Mantle shoes."

After college, Bob Fishel hired me permanently as his assistant. He took me under his wing and I was treated like one of the team. One of my first assignments was to arrange Old Timer's Day. It was an incredible treat to get to know the real heroes when they came back to the stadium.

Casey Stengel returned in 1970 after a ten-year exile. That was very exciting. He had stayed away for ten years after being fired, but now it was new ownership and it was time to mend fences so it was very nice. All the people who had done him wrong were long gone.

Because he was old, he had an older kind of American etiquette. When I say that, I mean, we would give everybody a present at Old Timers Day, and they were not fancy presents—they were fifty or sixty dollar gifts like clock radios or something like that. On the Monday afterward, when he got back to California, I picked up the telephone and he just started talking, not knowing who was at the other end. "Just wanted to say that Mrs. Stengel and I had a sple-e-e-ndid and mar-velous time in New York and thanks very much for my prize." He called it "a prize."

Joe DiMaggio would arrive in town on Tuesday before the game, and we'd house him at the Americana Hotel. Because I was the contact name on the instruction sheet, he would call me each day, about two or three times. He'd say, "Hello Marty, it's Joe." And he'd tell what his needs were, like tickets for the evening or he'd say, "Can you leave a couple of tickets for the doorman here at the hotel? I hate to impose." We'd do it, of course. It was always, "Joe, whatever you need. You call me twenty-four hours a day. I'll do anything you want." So then came Saturday, Old Timers' Day. I remember I was upstairs greeting the players as they came in, and as he came in, I stuck out my hand. I said, "Joe, Marty Appel." He walked right by me. He no longer needed anything from me.

Toward the end of his career, Mickey Mantle received a lot of fan mail. Ninety-nine percent of the letters read, "Dear Mickey, You're my favorite player. Can I have an autographed photo?" The other one percent I would save to go over with Mickey personally. This mail would include anything from Bar Mitzvah invitations to the Manhattan social scene, which he would never participate in. I remember an invitation to a party at David Susskind's duplex apartment on Central Park West. Sometimes a letter would include some nude Polaroid photographs.

When Mickey Mantle retired, it was sad because I knew him well, and it was very personal. He treated me so nicely so it wasn't just seeing a Yankee legend retire, it was seeing somebody leave that you wish were still around everyday. That was the sad part. Mickey just made you feel good to be around him. His personality was very easy, and he was very nice to people. There was none of that aloof super stardom. He had a reputation for being rude with the press if he didn't like them or if he was in a bad mood, but among his contemporaries, among the people who worked at Yankee Stadium, the ground crew, the clubhouse people, and of course, the players, the batboys, he was just "Mick." He was great.

With the other players who were the same age as I was, there would be sadness when the guys would get traded, and to be released in spring training was even tougher. I had to learn not to form close friendships because that was always gonna happen with players. The turnover became rapid after George Steinbrenner bought the team in 1973, and I developed high seniority very quickly, so I was the PR director at twenty four. I used to sit in at staff meetings realizing that I was almost the senior guy in the room. It was like fantasyland. I would be present when the roster would be discussed, and I would occasionally know a trade before a player did. I would be in the clubhouse, and I would look at the guy and think, "He doesn't even know that he's going to be with the Chicago White Sox tomorrow." That was really strange.

The sale was a total surprise, one of the best-kept secrets I've ever seen in sports. There wasn't even a rumor. There wasn't anything that tipped us off. I didn't even find out until the very morning of the sale. I was in my basement office at Yankee Stadium. Bob Fishel was in his office. The

> **The sale was a total surprise, one of the best-kept secrets I've ever seen in sports**

best-selling writer, Peter Golenbock, who was researching his first book, was in Bill Cains' office. Bob threw Peter out saying, "Too much top secret stuff is about to happen here, go home." Then we had to frantically put together a press release and call a press conference for midday at Yankee Stadium.

At that point, I didn't know anything about Steinbrenner, and certainly didn't appreciate how young he was, only forty two. Nobody had really heard of him, and the whole thing was stunning. The grounds crew guys, who always have their ears to the ground, were thrilled because they hated CBS ownership. They were the first to say, "This is a great, great thing." I was nervous because with a change of ownership you didn't know what was going to mean to your own career and whether Bob Fishel would stay.

We had the press conference, then a week later we had a second press conference to introduce all the partners, including Gabe Paul, which was a surprise to Mike Burke, and that started a chain of events under which five weeks later Mike Burke resigned and the team was wholly Steinbrenner's.

I hadn't been in the work force long enough to know how the politics work when new management comes in. I thought I was far enough removed that when they made changes they would be to department heads and not to underlings. Still, I was hoping the change would go well for Bob Fishel and he that he would look after me. That's kind of what happened.

After Steinbrenner bought the team, it started to improve. Sparky Lyle had joined the team, and Thurman Munson. It turned around almost overnight. We won in 1976, which was the same year that we returned to the newly-refurbished stadium. We drew two million people. It was as if none of those dozen years between pennants when we played sometimes to crowds of three or four thousand had ever happened. All of a sudden, Yankee Stadium was the festive place to be. Crowds were loud and enthusiastic, and the glory was back. It wasn't even a struggle to win that 1976 pennant. It came very easily.

In some ways, those losing years were more fun because there was less pressure on preparing for a World Series. There was no tension of winning a key series—the players just went out and played one game at a time, and each game was sort of a jewel of its own if you like baseball. It was a smaller organization. It wasn't building up to the size of organizations today. It was more of a family. It was just a great time.

I'm still a Yankee fan. The first thing I check every day is the Yankee box score. I watch most of the games on TV. My son and I went to two of the last Subway Series games. I loved the atmosphere outside the ballpark, how great everybody felt. Even between Yankee and Mets fans, who were easily identified by what they were wearing, there was a spirit of good feeling, not of tension. I think it was because everybody expected the **Yankees** to win and the teasing was good-natured. It felt so good just walking around outside the ballpark.

Football legend Lou Saban was president of the Yankees for one year. Former NFL quarterback, Jim Finks was General Manager of the Minnesota Vikings and the New Orleans Saints, and was president of the Chicago Cubs.

Former Mets GM, Bing Devine, was also General Manager of the St. Louis Cardinals—the baseball Cardinals and the NFL Cardinals.

# MICKEY MANTLE: CAUSE OF DEATH—LIFE

## Mark Rollinson

*Mark Rollinson, 52, grew up in Yonkers in the 1950s and 1960s, believing that the World Series was simply part of the Yankees regular season. Mark still lives in Yonkers where he works in laboratory accounting for the Ciba Specialty Chemical Corp.*

The first baseball game I ever attended was in 1956. I wasn't even five years old. I remember that the Yankees played the Baltimore Orioles. I remember entering Yankee Stadium. I remember the whole surroundings and being in awe of the fact that this guy, Mickey Mantle, who I had never seen any other way but in black and white, was actually, truly, a living person.

The Mick was right there out on the field. I remember spotty details of the game, but mostly what I remember is when the game was over, they would open up the gates and allow us to walk around the warning track. I thought that was the greatest thing in the world.

We walked out along the right field line past the Yankee bullpen and the auxiliary scoreboard, and we came upon the monuments. My brother, my dad, and my neighbor, John, were checking them out, and I was looking at them and saying to myself, "Gee, they buried three guys here. Who are these guys?" I went and read them—or tried to—and my brother was reading and telling me who they were. We lived in Yonkers on the Bronx line, and on the way home we were talking about the game. I said, "I never realized anybody was buried out there." They all looked at me and said, "There's nobody buried there. Those are just monuments. What's wrong with you?" As a four-going-on-five-year old, that was my perception. My brother has kidded me about that ever since.

When I was ten or eleven years old, I was down near the 353-foot marker in right field. That wall wasn't even three feet high in those days, and at the end of an opening in that wall there was a small chain link gate. The players would use it for filing out after the game. I was leaning over that fence and trying my darndest to get a ball that was on the ground. I tried to get my hand under the fence. I tried to get it over. Finally, I reached over, I got my glove on it, and the glove fell off my hand. Tom Tresh and Mickey Mantle were out in the field shagging fly balls—actually just talking with each other. For half an hour I yelled to them, "Mick, my glove. Mick, please, please. Mick, there's a ball in there, Mick. Could you please bring it?" I think just to shut me up, Mantle finally came over and gave it to me. He put the ball into the mitt, looked at me and said, "Here you go, kid." I was in my hour of glory.

One of my most memorable Yankee games happened more recently, when **Joe Girardi** hit that triple in the 1996 World Series. I never heard that amount of noise made in Yankee Stadium, and I've been to well over fifteen-hundred games. I've been in packed houses before, and final games of World Series, but when Girardi hit that ball…

You gotta remember that was Game 6, and we were down two games to none when we went back and won three straight in Atlanta, including the game when Jim Leyritz hit the three-run shot to tie it up at six. Then Wade Boggs walked with the bases loaded to score the seventh run. The Yankees held on to win that game, came back to New York and whacked the Braves on Sunday night. It was the greatest game. I was in section 24, seat 7, right down the third-base line about a hundred feet past the end of the tarp. I'm telling you, that place never shook like that in all the years. I felt that place bouncing and humming. I've been in Madison Square Garden in 1969 and '70 when the Knicks played—you talk about thunderous noises, especially in a confined space. Nothing was ever that loud. Everybody in the place just rocked. When Paul O'Neill came trotting in, it was like the

When Joe Girardi played for the Cubs, he caught a ceremonial first pitch from Mike Ditka. Girardi had a football curled behind his back. After catching Ditka's pitch, Girardi fired the football at Ditka which Iron Mike caught easily.

whole place exploded because we knew we had them right where we wanted them. We had taken a lead. We were up three to one now. We weren't gonna give anybody anything. Of course, I felt that way, too, in the 2001 World Series when Alfonso Soriano hit the home run late in the game to put the Yankees ahead, but it didn't come to fruition.

I did get to meet **Mickey Mantle**. I went down to Atlantic City with two friends when he and Willie Mays took a job greeting people at Bally's casino. I went the first day they were working to get their autographs after a golf tournament.

I had Mantle sign the original artwork of the Topps 1953, which is a painted series card. Back in the 1980s, Topps opened their archives, and from the original artwork they made two thousand lithographs. I bought one of those at a very reasonable price, and I had Mantle autograph that. I spoke with him for about ten minutes. Willie Mays, I love him dearly, but he disappointed me. He just kept his head down and kept on writing. He wouldn't really say much more than, "Hey, how you doin'?"

It was so strange when the Mick died. I had walked downstairs to the bathroom. There's a radio in there, and I always turn it on. I hit CBS at the top of the hour, and the first thing I heard was that Mick had died. I went down, sat on my bed, and...I'm crying now, because I was crying like a little baby that night. You feel attached to these people. It's hard to explain. I'm not part of their life, but for sure they were part of mine.

> Between walks and strikeouts, Mickey Mantle went the equivalent of seven full seasons without putting the bat on the ball.

# PHOENIX: THE VALLEY OF THE SUN... EXCEPT IN THE SUMMER WHEN IT'S THE SURFACE OF THE SUN

Mike Spelman

*Now living in Phoenix but raised in the shadow of Yankee Stadium, forty-five year-old Mike Spelman works for ADP, selling printing services to financial companies.*

In the 1960s, every kid, including me, wanted to be Mickey Mantle. By the time I was thirteen or fourteen years old, I wanted to be Bobby Murcer. The 44th police precinct, located on Sedgewick Avenue, used to have a Christmas party every year. One or two Yankees would always show up. Mantle and Maris never came, but guys like Hector Lopez and Roger Repoz came a lot. Whitey Ford showed up one year. He was a New York boy. One year Ralph Houk showed up. Al Downing came. Those were nice times.

I was a good ballplayer—in fact, I played almost up to the professional level, and I simulated the Yankees' batting stances and the way they played their positions, the way they stood in the outfield, silly things like that. I never did wear Number 7 when I was playing, but my son has been playing ball for about nine years, and I've always made sure he wore Number 7. He knows the whole story. One year, it was really great, my daughter played T-Ball and she actually got Number 7, too. Although we've lived in Phoenix for over five years, my son has the New York roots. He understands the history and the whole mystique of the Yankees.

My old parish, Sacred Heart Church, was located about six blocks from Yankee Stadium. When we were kids, Borden's Milk used to have a coupon on the back of the milk carton. If you cut out "X" number of coupons—I don't remember how many, twenty or twenty-five—they were equal to one ticket to a ball game. Us kids from the parish used to cut out the coupons and go together to games. Last year, we had a reunion. I saw people I hadn't seen in thirty years and we still talked about that.

July 8, 1969 was Mickey Mantle Day. He retired March 1 of that year at a press conference in St. Petersburg, Florida, where the Yankees trained at the time. He announced his retirement, then a couple of weeks later, right before the season opened, the team announced

> **We sat in the center field bleachers. It was a great day. I can't even tell you who was playing.**

plans to have Mickey Mantle Day. Tickets went on sale, but no one could get any. Somehow, my father got tickets through somebody at the Ward Baking Company. We sat in the center field bleachers. It was a great day. I can't even tell you who was playing.

The place was jam-packed to the rafters. It was the old stadium, and there had to be about 65,000 to 68,000 people there. It was a beautiful, warm, gorgeous June day. Mantle came out in a dark suit. The ceremony was held in the infield. Joe DiMaggio was there. All the players were there. The thing I remember most was the fact they put him in a golf cart and did laps around the ballpark. They drove him around the warning track and the infield and outfield cutoffs all the way around the park. I believe they did that two or three times. He just kept waving and waving and waving. To those of us who grew up worshiping the guy, we knew this was the last time we were gonna see him actually on the field. In a way it was horrible—the worst day of my life, but it was also just a wonderful day.

# SO SAY YOU ONE, SO SAY YOU ALL

In the old Bat Day days before they realized that giving a dangerous weapon to fifty-five thousand people was not necessarily a good idea, they would give you a real bat. Then they started giving out replica bats. They would give you a bat, and your bat would have the name of a Yankee on it.

I was a huge Roy White fan. On Bat Day one year, I got a Mickey Mantle bat, and I wanted a Roy White bat, and I found a kid who had a Roy White bat who was only too happy to trade me for my Mickey Mantle bat. A Mickey Mantle bat was probably worth about sixty Roy White bats, but I didn't know that. I just wanted a Roy White bat. We executed the trade, and my father just looked on aghast at his child undervaluing his assets. But it was worth it.

———VICTOR LEVIN, 41, Los Angeles

In September of 1961, I went to Tom's Superette, a little convenience store at the top of my street. I bought my one pack of cards. They used to cost a nickel and a nickel was a big deal. That was my allowance for the week. In this pack, I got a Mickey Mantle MVP card, all red. I was ecstatic. I don't know how, but if a kid ever came in contact with me and he had a Mickey Mantle card, somehow I had to get it out of him. I got some older ones that I didn't buy. They were someone else's and somehow I was able to trade, though I honestly don't remember the trades.

For about two years, I stapled all the cards to my bulletin board. When the players were traded and were no longer Yankees, I would take them down. I have a picture of all these now-valuable Yankee cards that I had stapled up on my bulletin board in my bedroom. When I look at the cards, I ask myself, "How did I get those cards?" But I remember that I just had to have them.

Mickey Mantle was my idol. I had pictures of him all over my bed. I remember when Mantle played at Fenway Park, I was disillusioned. I was probably about seventeen. I had a sign that read, "Mick is the greatest." He was sitting out in the bus, and I was probably about six feet away from him, and he didn't acknowledge any of us fans. Reading the Jim Bouton book *Ball Four* totally took Mantle away as an idol because it made me realize that he was a real person. For eight years, up until reading that book, Mickey Mantle had been like a god. Whenever he came up to bat, I expected him to hit a home run, win the game, or save the game in some way. I don't think I've ever had that feeling toward any other player since then. He really was one of the all-time greats.

————VINNY NATALE, 52, Accountant, raised in Cranston, RI

My very, very favorite Yankee was Mickey Mantle. I had so much faith and confidence in him. Before he hurt his knee, I was at a game sitting between home and first. I never in my life saw anyone run that fast to first base. It was unbelievable, because he wasn't a small man either. I couldn't believe he could move that fast. He thrilled me the way he swung the bat and the way the ball jumped off his bat. Anytime he was up, even when he struck out, I knew that he was going to help the Yankees. I don't feel that way about the Yankee players today. I love them dearly, but I don't watch a game and say, "He's going to hit a home run." I've never felt the same about any other Yankee since Mickey Mantle.

I was in Texas when Mickey Mantle became sick and he died. I watched the news about him on TV constantly. I wanted to go to the funeral in Dallas, but I heard there was a mob. I'm so mad at all the bad publicity he's gotten, hearing about how he could have been a better player if he didn't drink. God, how much better could he have been for me? He thrilled me so. There was not a lot of talk about him in Texas. Texans are really strange. They're so into the **Dallas Cowboys**. Even if there's a pennant race, if there's an exhibition football game, they couldn't care less about baseball.

————THERESA ARO, 67, Retired Credit Manager

Mickey Mantle was my idol. Based on that alone, when I was seventeen, I got a job as a vendor at the Stadium simply so I could watch Mantle play. I was the worst salesman they had because I didn't sell, I watched the games. They never fired me, but because I was such a

> It is true that NBA coach Pat Riley never played college football, but was drafted by the Dallas Cowboys. His brother, Lee, played seven years in the NFL. It is not true that Pat Riley combs his hair with a pork chop.

horrible salesman, they gave me popcorn, which is the worst item to sell in terms of commission. The popcorn used to be sold in a little megaphone and when you finished the popcorn, you punched out the bottom, and you had a little megaphone to scream and yell with during the game. I still have my vendor's badge to this day.

My closest contact with Mickey occurred when I was nine or ten while I was waiting outside the stadium players' exit one day. Bobby Richardson and Tony Kubek came out and signed autographs, and Mickey came out swinging his arms and didn't want to stop, and he elbowed me in the head. He didn't hurt me physically, but I was crushed emotionally. In one sense, I got to touch Mickey, on the other hand, he elbowed me in the head.

I love Billy Crystal. He does this comedy bit where he said his idol was Mickey Mantle. He said that when he was Bar Mitzvahed, he did his prayer in an Oklahoma drawl. I used to try to run like Mickey Mantle, even to the point when Mickey's legs bothered him, and he had a limp. Mickey had a way of running with his elbows tucked in near his rib cage, and I used to emulate that all the time. Later in his career, when he limped, I limped, too. Every time I played stickball and got up, in my mind, I was Mickey in the ninth inning of a tied game. I combed my hair like Mickey Mantle.

I still have on my dresser the statue of Mickey Mantle my dad bought me at my first game in 1956. I've been offered six hundred dollars for it as a collector's item, but I'll never part with it. It's plastic and about seven inches high, and Mickey is in his batting stance, holding his bat. It would be sacrilege in my own mind to even consider selling it. The Stadium to me is not a ballpark. It's tied up with my boyhood. It's more than a baseball park. It's my dad and my boyhood so I'll never let go of the little pieces of memorabilia.

———STEPHEN MASCIANGELO, 53, Retired School Teacher

My cousin had been a big DiMaggio fan and she moved right on to Mickey Mantle, so I became a Mickey Mantle idolizer. I have newspaper and magazine clippings, pictures, and autographs all over my little apartment here.

I have wonderful memories of Mickey Mantle at Yankee Stadium. He's absolutely my favorite player despite his frailties and everything that happened. I never met him. The closest I ever got to him was being on the other side of the fence where the parking lot used to be. We were throwing our programs over to the other side hoping for an autograph, which he didn't give us. We did get Mel Stottlemyre that day, if I remember correctly.

I can recall an Old Timers' game I went to when Mantle was still playing. It was one of his last seasons, either 1967 or '68. Jim Merritt, a big tall left-hander, was pitching for the Twins, and Mickey Mantle hit two home runs—the only runs the Yankees scored. One went to the left-field foul pole and one went to the right-field foul pole, so we were ecstatic even though we lost. Every kid says it seemed like every time you went to a game, Mickey Mantle did something.

I remember him playing the Los Angeles Angels, and he was definitely over his prime, limping, really having trouble. He couldn't hit the high fast ball anymore. He'd made an error earlier in the game to let a run in, and then he got up in either the ninth or tenth inning and hit a ball in the upper deck near right center, very high, just a walk-off home run. It ended the game. We couldn't even talk. We'd never seen a ball hit like that before or since. It wasn't a fly ball that came down. It was rising. It looked like it was out of that movie, *The Natural*, where Robert Redford's character hit the lights. You couldn't even clap or scream. It took the air out of you.

I saw him in a game against the Tigers. The Tigers were great in 1967 and '68, the year they won the pennant. The Yankees were definitely outmatched in the late 1960s. At this game, Mantle came up in the ninth inning of a tied game. He led off with a walk, which always disappointed everybody. You never wanted Mickey Mantle to walk. He got a base on balls. Somehow, he stole second. I don't know how he did it. Tom Tresh was the next batter, and he hit a base hit to left field. You knew there was no way Mickey Mantle was gonna score from second base. It was a hard hit ball. Jim Northrup was the left fielder. He picked up the ball and threw it home. From the angle high up behind home plate where I was sitting, it looked like Mantle had made the turn after the throw was already released by the left fielder. He's dead. He's gonna be dead at the plate. But something made the ball take a weird bounce over the head of Bill Freehan, the Tigers' catcher, and Mantle slid in with the winning run. It seems like a small thing, not a home run, nothing spectacular, but the place went crazy, absolutely wild. This was a man who was really physically deteriorating at that point. Somehow, that ball just took a high hop over the catcher's head. There wasn't even a play. Mantle just slid home with the winning run.

——JOE SANTOIEMMA, 50, Bronx native

*Richard Brewer*

When Mickey Mantle went public and talked about his liver problems and his drinking and how he wished he had everything to do over again and he told people, "Don't do what I did. Do what people tell you to do. Do the right thing," deep in my heart I was so sad for him because I thought, "Here's someone who was so talented and so neat a person." It really touched my heart when Mantle said that and then, later, when he died. What really touched me is that he was on a donors' list for a liver, and he insisted that he not be moved high on the list because he was famous. I think if he'd had the transplant earlier, it might have made a difference. I didn't know all about the drinking and philandering at the time he was doing it. But you know, most of the old-time players were like that. Babe Ruth was a rascal. That was part of the game. They were a pretty rough bunch.

——RICHARD BREWER, 66, Edmond, OK

In the 1950s, I was a real Mickey Mantle fan. Everything was Number 7. Whatever shirt we wore, whether it was a baseball shirt or basketball uniform or whatever, was always Number 7. Mickey Mantle's picture was all over the neighborhood. We saved Mantle cards and Mantle pictures. I grew up in an all-Italian neighborhood, and most of us were sports fans. People were mostly Yankee fans but there were Giants fans and a few Dodger fans. Every day we kids argued over Mantle, Duke Snider and Willie Mays. We all collected Yankee stuff. We'd argue, "Who has the biggest collection?" One kid would say, "Oh, I've got more Mays pictures than you have Mantle pictures. Come and see." That kind of thing.

——JOE FOSINA, 66, New Rochelle, NY

Mickey Mantle was my idol. He was the guy I loved. Any time he came up to the plate, I would stop whatever I was doing. I'd read about him every night in the papers. And, of course, I wore Number 7 on my jersey.

I loved Mantle because he was the first player I saw who could do magical things. He was this good-looking guy, blond, with muscles—he was everything I wanted to be, everything most kids wanted to be. He could do no wrong. He was always in the newspaper. We didn't have the information we have today so you'd have to read the newspaper to see what happened the night before. I'd always be hanging out on the front stoop with my friends when my father came home from work with the *Daily News*, which he brought home for my mother to read. I had to run to my father and kiss him because if I didn't kiss him, he would be mad at me. So I'd run and kiss him, and then I'd grab the newspaper out of his hand, and the first thing I'd do is go to the back page.

> **I loved Mantle because he was the first player I saw who could do magical things.**

Usually the Yankees won. I'd look up Mickey Mantle, see who was pitching, how many innings Whitey Ford pitched, and how many strikeouts he had. They had John Blanchard, Elston Howard, and Yogi Berra. I remember Blanchard hitting all those home runs. He was always a clutch home-run hitter. I took this all in in about sixty seconds, and then my father would go upstairs to my mother. When Mantle was fighting Roger Maris for the home-run record, I didn't really care who won. I just wanted them both to do well.

When Mickey died, it was hard because it was like a part of my life passed. I felt like it was the end of an era. It was the end of innocence for me because he was my innocence. He was my youth. He was the guy I thought could do no wrong. I didn't know what he was doing in his private life with women and drinking, and I didn't care. I loved him. I knew he played when he was hurt, and yet he still did these magical things. When he died, I felt the same way as when J.F.K. was assassinated.

I loved Moose Skowron, Whitey Ford, and Luis Arroyo, who was the guy who always saved his games. Ford would pitch six or seven innings and then he was done. In those days, most pitchers pitched a whole game, but not him. As a matter of fact, I was at Whitey Ford Day when they brought out Luis Arroyo in a Lifesaver carton. Whitey Ford went go over to the carton and opened it up, and Luis Arroyo came out. That was neat.

——JERRY FADEN, 57, Brooklyn native

*Maggie McDonald with Bernie Williams*

I don't even remember my first Yankee game because our family was always going. There were six kids in the family and our father was a big time, lifelong, obsessive Yankee fan. He idolized Mickey Mantle.

All of us kids would watch the games at night, and we'd talk baseball with my dad while my mother was out playing bingo or having coffee with her friends. At bedtime, he'd put us to sleep by having us lie down on the floor with our blankets and put on the Yankee game. We'd start dozing off as the game went on. This was just a constant in my family.

When Mickey Mantle passed away in 1995, I was on a backpacking trip in Europe with my older sister and some of our friends. Our parents told us when we called home. We weren't due home for another two months, and we told them to save the newspapers so we could read them.

We arrived home the first week of October, just in time for the '95 ALCS against Seattle. I looked through these two-month-old papers, reading about the funeral and the eulogies. Genevieve, my youngest sister, called "DenDen," looked at me and said, "It was the first time I'd ever seen dad cry." Mickey Mantle was our father's childhood idol. He didn't have a very good father figure. His father left when he was very young. I think maybe that affected his feelings about Mickey Mantle. He'll tell you everything about the Mick. He knows his life story. It was hard to lose him.

——MAGGIE MCDONALD, 30, Brooklyn

After Joe DiMaggio, Mickey Mantle was our guy. In the early 1950s, my friends and I made a sign out of brown wrapping paper, and about eleven of us in two cars went with the sign up to the Stadium. I know we were the first ones to make a sign that said, "Mickey, we love you." We sat in the lower deck of right field, and from center field, Mickey waved to us. Everyone in the Stadium was looking at us.

The Yankees won the game, and afterward, we tried to see him by the clubhouse. A limousine pulled up to pick him up, and there were cops who were pushing us away. Mickey came out and he saw us, and he acknowledged the fact that we were the guys that had brought the sign. He told the cops, "It's all right. Let them go." He shook all our hands and said, "Thanks. I appreciate it. You guys are great."

Was he a ladies' man? He was some ladies' man because the girls lined up along the bullpen in right field and the little low wall and they would wave at him and he would wave back, shake his head, and make dates with some of them.

——CHARLIE FUOCO, 69, raised in the Bronx

Mickey Mantle could have pitched an inning or two with a knuckle-ball. He had a great knuckleball—you couldn't catch the thing. It was one of those that we called a sideline knuckleball. It was good on the sideline. It would have been almost unhittable.

——JIM BOUTON, 64, Former Yankee

Growing up, my favorite Yankee, without question, was Mickey Mantle. When we went to games, anything Mickey Mantle did caused us to cheer loudest. Anything he did, we'd cheer. He came up to bat, we'd cheer. He would make a play, we'd cheer. He would tie his shoe, we would cheer. It was "All Mickey, All the Time." I remember him always talking to Whitey Ford, and I always thought Mickey was so much more "our guy" because he seemed so much younger than Whitey.

——LORI SCHWAB, 44, Marketing Consultant

There was something about Mickey Mantle. It was everything about him—his youth, his appearance, his sort of generalized American boyishness. And then, the power and promise embodied in his physical strength, the way he held the bat that translated for me into kind

*Roy Peter Clark*

of a mythology which became greater over the years, even after it turned out that he had quite a number of fatal flaws.

My mom is right-handed and my dad is left-handed, so I grew up throwing right-handed and batting left-handed. Because Mantle faced mostly right-handed batters, I could definitely make that connection. I couldn't hit with power, but in my final year of organized baseball in the Babe Ruth League, when I was about sixteen years old, I did play center field for the All-Star team.

When you grow up Catholic and passion is frowned upon, you exercise it in any legal way that you can. I guess in my case it was rock and roll music and the New York Yankees.

I went to St. Aidan's, a Catholic grade school, in Williston Park on Long Island, where you were constantly reminded of your "sinfulness." It was during the era when we used to collect, trade, and flip baseball cards, which was a form of gambling, a kind of competitiveness. Mickey Mantle was my idol.

I was about a sixth grader when I saw a Mickey Mantle card that I wanted badly. In the schoolyard, some kids were flipping cards, and the cards were scattered all over the asphalt. I took a piece of bubble gum, which you weren't allowed to chew, and I stuck it on the bottom of my shoe. Then I walked past their game, and in a moment of confusion when an argument was ensuing, I stepped on the card and it attached itself to the bottom of my shoe.

I basically illegally, acquired a Mickey Mantle card. I had coveted it, but it was only a venial sin, not a mortal sin because I couldn't help myself. The power of the Mick, the desire to possess him was too great. I didn't invent this way of stealing cards. There was a wave of this kind of petty crime. There were techniques that would minimize the stickiness of the gum so the card wouldn't be damaged.

——ROY PETER CLARK, 54, raised on Long Island

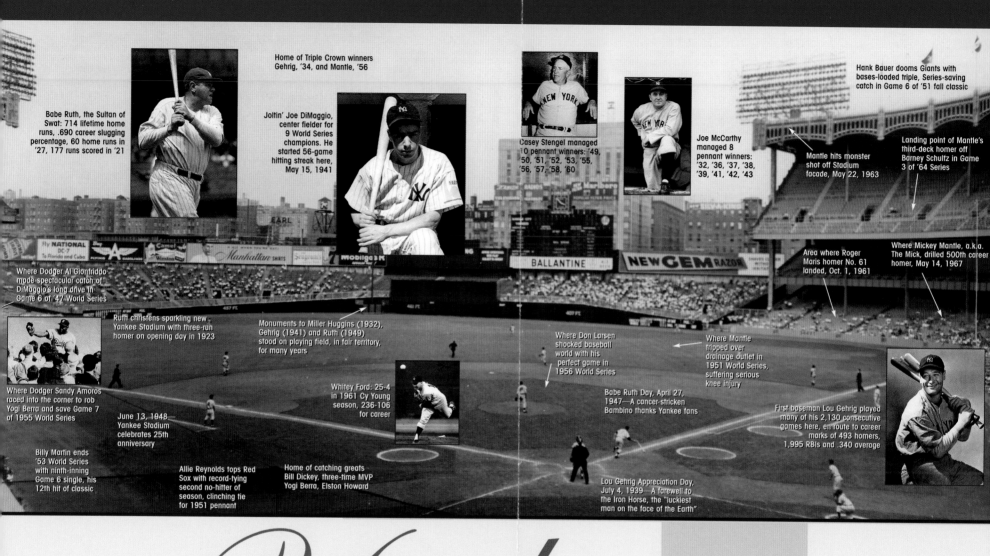

Home of Triple Crown winners Gehrig, '34, and Mantle, '56

Hank Bauer dooms Giants with bases-loaded triple, Series-saving catch in Game 6 of '51 fall classic

Babe Ruth, the Sultan of Swat: 714 lifetime home runs, .690 career slugging percentage, 60 home runs in '27, 177 runs scored in '21

Joltin' Joe DiMaggio, center fielder for 9 World Series champions. He started 56-game hitting streak here, May 15, 1941

Casey Stengel managed 10 pennant winners: '49, '50, '51, '52, '53, '55, '56, '57, '58, '60

Joe McCarthy managed 8 pennant winners: '32, '36, '37, '38, '39, '41, '42, '43

Mantle hits monster shot off Stadium facade, May 22, 1963

Landing point of Mantle's third-deck homer off Barney Schultz in Game 3 of '64 Series

Where Dodger Al Gionfriddo made spectacular catch of DiMaggio's long drive in Game 6 of '47 World Series

Area where Roger Maris homer No. 61 landed, Oct. 1, 1961

Where Mickey Mantle, a.k.a. The Mick, drilled 500th career homer, May 14, 1967

Ruth christens sparkling new Yankee Stadium with three-run homer on opening day in 1923

Monuments to Miller Huggins (1932), Gehrig (1941) and Ruth (1949) stood on playing field, in fair territory, for many years

Where Don Larsen shocked baseball world with his perfect game in 1956 World Series

Where Mantle tripped over drainage outlet in 1951 World Series, suffering serious knee injury

Where Dodger Sandy Amoros raced into the corner to rob Yogi Berra and save Game 7 of 1955 World Series

Whitey Ford: 25-4 in 1961 Cy Young season, 236-106 for career

Babe Ruth Day, April 27, 1947—A cancer-stricken Bambino thanks Yankee fans

First baseman Lou Gehrig played many of his 2,130 consecutive games here, en route to career marks of 493 homers, 1,995 RBIs and .340 average

June 13, 1948— Yankee Stadium celebrates 25th anniversary

Billy Martin ends '53 World Series with ninth-inning Game 6 single, his 12th hit of classic

Allie Reynolds tops Red Sox with record-tying second no-hitter of season, clinching tie for 1951 pennant

Home of catching greats Bill Dickey, three-time MVP Yogi Berra, Elston Howard

Lou Gehrig Appreciation Day, July 4, 1939—A farewell to the Iron Horse, the "luckiest man on the face of the Earth"

# STADIUM *Yankee* 1923-73
## PRE-RENOVATION

Joe Torre has managed five pennant winners and four World Series champions— '96, '98, '99 and 2000

Home of George Steinbrenner's Bronx Zoo

Remodeled Yankee Stadium opens April 15, 1976

Landing area for Brett's third-deck homer off Goose Gossage—the deciding blow in Game 3 of '80 ALCS

Shortstop Derek Jeter, the main cog in Yankees' 1996-2001 pennant and championship machine

Where 12-year-old Jeffrey Maier made the catch of his life on Jeter's home run in Game 1 of 1996 ALCS

Tino Martinez, Scott Brosius hit two-out, two-run, game-tying home runs in ninth inning on consecutive nights to stun Diamondbacks in Games 4 and 5 of 2001 Series ... Jeter, Alfonso Soriano provide game-winning hits

Monument Park

Where Chris Chambliss hit ALCS-winning home run in 1976

Opening day '78: Roger Maris returns to Stadium for first time since '66 trade to Cardinals

Thurman Munson hits ALCS-turning home run into bullpen vs. Royals in 1978 Game 3

Area patroled by '85 A.L. MVP Don Mattingly from 1980-95—one of most popular players in Yankees history

World Series playground for always-controversial Reggie Jackson, a.k.a. Mr. October

Where fiery Billy Martin was hired and fired as manager five times by George Steinbrenner

Louisiana Lightning: Ron Guidry dominates with 25-3 record, 1.74 ERA in 1978 Cy Young season ... strikes out 18 Angels June 17

Where Roger Clemens threw broken piece of bat, narrowly missing Mets star Mike Piazza, during intense and confrontational Game 2 of 2000 Subway Series

Jackson's three homers on consecutive pitches finish off Dodgers in Game 6 of '77 World Series

Chicago's Tom Seaver wins 500th game, Aug. 4, 1985

Site of K.C. third baseman George Brett's Pine Tar tirade, July 24, 1983

Wade Boggs gets victory ride on police horse after 1996 Series-clinching victory

May 14, 1996: Comeback-minded Doc Gooden no-hits Mariners

David Wells fires first regular-season perfect game in Yankees history, May 17, 1998 ... David Cone spices up "Yogi Berra Day" with another perfect game, July 18, 1999

Last game of century takes place at Stadium as Yanks complete sweep of Braves for 25th World Series championship, Oct. 27, 1999

STADIUM

Yankee

1976-Present

POST-RENOVATION

# Chapter 7

# When the Yanks Call, Ya Gotta Accept the Charges

## Take this Job and Love It

# HE TOOK THE YANKEES
# TO THE CLEANERS

## Joe Fosina

*Lifelong New Rochelle resident Joe Fosina, 66, was fortunate to be at the right place at the right time. The company this diehard fan works for cleans and repairs the Yankees' uniforms.*

*Joe Fosina (middle) with Yankees players Ramiro Mendoza and Mariano Rivera*

I work for Raleigh Athletic in New Rochelle. The company has cleaned and repaired the Yankees' uniforms since 1945, when Pete Sheehy, the Yankee equipment manager, found what was then a little company to do it. Back in those days when the uniforms were wool, they had to be pressed every day. Otherwise, they looked wrinkled.

In 1978, I was working for the company as a salesman for the Connecticut region. Our customers are mostly high schools, colleges, and a few pro teams. The salesman in the Bronx died about that time, and the boss said to me, "Well, you've got to handle all our Bronx customers." I said, "That's fine, but I get the Yankees, too." He said, "Well, we've been handling that as a house account." I said, "No way. If I get the Bronx, I get all of them." He said, "Okay, take it." So I've been handling the Yankee uniforms for twenty-four years.

When the Yankees are at home, I'm at the Stadium every day. I'm in the clubhouse every day. I put the armbands on the uniforms when Roger Maris died, when Thurman Munson died, and when Mickey Mantle died. We have a factory and I bring the uniforms in and our seamstresses sew the black armbands on.

I'll never forget when Thurman died. I was on the football field coaching Pop Warner football, and my wife pulled up in the car. I panicked because she never came to the football field unless there was an emergency. She said, "The Yankees called, and you've got to call them right away." I said, "Why?" She said, "I have no idea."

By the time I jumped in the car and went home, the announcement that Munson had died came on the radio. The Yankees called me and said, "Mr. Steinbrenner wants something done with the uniforms for tomorrow's game." I drove down to the Stadium and we worked up different ideas. We tried out a Number 15. We put on a black armband. We did different kinds of things and settled on the black armband.

If you watch the Yankee games when they play at home, you'll see, say, Bernie Williams slide and rip his pants. In that case, we'll pick his pants up after the game, and the next day one of the ladies will sew them, and Williams will get them back. We try to hold the uniform together for a whole year. Those players who are superstitious, like Paul O'Neill and Bernie Williams, wear the same pants all year. We patch them and do all kinds of things. Jason Giambi doesn't like to change his pants. Guys like him will say, "Joe, man, you've got to get these pants back for tomorrow, right? These are my game pants and the others I'll practice in and work out in, but when the game comes I want these pants on." I say, "Yeah, I understand."

Not all the Yankee players feel this way. A guy like Derek Jeter doesn't care. He takes whatever's in his locker. He's got two or three pairs that he wears. We clean them, we repair them, we put numbers on when they make trades. For years and years, the Yankee uniforms were made by Wilson, but they're made by Russell Athletic now.

The way the players wear their pants runs in circles. Bobby Murcer was the first Yankee to roll his pants tight down his legs. We used to taper them for him. After he did that, you started seeing a lot of players who liked the tapered look. That's changed in the last couple of years. Now, the players are going to a more baggy, bell-bottom look.

I love being at Old Timers' Day. To see the old players come back in the clubhouse early in the day, sit around and tell stories about when they were playing in the 1950s and 1960s, is marvelous. Even the current ball players absolutely love to listen and talk to those guys.

On Old Timers Day, I go to the ballpark in the morning to take care of business. I stay in the clubhouse usually from three to five o'clock, when the players start to get ready to play. Then I go home and watch the game on TV like everybody else.

I love to sit and talk with Yogi Berra, Moose Skowron, Hank Bauer and the other guys. Most of them tell the old "war stories." In the days when they played, they didn't have six pair of gloves in their lockers, and they notice things like that. They see the differences in the equipment. They'll tell you that they had one pair of shoes, which they had to buy themselves. The Yankees provide most everything for the old timers to wear on that day.

Don Larsen comes a lot now, and Yogi will sit around and just shoot the breeze. As a fan, I get excited at the chance to be with the players because everybody else goes home and watches games on TV, and I talk to Jeter every day, or to Bernie Williams or Roger Clemens. I watch the game completely differently than the average fan does because I have a personal interest in everything they do. Mariano Rivera has become a family friend. We spent a week with him in **Panama**. Now I worry if he gives up a hit or gives up a run. I watch the game so much more intently. When I walk in the clubhouse the next day, if I know if a guy lost or didn't do well, I'll take a different approach to him. So as a fan, I take the losses a little harder.

Rod Carew was raised in the Bronx but was born unexpectedly on a train in Panama. He was delivered by an American doctor, Rodney Cline, a passenger on the train. Rod Carew's full name is Rodney Cline Carew.

# YANKEE PAN DEMONIUM

### "Frying Pan Fred"

*Life-long Yankee diehard Fred Schuman has found his way into Yankee hearts with a kitchen frying pan. Fred, 77, is a retired truck driver and lives in Manhattan.*

The Yankees themselves have labeled me "Number One Fan." I have letters from them saying so. They're written on the actual Yankee letterhead and signed by Mr. Kraft of the Yankees public relations department, so I can prove it.

It all started in 1988 when I had gone to a game about the time I retired. I was very disappointed. The Yankees were in last place, so I suggested to the management that if they would give me an opportunity, maybe I could wake up the fans and maybe the fans could wake up the Yankees.

I remembered that as a kid growing up in the Bronx in the 1930s, we used to celebrate New Year's Eve by banging pots and pans in the apartment hallway and waking up the neighbors. I made some signs and attached them to a stake, drilled a hole through the wood and attached a frying pan to it. The first year was a little rough. I could only get the kids to hit the frying pan. They loved it. But the grown-ups—I can't even repeat the language that some of them used to tell me to get lost. Boy, did they give it to me good.

After the first year, on the following Opening Day, the grownups started to ask, "Could we have an opportunity to hit the frying pan? Could we have an autograph? Would you sign our ball?" The grownups started to come around. Evidently, they saw the kids were having such a good time they wanted to have a good time, too. Also, what I was doing seemed to have helped an awful lot. The Yankees did improve. Let's face it, they were in last place, they had to improve. Gradually, year after year, it progressed to the point where it was not exactly embarrassing, but the fans would say things like, "Freddie, you're an icon. You're the Number One Fan. We love you."

When I first started taking around my frying pans, I bought my tickets every time, and I didn't have the same seat for every game. Now the Yankees don't charge me to go in. And if there's a situation where I would have to pay for something, Modells is my sponsor. No matter what I spend for the ticket, Modells reimburses me. That also started in 1997 or '98.

> **I never stole any frying pans from my wife. I just "used" them.**

I begin in the upper tier for the first three innings. Then I go to left field, center field, and right field. If every single seat is taken, I don't sit down. I will sit down if somebody vacates a seat for a moment. Then when the fourth, fifth and sixth innings come around, I will be in the loge section. For the seventh, eighth and ninth innings, I will go down to field level.

I never stole any frying pans from my wife. I just "used" them. Actually, I have used six different frying pans over the course of years. They get dented. People hit them with such force that while they are originally flat, they become concave. I don't really buy frying pans. People give them to me. The frying pans that are made out of steel make the most noise. Aluminum frying pans make noise but not as loud, plus they cave in faster than the chromium steel ones.

I have one particular frying pan that Mayor Giuliani used to call "the lucky frying pan." For some reason, when he hit it and when I hit it and when the fans hit it, the Yankees seemed to win. In 2001, the mayor took me out to Arizona with him for Game 7 of the World Series. In the eighth inning, Mayor Giuliani said, "Freddie, do your magic." I started to hit the frying pan and, lo and behold, Alphonso Soriano hit a home run. Unfortunately, we lost out to Arizona, but I did my fair share.

# FUZZY IS NOW "COMIC BOOK GUY" ON *THE SIMPSONS*

Phil Panasci

*Phil Panasci, 48, loved* **Roger Maris** *over Mantle, treasures memories of the Yankees' lean years of the early 1970s, and after growing up in the Wakefield section of the Bronx, now lives with his family on Cape Cod, where he is in the messenger service business.*

In the 1980s and '90s, I probably went to fifteen or twenty games a year, and I knew people and saw people who went to literally every game. There was a subculture of "weirdo" baseball fans. One guy had been to every single Yankee game for twelve years straight. He was a total weirdo, a total nerd. He wasn't interesting at all. But there was a whole bunch of these guys. One guy was named Fuzzy, and he was really famous. Fans who would go often to Yankee Stadium or Shea would know who Fuzzy was. He would always be in the same place, sitting in Section 1. He was a middle-aged guy, short, squat, hairy, balding, bearded, not appealing at all. And he talked in a fast, scratchy, loud whisper.

You'd hear these guys having a contest about who went to more games that year. They'd include major and minor league games. They'd try to do it all—go to a minor league game in the afternoon and then go to a major league game at night. That's all these guys did. In the current marketplace, these guys are shut out. They can't go to

Roger Maris' original name was Maras. Tired of fans deliberately mispronouncing his last name, he changed it in 1955. An outstanding high school football player in Fargo, ND, he went to Oklahoma on scholarship to play for Coach Bud Wilkinson. He quit after two weeks.

every game anymore. Teams want the kind of people that go to one game a year and spend a lot of money, so you don't get these hardcore nuts anymore. Now you go, and it's kind of boring.

One of my most memorable baseball days occurred in the 1985 season. The Mets were on the verge of becoming a really good team, and the Yankees were sort of on the way downhill, but that season was probably the first time—and after that it didn't happen for a long time—when the Yankees and the Mets were both in a pennant race at the same time.

It was September, and they were each playing the team they had to beat at home on the same day. It was an exciting time. There was an afternoon game at Shea Stadium and a night game at Yankee Stadium. I remember people playing hooky from work to go to both games. They were both really exciting, come-from-behind victories for the home team.

It was one of those magical baseball days. Ultimately, neither of them made it to the World Series that year, but that day was just a great, great day. It was fun. Seeing two games in one day is wild. Years later, my friends and I still refer to it as "Baseball Thursday."

Every year for the first game of the World Series, regardless of whether the Yankees are in it or not—though obviously in recent years the Yankees have been—I get together with a couple of friends and we spend the whole day just walking around the Bronx. Only one of us lives there anymore. We start early in the morning. We visit our old neighborhoods, go past our old schools, all our old haunts. We end up back at my friend's place in Riverdale, and we watch the first game of the World Series together. We have this bond. We're three friends who've known each other for forty years, and though we now live in different places, we manage to get together for that special occasion. It's really nice and fun. Basically, we just laugh all day.

# THE YANKEES FILL THE POTHOLES OF HIS SOUL

Louis Dituri

*Forty-nine-year-old Louie Dituri put his money where his mouth is. At his restaurant across from Yankee Stadium, Yankee Eatery, his patrons do, too.*

I grew up in Oakland, California. A lot of people don't realize that a lot of famous Yankees came from the San Francisco Bay area: Joe DiMaggio, Billy Martin, Frank Crosetti. In 1962, I was in third grade, and my teacher was a big Giants fan, so she allowed us to listen to the World Series during class. It was the last game of the Series when McCovey lined out to Bobby Richardson. The teacher came up to my desk after the line drive, and she looked me in the eye and asked me the question very poignantly, "How can you live in California and be a Yankee fan?" Then she walked off. Of course, I was laughing inside because I wanted to say, "We win."

My brother Phil and I always felt misplaced growing up in **Oakland**. We felt we were supposed to live in New York. Now we know why. You go to New York, you walk around Manhattan, and you feel at home. You never think that you're a stranger or someone visiting the city. Then, of course, we'd looked at Yankee Stadium on television all our lives. CBS owned the Yankees when I was growing up, so out in California we were able to watch the games every weekend. Being around Yankee Stadium was just something I always dreamed about doing.

> Late Oakland A's owner, Charles O. Finley, grew up in Northern Indiana and loved Notre Dame. When he bought the A's, he changed their colors to Notre Dame's green and gold.

Starting in the early 1990s, my brother and I would travel to New York about twice a year and spend every day of every trip at Yankee Stadium watching Yankee games. We had gotten tired of going to the Oakland Coliseum. There just weren't many Yankee fans, and we never felt at home. So after making these trips for about three years, I suggested to my brother, "Phil, we've got to find a way to get paid to do this rather than having to pay."

Around 1994, I was in New York attempting to buy a technology company that was in bankruptcy. After the court hearing ended, I had about a day and a half to kill so I said to myself, "Well, I'm gonna go hang around Yankee Stadium." What better place to be if you're in New York but Yankee Stadium?

**Since we've owned Yankee Eatery, the Yankees have won four World Series— three in a row—**

In the past, my brother and I had eaten at this restaurant, Yankee Eatery, because the food was so much better and cheaper than inside the Stadium. I went inside and saw the guys preparing for the season. It was a strike year. I just walked up to the counter and one of those lights went on in my head. I said, "Hello. My name's Louis Dituri. I'm from California. If you're ever interested in selling this business, let me know." The owner said, "Sure, we can talk I guess." I said, "Well, think about it."

I was on my way back to the subway, which is less than fifty yards from the restaurant, when the owner called me back. I returned, and he said, "We need to talk." I told him, "Well, I am going to be back in two weeks. Why don't we talk about it then?"

Well, lo and behold, Phil and I now own that restaurant and have since 1996. I remind you, 1996 was the first year the Yankees got back into the World Series. Since we've owned Yankee Eatery, the Yankees have won four World Series—three in a row—and were a couple of outs away from winning four in a row. We've seen post-season game after post-season game. When that poor guy ended his eleven-year history owning the restaurant, he'd seen only two post-season games. So now I get to spend the baseball season here in the Bronx. If the Yankee's are home, we're there.

I've had several offers to buy the restaurant, but I always tell people, "Look, everything I get out of this restaurant is extra because I came here to be by Yankee Stadium. That was the reason for coming here."

I rent a room during baseball season from a great family that I met in the early years. They are avid Yankee fans, but the interesting thing is that they are from the Dominican Republic. I speak no Spanish, and they speak no English. We get along like a family, especially when the conversation has to do with the Yankees. I could say to Rosie, "The Yankees win. The Yankees win." And she'll know what I'm talking about. It's a lot of fun. She'll do the same when I walk in after the game if she's awake. She'll stand there and say, "The Yankees win. They're so good. They're so good."

Some of the players will come into the restaurant from time to time. David Cone came in the day that the joint that held together two pillars in Yankee Stadium fell, damaged the concrete below and a couple of seats, and they had to close Yankee Stadium for a period of several weeks. He spent about twenty minutes signing autographs for everybody who came in, talking, and allowing us to ask him questions about his career. He was having a slow start, and he was down on himself saying, "I want to get going." Everybody was saying, "We know you're gonna get going." He said, "If I could just get myself going, we'd be doing great." We kept saying, "Aw, we're not worried about it. You'll be there." He ended up having a good year.

Pat Kelly would come in sometimes and just grab something real quickly, like a hot dog. If he didn't come in, he'd wave. A few of the players enter the Stadium through the back, and pass by us on their way. Another one who used to come by and say hello was Ruben Sierra, although he never stopped to eat. Then Gene Monahan, a Yankee trainer, would come in every once in a while. We have a little counter that you can stand at on the sidewalk and get a hot dog or something, and he'd eat there. What was interesting is whoever was standing beside him, Monahan would always buy them a hot dog, too.

A couple of years ago, I met Bobby Murcer. The significance of my meeting Bobby Murcer is that when I was younger, I first wanted to be Roger Maris because he was left-handed like me, but once Roger Maris was gone, Bobby Murcer came up. Of course, he was supposed to replace Mickey Mantle, but in any event, he was left-handed, and so I kinda latched onto him. When I met him two years ago, I told him that story, and he said, "I don't think you wanted to be me." I said, "Well, I really did want to be you." Then I told him, "You know Bobby, one of the worst days on my life was when they traded you to San Francisco for Bobby Bonds."

In 1996, the Yankees were humiliated by the Atlanta Braves in the first two games. This guy who calls himself "Super Yankee Fan," came into the restaurant, and he was practically crying after we lost the second game. But being the positive guy that I am, I said, "Herman, what's the matter?" He said, "Man, we're not gonna win. We can't beat these guys." I said, "Herman, I'm gonna tell you what I told a friend of mine when the Dodgers played the Yankees and the Dodgers won the first two games of the World Series. 'This is called a series. We've only played two games. So don't give up yet.'"

He just kept hanging his head and doubting that we could ever come back, and he looked up at me, and I said, "Herman, are you gonna be here Saturday?" He said, "What for?" I said, "Well, we're gonna paint '1996 World Champions' on that wall right there." He said, "We're not gonna beat Maddux. We're not gonna beat Glavine." And he just rattled off all the pitchers' names.

Well, what happened Saturday? The Yankees went to Atlanta, won three in a row, and came back to New York and won it there. Herman, the Super Fan, gave up. But Louie, the real fan, never gave up.

# FRIENDS DON'T LET FRIENDS CATCH JIM BOUTON...UNLESS IT'S ON TELEGRAPH HILL

### Eddie Miller

*Like a lot of Yankee fans, seventy year-old Eddie Miller didn't have much money growing up in the South Bronx as a child of the Depression. But rooting for the Yankees softened the bumps. Now living in Florida, the actor and softball star got an early dose of reality when he and his buddies hung outside Henry's Bayview Inn to catch a glimpse of their favorite players.*

I grew up four blocks from Yankee Stadium. In 1947, when I was fourteen, my dad lost his job as a sign hanger on billboards, and my mother got sick. It was really a tough time. My brother was sent to stay with an aunt, and I went to live with my grandmother in Throgs Neck, then the suburbia of the Bronx. My grandmother lived in a beautiful bungalow colony, a block off the water. It was another world, with trees and open lots and places to play ball.

In Throgs Neck, there was a place called Henry's Bayview Inn, a very popular, late night bistro-restaurant. The Yankees would come up there and hang out to get away from all the fans down in the South Bronx. We got word about it from the boss's son, who used to tell us, "The Yanks are in here."

It was great. We'd go down there and see fifteen or twenty kids standing outside just waiting for the players to come out. None of us kids rooted for the Dodgers because we were Bronx kids. Brooklyn was another world. We didn't care about Brooklyn.

We couldn't go inside Henry's because we were too young. Some guys would stagger out. The Yankees I remember distinctly were Joe Page, who had a reputation for really boozing, and Allie Reynolds. It wasn't like they were drunks or anything. They were just feeling good, having a nice time. I don't remember them ever being with their wives though. It was kind of like a place where guys go to hang out. They didn't go that often. Maybe in a period of a month, we'd see them once or twice.

One night, Joe Page came out, and I asked him for his autograph. He was a little sloshed. He wrote his name like this: J – o – o – o – e – P – a – a – a – g – e. I wish I still had that autograph. I have no idea where it is. I had a scrapbook filled with Yankee stuff, and I have no idea what happened to it. Oh, I wish I had that thing.

I remember meeting Mel Allen, the Yankee voice. He was The Man. He was coming out from Henry's and said to me, "How you doing there, little fellow?" or something like that, with that beautiful Mel Allen voice of his.

I started to fully appreciate the Yanks about 1949 when I was sixteen years old. That year, I had a chance to go see the second game of the World Series with a friend, Harry Hink. We went to Yankee Stadium the night before the second Series game against the Dodgers, and we had to stay there all night to get a seat. We went to the bleacher line where we were about third in line. I remember sitting down on this slab of concrete and staying there all night. Since we lived so close, our parents would walk by and take a look to see if we were okay, but by that time there was a long line of people. I think it cost us fifty cents or seventy-five cents for bleachers seats. Preacher Roe was pitching against Vic Raschi. The Yankees won 2-1.

Phil Rizzuto later became my hero because I was an infielder in the sandlots. At that time, he was the little guy. He won the MVP in 1950. I used to wonder how wonderful it must be to play alongside him. Then, years later—I was a player/manager for the CBS All-Stars, a charity softball team, in the 1970s when CBS owned the Yankees. Rizzuto was working for CBS at the time, and he played in one of our games out in New Jersey. This was about 1971 or '72.

So here I was on the softball field with Phil Rizzuto! We had our infield practice, and I'm feeding him the ball on double plays, and he's playing short and I'm playing second. He was probably fifty then, but he was still good enough for softball. We played a pretty good brand of softball, so it wasn't the ground balls that bothered him. He could field them. But when we threw the ball around, he kept taking the glove off and saying things like, "My God, you guys are going to break my hand," and "Boy, you guys really throw that ball around really fast."

I just kept thinking to myself, "Isn't this great? This guy was my hero when I was a kid, and now I finally get a chance to play alongside him in a softball game." We even made a double play! How many guys in their life can say they made a double play with Phil Rizzuto, a Hall of Famer? I've got that on video. It was great, sensational.

**How many guys in their life can say they made a double play with Phil Rizzuto, a Hall of Famer?**

I talked to him and told him how I had felt about him as a kid. He loved it. He was a sweet guy. I remember asking him who was the best second baseman he ever played with. He didn't want to hurt anybody's feelings so he said they were all pretty good, but he told me he really enjoyed playing with Jerry Coleman. I said, "Well, what about me, Phil?"

In the late 1970s, I was still managing the CBS team when I was voted to become Commissioner of the League. At the time, Jim Bouton, who had been a Yankee, and Ron Swoboda, who had been a Met, were both working for CBS as newscasters. Bouton was doing the six o'clock news. Swoboda was doing the eleven o'clock news. CBS wanted to do a little human-interest story. Could Bouton strike out Swoboda?

So we all went up to Shea Stadium—myself, Jim Jensen, CBS' star newscaster, and some of the guys from the team, including Duke Carmel. In his book, *Ball Four*, Bouton was very unkind to Duke, who had come up as a rookie with the Yankees from his minor league team where he'd had hit fifty-nine home runs in one season. When he came up to the Yankees, he couldn't get a hit. He just could not get it.

Now we're all up in Shea Stadium, and they've got the camera guys there to do the story. The umpire they'd gotten had spent many years in the sandlots. Bouton was gonna pitch, but they couldn't find anybody to catch because Bouton threw a knuckleball. I used to be a catcher so I said, "Give me the stuff and the mitt, and I'll get behind the plate."

So I'm gonna catch Bouton, and Swoboda's gonna hit. I'm calling the signals for Bouton, what to throw, etc. Swoboda gets a few hits, and then he strikes out a couple of times.

When it was over, Bouton started teasing Duke Carmel, "Hey Duke, get in there, take a couple of swings." Now I know Duke Carmel real well because we had played together when we were kids. Duke came over to me and whispered, "Hey you, how long we know each other? A long time, right?" I said, "Yeah, of course, Duke." He said, "I want to know every pitch that's coming." I said, "Duke, I can't. This is like the honor system. I'm the catcher, he's the pitcher. I gotta give him the signs. Nobody is supposed to know them but me and him."

Duke said, "I don't want to hear that ———. I want you to tell me every pitch." So I said, "Okay."

Now I'm calling the sign, the umpire's right behind me at home plate, and I whisper to Duke, "Curve ball." Whatever Bouton is throwing, Carmel is popping them into the stands. He's hitting home runs all over the place. It was funny. The umpire kept saying, "You guys are slime. You guys should be ashamed of yourself." I knew the umpire from all the years playing sandlot ball. I said, "You shut up. Come on, we're having some fun here."

When it was over, Bouton came in scratching his head. "Man, this guy was really rapping me." I didn't say a word.

# Chapter 8

# The ERA of the
# E.R.A. and the ERA

## Earned Runs And Equal
## Rights In A Woman's World

# ACTUALLY, THERE WERE FOUR ALOU BROTHERS IF YOU COUNT BOOG

## Amy Shapiro

*Amy Shapiro, 52, has climbed the ladder to the executive suite in the man's world of pay-television entertainment. However, as a child of the 1950s, growing up in Norwalk, Connecticut, Amy found baseball to be an impenetrable bastion of male intimacy.*

When I was growing up in the 1950s, fathers didn't take little girls to baseball games. My dad, who was more of a Giants fan, always took my brother Walter, who is three years older than me, to baseball games. The Yankees were a big deal. My grandfather was a Yankee fan. My uncle was a Yankee fan. My mother's whole family were total Yankee fans. My mother was a Yankee fan, too, and watched the games as soon as we got a television, but she and I never talked about the Yankees. I remember as a child we would all sit around the radio and listen to the games. I thought that Mickey Mantle and Whitey Ford was one word. I'd constantly hear about "MickeyMantleandWhiteyFord."

I always felt that baseball was something Walter and my father shared. They talked about it all the time. I use it as an example of how things have changed. I don't know of any of my girlfriends, regardless of whether they were Yankee fans or not, whose fathers took them to baseball games. Strangely enough, all my girlfriends are huge baseball fans, and they all have husbands and boyfriends who are nuts about baseball, too. Fathers just didn't do it back then. They took their sons to baseball games—they didn't take their daughters. That's just the way things were so I didn't resent it then, but I think I did resent it later on in my life.

Walter played baseball and was an avid fan. We had a marvelous collection of baseball cards. He could do baseball averages in his head. I was always dancing around the edge. At an early age, I just thought baseball was really interesting and fascinating.

I loved Mickey Mantle and Whitey Ford. I loved Mel Allen's great voice. I remember Yogi Berra, Phil Rizzuto—I could actually name all the teams that were in the American and National League in the 1950s before expansion. I wasn't conscious of listening to these details so it wasn't until I was an adult that I realized what an impression the Yankees and baseball had made on me. I said to myself that my interest had obviously been going on for a very long time, and I just didn't realize it. It wasn't until I was in college in **Baltimore** and my best friend and I both admitted that we were avid Yankees fans that I was verbal about my love of baseball.

Around this time, I started knowing the whole lineup of the Yankees and started becoming very, very conscious of everything about baseball. That was about the point where my father and I realized we had this in common. If I would be visiting in Connecticut and there was a baseball game on television, or if I would start reading the sports pages, it became very natural for me to talk to my father about the game. It became apparent to him and to my brother that I loved baseball. I don't think my father had realized it before that time.

Then I moved out to Los Angeles, and I would turn down box seats for the Dodgers because I hated the Dodgers so much. I hated them because they left New York and were the rivals of the Yankees. There were a lot of Yankee fans in L.A. Most of the people I worked with at Universal Pictures as vice-president of pay-television films were from New York and we were all Yankee fans.

I guess I channeled my love of the Yankees out there by hating the Dodgers. That was the communal rivalry. Obviously, we couldn't go to the Yankee home games, and we were only able to get the scores if we got home delivery of the New York Times. I knew why I hated the

St. Mary's Industrial School for Boys in Baltimore —now called Cardinal Gibbons High School—was known as "the House that Built Ruth."

Dodgers, but I was curious as to why other people hated the Dodgers. We were all roughly the same age. The answer was if you were a Yankee fan and had grown up in a Yankees family, you hated the Dodgers. Then, also, there was the double whammy of their being traitors by leaving New York.

> **One of my neighbors walked by and said, "How come you're not outside? It's a gorgeous day." I said, "I'm watching the baseball game."**

A lot of people talk about how laconic Dodger fans are. They don't root or anything, and they leave in the seventh inning. Well, in 1981, the Yankees were playing the Dodgers in the World Series. I had this one-bedroom apartment. LA apartments have these open catwalks so I had my windows open and the drapes open in the living room and was on the floor watching a daytime World Series game. I was home because it was the High Holy Days. One of my neighbors walked by and said, "How come you're not outside? It's a gorgeous day." I said, "I'm watching the baseball game." The neighbor looked at me as though I was totally weird. If I'd been in New York, nobody would have thought it was strange.

I'm now living in Westport, Connecticut, about ten minutes from my dad, who is ninety-three. I tried to get reception at my house with a satellite DirecTV, but I couldn't get a clear picture, so I gave the satellite dish to my dad. I was determined that one of us was going to get DirecTV. It's a lot of fun to watch the games with him. It started when I moved back because I was living at home for a while. It became this sort of bonding thing with my dad, which I hadn't really had before—ever. All of a sudden, I was able to talk to my dad. We'd sit there and watch ball games.

My dad remembers a time before Yankee Stadium was built, when the Yankees were playing in the Polo Grounds. He lived in Coogans Bluff and remembers looking down into the Stadium and watching the Yankees play without paying for the game. He also remembers his older brother, my Uncle Joe, putting together a crystal radio to listen to the World Series broadcast on radio. It was 1922 or '23. The

Yankees played the Giants, and Uncle Joe put the crystal radio into a bowl so it would resonate and more than one person could hear. It was my father's job to listen to the score on the radio and run downstairs and tell all the neighbors what it was.

If a Yankee game is on the network, I'll have my father over to my house to watch or I'll go over to his. Also we've been able to go to a couple of games together. It's really cute. Walter and my dad sit together, and you've got these two heads together, and they're both fascinated by statistics. My father was a city planner and only retired a few years back, and he always wants to know how my brother is calculating the batting averages.

Because my memory is almost as good as my brother's, I'll say to Walter, "Weren't there three **Alou** brothers?" He'll look at me and say, "I never knew you were paying attention." I say, "I was."

I took my best friend's son, who is a student at New York University, to a game this year at Yankee Stadium. He grew up in Washington, D.C., and his family has lived in Colorado for about eight years so he'd never been to Yankee Stadium. We were sitting there watching the game and he said to me, "How old were you when you first came here?" I said, "I was about forty-three." He looked at me and I started telling the story about how my father always took Walter to baseball games and not me, and that fathers really didn't take little girls in those days.

He looked at me blankly. I thought, "How absolutely marvelous." This kid obviously could not understand a time when fathers wouldn't take their daughters if they were interested in baseball.

| **Graffiti seen in a Nebraska truck stop, 1973:** | |
| --- | --- |
| (Written on wall) | *The answer is Jesus.* |
| (Written below) | *What is the question?* |
| (Written below) | *The question is: What is the name of Matty Alou's brother?* |

# THE WORLD WAS DIFFERENT WHEN SHIRLEY WAS YOUNG. FOR ONE THING, IT WAS FLAT.

Shirley Clark

*Formerly of lower Manhattan and then a resident of Long Island, Shirley Clark, 83, is every Yankee fan's dream daughter, wife, mother, sister, and aunt.*

About 1940, I was living in lower Manhattan. It wasn't "the suburbs" as we call it now. We used to call it, "the tenements." We were poor girls. I would go with my girlfriends to Yankee Stadium on Ladies' Day. We would always sit between first and home. I had a little camera. I once took a picture of DiMaggio from way up, and he was just so tiny. I kept it for so many years, but I've lost it. DiMaggio had a way of being at bat, what they called the "Eagle Spread." I got that in my picture, and I just was thrilled.

I had a famous record by Les Brown about Joe DiMaggio, "We Want You on Our Side." I had it for years and years and years. My youngest sister had hers and my brother Peter had his but in moving around it's gone the way of other things, like that little tiny photograph.

So many people at that time were interested in baseball. When I was twenty-one, during the 1941 World Series Yankees against the Dodgers, there was the game where Mickey Owen dropped the ball and the Yankees ended up winning. I thought our apartment building was shaking. You felt it was shaking because you could hear in all the apartments people just screaming and yelling. The Series was played during the daytime, during work hours, but everybody was listening to their radios.

I never did meet any Yankees, but it didn't matter, though I was disappointed once that I didn't get to meet Joe DiMaggio. It was in

**1942**, during the war, after my husband and I were just married. We were stationed out on the West Coast. My husband got leave so we could go from **Oregon** down to San Francisco. All that was on my mind was, "I'm going to Joe DiMaggio's place on Fisherman's Wharf." I was sure that Joe DiMaggio was going to be there, but, of course, he wasn't. It wasn't as though he was going to say, "Oh you're the young lady who took the photograph of me in 1940." I was disappointed he wasn't there, because I was a fan of his like other people were fans of Frank Sinatra.

I was such a fan of Joe DiMaggio's, and when he married that girl in show business, I thought to myself, "Oh dear, wouldn't it be nice if he married a little Italian girl, a real Italian girl." But of course, that's what they do. That's their lifestyle. This was not **Marilyn Monroe**. This was his first wife, the one he had his son with, Dorothy Arnold.

I never did get to take my kids to Yankee Stadium. By the time I had my family, the games were on television, and we got our first television set in the 1950s. Whitey Ford came from out here on Long Island. For my seventieth birthday, one of my sons went to a baseball fair, and bought me a picture of Joe DiMaggio. In the frame is a cocktail napkin with his autograph. It was from the Starlight Room at the Waldorf Astoria Hotel.

My one son is a great fan of Mickey Mantle's and this past Christmas, I bought him the Hallmark Mickey Mantle ornament. One of my sons and his wife took me to Shea Stadium for my birthday because the company they worked with had a box. I'd never been to Shea Stadium, and I felt like I was being a traitor. It seemed strange for me to be there.

The 1942 Rose Bowl game between Oregon State and Duke was played in Durham, NC because of fears that the Rose Bowl in Pasadena could be attacked like Pearl Harbor was three weeks earlier.

To accentuate a wiggle in her walk, Marilyn Monroe would cut a quarter of an inch off one of her heels.... The combination on Monroe's jewelry box was 5-5-5.

# THESE TEN THINGS ARE THE SEVEN SIGNS THAT YOU'RE HOOKED ON BUCKY DENT

Ilene Snider

*Her husband aside, Ilene Snider, 37, is a one-man fan. Though the Bronx-born Snider lives in Northern California, where she is the Executive Assistant to the San Francisco Giants Chief Operating Officer, Larry Baer, she still holds a candle for Bucky Dent.*

When I was a teenager, I actually became a die-hard Yankee fan to the point where my whole life was baseball. At home growing up, it was just me and my mom. I didn't have any brother to take me to games. I constantly read about baseball, studied it. The only books I read were baseball books.

I had the maddest crush on Bucky Dent. He's just gorgeous. My grandfather used to take me to the Yankee games when I was a little kid. In 1977, the White Sox and the Yankees made a trade, and the Yankees got Bucky Dent. I was a baseball fan but not hard core. I was twelve and didn't really care that much. Then I saw this Bucky Dent.

I was one of those girls who loved Donny Osmond and David Cassidy. I definitely liked boys. I thought Bucky was so cute. I thought he was gorgeous. So in 1977-78, I started following the Yankees to see how this really good-looking guy was doing, and I started going to the games with other kids. I was probably thirteen, and a couple of us would take the train to Yankee Stadium. I would go thirty to forty times a season, and I always wore the same outfit—red pants, which were hysterical, and then I had this little white T-shirt. The shirt said, "I (heart) Bucky Dent." I would wear that same outfit, and I would carry a sign that said, "Bucky makes a Dent in my heart." I'm sure he noticed me every once in a while because I would be taking pictures right down where he would be shagging balls on the sidelines.

When I met Bucky in 2000, I asked him if he remembered me, and he didn't, which was devastating to me. All the girls loved him. He was it! He became a pin-up guy. He did that Dallas **Cowboy Cheerleaders'** movie, which I watched a billion times. He came out with a couple of posters, and I covered my room with them. I've been looking on-line for years trying to find one of those posters, but I haven't been able to. Nobody has one, and if they do, they ain't giving it up.

I used to hang out in the bar in Yankee Stadium. The bartenders would make fun of me because I was wearing my Bucky Dent clothes. They'd be telling me Bucky Dent was gay. They were so mean. One guy said, "You know Bucky Dent's gay, right?" I said, "No, he's not. There's no way." He said to me, "You remember that fight between Goose Gossage and Cliff Johnson?" I said, "Yeah," because that was a big deal. This guy said, "What do you think it was over?"

The people I work with at the San Francisco Giants make fun of me because they know I still love Bucky Dent. He's my computer screen saver. I have pictures of him everywhere. I am married, but my husband knows about my obsession. In 2000, Bucky was coaching for the Texas Rangers. The Giants were playing an interleague game against them, and the Rangers were coming here to San Francisco. I was so excited, feeling, "Oh my gosh, he is actually going to be in this very building while I'm here. This is insane. I could actually meet him."

I'm not one of those autograph seeker types to go down to the field and say anything to him. I was sitting up at my desk, and the Rangers were on the field taking batting practice. Our assistant general manager was down there, and he called me from the field and said, "What are you doing right now?" I said, "Nothing in particular." He said, "Well, get down here. Someone wants to meet you." I almost died! I had a feeling who it was. I was freaking out. I was running to the

When the Dallas Cowboy cheerleaders were created in 1972, each earned $15 per game—the same amount they received last season.

bathroom making sure I looked all right. I was saying, "Is my hair okay?" I was so nervous.

I went down, and we talked for about ten minutes. I told him of my absolute obsession with him. He asked me, "After I left, who was your guy?" I told him, "Dave Righetti." Bucky asked me, "So now what? It's Derek Jeter, right?" I said, "No. After Righetti, there was nobody else. I got over my silly schoolgirl crushes."

We talked a little bit more, and he said, "Hey, I've got something for you. Come with me."

We walked over to the dugout, and he had a picture of himself when he hit the home run in 1978, autographed by him and by Mike Torrez, who threw the pitch. He must carry these around with him. Some of my friends from the team were down on the field at the same time taking pictures with Pudge Rodriquez, so I called them over, because they had a camera. I asked Bucky if he'd take a picture with me, and he did. It's sitting on my desk right now. That was a seriously top-five moment in my life. It was the culmination of how I became a baseball fan. That cute guy made me a baseball fan.

So I just became this crazy baseball fan. I had to date Yankee fans. I would never date a **Mets** fan. In college, I majored in journalism and wanted to be a sports writer so I could meet baseball players. I just wanted to be part of baseball. But the more I studied journalism and the more reporting I did, I realized that I was the enemy. I wasn't part of the team, and I didn't like that. From that point on, all I ever wanted to do was work for a Major League Baseball team. So I kind of credit Bucky Dent for getting me to the San Francisco Giants.

In my original interview with the team, I didn't want to sound like an obsessed fan because no one really wants that in an employee. I didn't want them to think I was this crazy obsessed girl that was gonna want to be on the field around the players all the time. That's not a good thing, and I'm actually not that way at all. I see the

> After the Mets had played their first nine games in their inaugural 1962 season, they were 9½ games out of first place.

players, but I don't go down there. I'm never down on the field unless I have a purpose for being there—like to meet Bucky Dent.

I've been married for six years, and my husband is not a Yankee fan—he's a Yankee hater. It hasn't been easy. But he's pretty good about it. I have Yankee stuff all over our house. When we met, we were living up in Washington state, so he was kind of a Mariners fan. This was a major problem because the Yankees and Mariners played each other in the 1995 playoffs. It was a battle.

> **I've been married for six years, and my husband is not a Yankee fan—he's a Yankee hater. It hasn't been easy.**

At the time, I was managing an apartment complex in Tacoma, Washington, and we had a rec building that had a giant, wide-screen TV. I decided I would have a party and invite all my friends over to watch Game 7 of the playoff series. There were probably twenty-five of us in the room. My husband and my friends were all Mariners' fans. I was the only Yankee fan in the room, and they were fighting me throughout the whole game, making fun of me and being mean, awful, awful, terrible to me. I fought back. I was so loud and obnoxious.

The Mariners won and eliminated the Yankees from the playoffs. All these people were sitting in this big room watching the TV, being so excited for this final moment when the Yankees lost, that they turned around and just went off on me. When they looked at me, they realized I was bawling. They all just looked at me and acted like, "Humph, this isn't going to be any fun." They got up and walked out, just left, because I was bawling. That loss was really hard.

If the Giants and the Yankees ever faced each other in a World Series, it would be a bad situation for me. I've never, ever, ever in my life rooted against the Yankees—never, ever. I can't even imagine. But to win and go to the World Series is every baseball team's goal, and that's what everyone here at the Giants wants. That's what everybody here is working for. It would be very difficult. I would have to root for the Giants.

# SHORT STORIES FROM LONG MEMORIES:

## EQUAL RITES

*Arianna Patterson with her daughter.*

I was always the kid who was more into baseball than my friends. I watched the Yankees on TV on the sly. I always loved baseball, but when I was a teenager and the other girls weren't into baseball, I went through a period when I stopped following it. I picked it up again as an adult, but what's funny is that my ex-husband hated sports. I used to watch baseball when he wasn't around, or else he would watch the History Channel downstairs and I would watch baseball upstairs. It was quite a role reversal.

Now when I go to a game, I drive into Manhattan to meet my boyfriend, who lives on the Upper East Side. I park near his apartment, and we take the Number 4 subway straight up. We go on spring training trips together. We get tickets for games throughout the season. It's a big shared experience for us. It's a way of me connecting to my feelings of childhood, and being able to pass down to my daughter the spirit of the game. She loves Derek Jeter. She asks us to get seats at third base so she can get the best view of his bod.

———ARIANNA PATTERSON, 46, West Orange, NJ

I have a special Yankee cap that George Steinbrenner sent me and I won't wear it in the house when I'm watching a game because it might jinx the team. I keep all my Yankee hats in my closet.

My friend Rae and I were at a game and she asked if she could wear my Yankee hat. She said, "I'll let you wear this brand new Ranger hat." I said, "Okay." I thought, "Good, I don't want to wear the hat. They'll lose if I wear my hat." I had this superstition because they lost one time when I went to the game wearing that hat, so since then, I don't wear it, I carry it. Well, the Yankees won that game. Rae said, "You know. I didn't want to tell you, but I wanted you to wear the Ranger hat so the Rangers could win. I thought if I took the Yankee hat off your head, it would give them bad luck." I said, "It's the opposite." You don't reveal to people these game superstitions. So when the Yankees won, she was so mad. I said, "Oh, you didn't know that I feel that if I wear the Yankee hat, they lose."

——THERESA ARO, 67, formerly of Dallas, TX

*Libby Roper*

In the 1970s, I went to work for the Federal government. In Washington at the time, there was still a stigma to being a woman. Though I was hired as an international economist, I was basically a secretary.

One day, I had a video presentation for my boss and my immediate supervisor. We were in a room waiting for the audio-visual technician to fix the projector. Somehow, we started talking about baseball. Also in the room was a woman friend of mine, who worked at the Department of Commerce and had a garbage can for a brain. She remembered the world's most trivial stuff.

She started throwing out baseball trivia. I was sitting there with these two men and we were waiting and waiting, so I also started throwing out trivia questions like, "Who are the three major league players who've played in four decades?" "What's the distance between home plate and first base?" Of course, I knew the answers because I'd asked the questions. One of the men turned around and looked at me, and asked, "Okay, what's Reggie Jackson's lifetime batting average?" At that time, I knew about five lifetime batting averages and Reggie Jackson's was one of them. So I answered correctly. The man's mouth dropped. He was just aghast. I thought, "Oh thank God, he picked one of the five I knew." Luckily, the video projector then started to work.

——LIBBY ROPER, 52, Evergreen, CO

Three years ago, my friend, Barbara, and I were walking down into the subway after leaving Yankee Stadium. A guy walked in front of me, walked down the steps and stepped in front of us. I was thinking that he looked a lot like Chuck Knoblauch, who at the time played second base for the Yankees. I looked at him for a few minutes, and then I turned to Barbara and grabbed her and whispered, "I think that's Chuck Knoblauch." She looked at me, looked back at him and looked back at me again and asked if I was sure. I said, "It looks just like him."

We got into the subway tunnel and Barbara ran over to him, looked him straight in the face and asked, "Chuck?" He turned and looked down at her and said, "Yeah." She started screaming. I always get embarrassed when I meet celebrities so I would have been excited just to be able to say, "I saw Chuck Knoblauch in the subway," but Barbara grabbed my camera and asked if we could take a picture with him, and he said, "Yeah, sure."

We couldn't find anyone to take our picture, so after standing there about two minutes, she grabbed the arm of a police officer who was walking by and begged him to take our picture. He said, "Well, I have to go do something right now. I'll be back in five minutes. I'll come take your picture then." Barbara said, "No, no, no, you have to do it right now." She grabbed him and wouldn't let go of him until he took our picture. We thanked Chuck Knoblauch, and he went on his way.

I have the picture on my desk here at college in Worcester, Massachusetts. Not many Red Sox fans have seen it and most of my friends don't even know who Chuck Knoblauch is.

———RACHEL VAN-RAAN-WELCH, Worcester, MA

I remember having a crush on Joe Pepitone. On one Bat Day, I got Jake Gibbs' bat, so he was my favorite for a long time. I always had a thing for catchers. I really loved them all. Our family went to a lot of Yankee games, so I especially remember the Bat Days and Ball Days and Picture Days and Photo Days. It's interesting that I knew all the Yankees and hardly knew any of the other teams. I always say, "I'm a bigger Yankee fan than I am a baseball fan."

When I was a girl, trading baseball cards was a really big deal. My brother, who is three years older, and I had a great partnership. We considered our baseball cards the "family" collection. When we went to school, we would each trade accordingly. He trusted me to trade the right way. We probably had our own, personal favorite cards, but when it came to trading outside the home, then we would consider ourselves as a family. We did not compete with each other.

One year, the Yankees won the championship away from New York, and my family went to the airport to greet them when they came home. It was weird because it was a weeknight, a school night, so that shows you how devoted we were. My brother and I were never allowed out on school nights, so the fact that my parents took us to the airport was really quite amazing to me to begin with. When we arrived, there were lots of smiling, cheering people. And when the Yankees appeared, they were all smiling, too. The scene was not as chaotic as I think it would be today. I remember getting close to a bunch of the players. I touched their shoulders, but there was no crushing or anything like that. It was just a real happy scene. I couldn't believe I was there, and that we were allowed to stay out so late.

———LORI SCHWAB, 44, raised in Queens

My grandparents were Italian immigrants and all the Italian Americans were very proud of the Italian baseball players. When Italians first came to this country, they were called all kinds of awful names. The cops used to come around and beat the boys with nightsticks. I remember one time we were watching a game and Don Drysdale was pitching. A commercial came on for a men's hair product. The advertisement said that the product was not greasy. Several times the phrase, "Grease ball" was said. My grandmother got up all excited and said, "Who's saying that?" I had to explain to her that when a ballplayer greased up a ball, it's an illegal pitch. She was all right once I convinced her the commercial wasn't poking fun at Italians.

———THERESA ARO, 67, raised in Manhattan

When I was about ten, I was absolutely convinced I was going to be the first female Yankee, the female Thurman Munson. You couldn't tell me any different. I started playing when I was young, about six, and I played one year on third base, but then halfway through the next season, my coach put me behind the plate. I thought, "This is great. I'm a catcher now." I tried to play like Thurman, to play hard, play rough.

It's strange, but I have no recollection of when Thurman Munson died. I would have been six at the time, but I just have no recollection of his death. My father and I were talking about it on the anniversary a year or so ago, and my mother said, "When I first heard the news, my first thought was, 'I'll call Margaret. She's going to be so upset. She's such a Thurman Munson fan.'" And yet I don't recall it at all.

Thurman Munson and I actually have the same birthday, June 7. So, of course, when I played softball all through high school, I had to wear Number 15.

When I was around eleven or twelve, I'd go to school in my Yankee hat which I still have around here somewhere. I was very much a tomboy, and I would put all my hair up inside the hat. I lived in it until the "NY" was flopping off and the bill was coming undone.

I used to get quizzed a lot by the boys in my class. We would be on a class trip, and I'd have my Yankee jacket on. Boys would say, "Oh, you're a Yankee fan. Name me five players." **"Who's on first?"** "Name me the pitcher rotation," that type of thing. Once I'd passed the test, they would leave me alone. I went to the same school with the same kids for years so after a while, they let me be.

——MAGGIE MCDONALD, 30, Brooklyn

In 1955, my schoolmate, Lucille Behrmann, asked me to join the Phil Rizzuto Fan Club. There were about eight of us girls in the club. We were seventeen and we all went to Dominican Commercial in Jamaica, New York, an all-girl Catholic high school.

Our friend Rosalie was in the club, but she got in trouble with her mother, and wasn't allowed to go to the ballpark any more. I went frequently, but she only went to one game. I don't think Rosalie was a real baseball fan anyway, it's just that Lucille wanted all of us to join the club. Lucille was a huge Phil Rizzuto fan. I was a Yankee fan, and we loved Phil Rizzuto, because he was the greatest. We thought the Yankees were wonderful.

We didn't pay for our tickets because the Club was given them. That's why most of us joined—so we could get free tickets! It was like if you belonged to the Bing Crosby Fan Club, you got free tickets to his concerts. As president of the club, Lucille always had the tickets.

Phil Rizzuto came over mostly to Lucille Behrmann. We girls would giggle—I always giggle. We always sat next to the bullpen, way out in right field. Phil would walk outside the outside of the

In the Abbott and Costello routine, "Who's On First?" the name of the team was the St. Louis Wolves. Only two major leaguers were mentioned in the full skit: Dizzy Dean and his brother, Paul.

Dr. Larry Lieberman (see page 154) shows his Mickey Mantle shrine at his dental office in Palm Harbor, Florida.

Fryin' Pan Fred Schuman
(see page 181)

**Ron Guidry (L) and Yankee fan, Mike Lobell (see page 65), at Guidry's Louisiana home in 1992.**

Dan McCourt, right, (see page 136) with friends in Box 622 at Game 4 of the 2001 World Series.

**Marty Appel patrols left field at Yankee Stadium in 1974.**

Yankee Stadium

Circa 1947

Yankee fan, Joe Fosina, (see page 178) is flanked by Bob Watson, Charlie

*Lucille Behrman, President of the Phil Rizzuto Fan Club, 1956.*

fence and visit with us. He never flirted. He was very businesslike. All the players were. They would come over and say, "How are you? Welcome." They were very formal.

After I graduated high school, I went to work in the export department for the Liggett and Myers Tobacco Company in Rockefeller Center. I was in charge of the baseball pool. We'd collect a dollar from everyone, and they'd bet on an inning. Whoever got the most runs in that inning would win the pool. It was nice.

———LILLIAN MCCLELLAND, 64, St. Petersburg, FL

Bucky Dent was my favorite player for the first five years of my being a fan. He was such a handsome guy—it's the same as all the girls now being in love with Derek Jeter. Even though Bucky wasn't a great hitter, I just liked the way he played shortstop. I had his poster in his cut-off shirt. As a thirteen-year-old, I was interested in the players' personal lives, so I knew what Bucky's wife's name was and his kids' names.

As I got older, I became less like the typical "girl" fan and more like a guy, in that I just truly love the game. I love the strategy. I'm not a groupie kind of fan or a big autograph person. I would never stand outside and wait for players for three hours to get an autograph. Since Dave Winfield, I haven't had one favorite player. I loved Don Mattingly, but everyone loved Mattingly. He was such a true Yankee. I love the sport more than the individual players. Baseball to me is like therapy. It's very relaxing. I can center myself. I can focus on the game and forget everything else that's going on in my life, good, bad, or indifferent. People who say that baseball is boring don't have a clue. Every game is different. It's the one game where the clock doesn't run out.

———LISA DUNLEAVY, 37, Manhattan

# Chapter 9

# Fandemonium

*Lisa Dunleavy*

I'll never forget going to my first game at Yankee Stadium the day of Thurman Munson's funeral. I remember it like it was yesterday, just the feeling of being there when I'd seen the Stadium on television for years and years. To walk up the ramp, and then get to the upper deck, take the escalators up to the top, and then walk out to the field and see how green it was amazing, and then for it to be such an emotional game. I went by bus with a group of about a hundred adults and children from my hometown. I remember Bobby Murcer's impact and how emotional he got when he hit the double in the ninth to win the game and the players all jumping around and hugging him. Everyone loved Thurman Munson.

Actually, one of the nicest memories of my life is related to Munson's death. In 1995, I worked for a PR firm that had some sports-related accounts. One of the accounts I worked on was the annual Thurman Munson dinner, which benefits an association for helpless and retarded children. Mrs. Munson comes in every year, and they take a bunch of athletes and honor them. It's a big fund-raising dinner. I'm not crazy about meeting players. I'm always afraid they're gonna be jerks, and I'll be disappointed, but I sat with Mrs. Munson and told her how much her husband had meant to me and that I was such a big Yankee fan, and that my very first game was the day of his funeral. She actually started to cry. She said, "Thank you so much for sharing that with me. I love to hear remembrances of Thurman, even to this day, that's why I always love coming."

She always came back from Canton, Ohio to New York for Old Timers' Day. She'd get a standing ovation every year. She said she always loved coming back to New York. Even twenty-four years later people on the street would come up to her and tell her how much her husband meant to them, and that means so much to her. Living in Ohio, she doesn't have people do that. It made me feel good that she actually cared about my story about it being my very first game.

———**LISA DUNLEAVY**, 37, Manhattan, ESPN Sales Director

In 1983, I pitched in the British Baseball League, an amateur league with Brits, Canadians and Americans. One day, I was pitching and a guy came up wearing a New York Yankees uniform and a mustache. I said to myself, "That guy looks familiar!" I called time out and looked at the roster, and next to his number it said, "American" and his name was John Munson. I called time out. I went over and asked my coach about him. "Yep, it's Thurman's brother," my coach told me. "He's in the Air Force."

The guy looked like Thurman and he was digging away just like his brother always did. The first pitch I threw to him, I hit him right on the hip, but it was such a soft pitch that he looked at me funny. I called time out. I said, "I'm sorry there, John. I'm an old Red Sox fan." He laughed and said. "That's all right!" I told him, "When I was a batboy for the Orleans Cardinals in the Cape Cod League back in '66, I saw your brother play a lot." He said, "No kidding! Let's have a beer at the end of the game." So, at the end of the game, Johnny Munson and I got together for a while.

—SHAUN KELLY, High School Teacher, Greenwich, CT

I am somebody who has trouble sleeping at times. I've gone through all the routines you hear about to help a person get to sleep. Obviously, counting sheep is the one that comes to mind most often. I'm not even quite sure where it started, but somehow I created a variation where I count Yankee uniform numbers, either the Yankee that's currently wearing the number or the retired Yankee that had it.

As I'm drifting off to sleep, I'll say, "One–Billy Martin. Two–Derek Jeter. Three–Babe Ruth. Four–Lou Gehrig. Five–Joe DiMaggio. Six–Joe Torre," etc. Usually, when I hit around the fifties, I fall asleep. The Yankees have had so many retired numbers that you can go into the 1950s and still come up with names to fit to numbers. Most of the time, I'm dozing by the time I hit Ramiro Mendoza, Number 55.

Obviously, everybody knows certain numbers. Everybody knows three is Babe Ruth and four is Lou Gehrig. Some of the numbers don't seem to get chosen as often. I think the last Yankee to wear Number 13 was Michael Coleman. He was an outfielder they had picked up early one year and was subsequently sent down to the minor leagues and is now back with the Red Sox.

I doubt that they don't give out the Number 13 because of superstition. Some players may just decide not to wear it. The last prominent one before Coleman was Jim Deshaies. He had Number 13. As I get into some numbers that haven't been in circulation for a while, I have to think hard, "Okay, who was the last guy to wear Number 27?' That was more than four years ago: Oh, that was Allen Watson."

I probably started doing this around 1991. Friends ask me if I do it in my own voice, or do I do it in the voice of Bob Sheppard, the great Yankees P.A. announcer. I always count in my own voice. I've been asked the question more than once so it's obviously something that people think about. Usually when people talk about not being able to get to sleep, if I know they're a baseball fan, I'll usually share my story with them. I have an acquaintance I met through the Internet who is a Red Sox fan, and she's tried it, and she says it's worked for her.

——STEVE LOMBARDI, 40, Middletown, NJ, Founder NetShrine.com

One thing about being a self-employed writer is that I don't have a lot of money to throw at my Yankee fandom. You see some folks at the Yankee Stadium and they've got their replica jerseys and they're driving a car with a Yankee license plate on it. I think to myself, "God, a replica jersey costs $99.99 or something like that." For me, that's the budget for an entire trip to Yankee Stadium. I live two hundred miles from the Stadium. I have to drive four hours, buy tickets, hot dogs, whatever, and then drive all the way back, pay the tolls and gas. I'd love to wear a jersey, but I'd rather spend that money going to a game at the Stadium.

I think partly what attracts me to baseball is the drama of it. I don't watch soap operas. I'm very disillusioned with Hollywood movies. How many times have you gone to a movie and two-thirds of the movie is good, and then the last third is drek? You wonder, "What happened in Act 3? Did a focus group change the ending?" I used to watch *The X-Files* and, finally, I felt that the writers were just playing around. But I still need something that's has drama and human interest in it. Baseball's perfect. Here you've got the whole season. This long unfolding epic. There are all these different characters running around. You don't know what's going to happen, and what's going to happen hasn't been determined by a focus group or some executive.

——CECILIA TAN, 35, Cambridge, MA, Science Fiction Writer

The game after September 11 was unbelievably moving. I was distressed, though, because the Stadium wasn't full. People were frightened and stayed away, but also, a lot of people weren't let in by the security guards because they had come from work with their briefcases and bags. What was memorable was the silence of the fans on their way home. There was much more stillness than there had ever been. I think just everybody was just very moved, still distressed about everything.

There are no fans like New York Yankee fans. They have the most cutting sense of humor in the world and find the strangest things funny. Remember when **Darryl Strawberry** was missing? I was at a game during the week that he was missing, and I was in the tier-reserved section, which to me always has the loudest and most aggressive fans, always making the motion wave, which I love the best. They're the rowdiest. They don't give anybody a break. Nothing is sacred. Nothing is untouchable. And forget what they do to a fan from the opposing team. That person is harassed the whole time.

There was a guy who kept getting up during the game. He was a tall, black man who had a shaved head. Every time he got up, the whole section would start to chant, "D A R – R Y L. D A R – R Y L." They were relentless throughout the whole game, and the section just kept getting bigger and bigger and bigger. To me, this epitomized Yankee fans. It's their sense of humor, their zest for life, their love of the team. They loved Darryl. The guy just laughed. He stood up, and he took a bow. He was great. He had great humor about it.

I felt at that moment that I really loved New York. I love New York for all its passion and all its zaniness and it's honesty and sense of humor through everything. Fans were really distressed about Darryl. Fans were really hurt. They felt that the number of chances he was given and the number of chances they gave him, the support when he'd come out on the field was totally open. It was as though when he came on the field, everybody forgot what he had been through. He has a sickness and yet when he disappeared, they were able to keep their sense of humor about it no matter how hurt they were.

——ARIANNA PATTERSON, 46, West Orange, NJ

> Who is the most famous person to pinch-hit for Darryl Strawberry? Homer Simpson, on an episode of *The Simpsons*.

A couple of years ago, my girlfriend and I drove up to **Oakland** for the weekend and watched both playoff games. The Yankees lost the first two games of the series, and it was so much fun because I'm never in that situation where I'm a defiant ——, but that weekend, I was sitting there wearing all my Yankee gear and making sure that everybody knew exactly where I was from. The funny thing is that New York is the one place where you really can't get away with doing that. If you show up in A's gear, someone is gonna kick the —— out of you. I've seen it too many times. They really will pick a fight. In Oakland, people were deliberately bumping into me and occasionally even cursing at me. No one actually tried to start an altercation, but it was great because A's fans were carrying brooms and all the people were talking so much yang about sweep, sweep, sweep.

I remember honestly feeling like all the Yankees had to do was win Game 3. For whatever reason, I guess I'd just seen this team do so many incredible things over the last five years that all they had to do was win that one game.

At the end of that game, there was that one Derek Jeter play that I imagine people will be talking about for a long time: left-fielder Shane Spencer overthrew two cut-off men, and Jeter ran all the way across the diamond, picked up the ball on two hops along the right field line between home and first, and back flipped it to Jorge Posada to stop the tying run at the plate in a 1-0 game.

Back at the hotel, I refused to turn off the light. I made my girl-friend sit up until *SportsCenter* came on at two in the morning just so I could watch the replay.

——VAUGHN SANDMAN, 27, Los Angeles, Television Writer

I could have seen Doc Gooden's no-hitter in 1996, but I had to coach a Little League game. I had gotten free tickets as a rainout giveaway, so I gave the four tickets to a couple of kids from another team that weren't playing that night. Obviously, I didn't know Doc was going to pitch a no-hitter. They go to the game, they see a no-hitter. After, I grabbed one of the kids. I said, "Look, do me a favor. Give me back the

> Tom Hanks once sold Coca Cola for the Oakland A's....Mrs. Fields of cookie fame once was an A's ball girl...and M.C. Hammer was a batboy.

four stubs. My friend knows a friend, who knows a friend, who knows a friend who works in Yankee Stadium. I'll try to get them signed by Doc Gooden."

A couple of weeks later, my buddy came back with the stubs. He said, "Look, my friend made a mistake. He accidentally put the stubs in the wrong locker room. Cal Ripken, Jr. signed the tickets."

*Joe Santoiemma*

I said, "Oh, that's such a mistake. I think I'll accept that. No problem. Give me the tickets!" Later on, I got Doc Gooden to sign the same stubs. I gave two back to the kids who went to the game, and I kept one for my son and myself.

When Arizona won the 2001 World Series, I was over at my brother-in-law's house. We were watching, getting ready to celebrate, the champagne was out, and the Diamondbacks scored the winning run with that little bloop hit. Nobody said a word. My twenty-one-year-old son and I just walked out and waved thank you. Not a word was said. There was dead silence, like a funeral, and I'm fifty. I'm just as bad now as when I was young.

———**JOE SANTOIEMMA**, 50, New Rochelle, NY, Stay-At-Home Dad

One of my good friends lives in New York and works for a liquor importer. After the ticker tape parade in 2000 following the Subway Series, Mayor Giuliani held a reception back at Gracie Mansion at about four o'clock in the afternoon. All the players and Yankee personnel were invited.

My friend Charles, whose company was providing the champagne for the party, had called me a couple of weeks before. He said, "I'm pretty sure I can get you into this. Get a plane ticket, let's assume it's going to happen, but if for some reason it doesn't, you can't be disappointed." So I said, "Okay, it's worth a gamble. Let's do it."

So I came to New York. It was a cold, blustery October day. I watched the ticker tape parade where the players were up on the trucks and the floats and the team got the Key to the city. I made my way to Gracie Mansion and was able to get in. That's where the fun

*Pat Cantwell*

began. The party was held under one of those huge tents, about eighty feet by sixty feet, on the lawn of Gracie Mansion. There were a couple of hundred people there. Various restaurants in New York catered the food and beverages. The players didn't show up because they were out doing their own thing but that was okay. George Steinbrenner, the coaches, Joe Torre, the announcers, Michael Kay, and of course, Mayor Rudy Giuliani were all there so I have this incredible set of photos. There's me and George shaking hands. There are other pictures of the actual World Series trophy. But the real kicker is that I have a baseball autographed by George Steinbrenner, Joe Torre, Rudy Giuliani and Michael Kay—all four names on one ball. It's in a drawer somewhere. I've got to get one of those plastic cases.

——PAT CANTWELL, 43, Santa Barbara, CA, Radio Station Ad Salesman

The monsignor at our church recently retired after fifty years as a priest. He was a diehard Yankee fan. He was born and raised in the Bronx and has been the pastor at many churches in the Bronx. After his final mass at the church, there was a reception for him. I made up a Yankee shirt with the Number 50 on the back. I brought it to the Yankees clubhouse and got whoever was there at the time to sign it, about ten or twelve of the players. After Mass, we went to the reception, and there were a lot of presents on the table. I went to him and said, "I'm not more important than other people, but you do have to open this one." He opened it, and the place went crazy because here was a big Number 50 on the back—a real Yankee shirt, and it was signed on the front by at least half the team. He became pretty emotional about it.

——JOE FOSINA, 66, New Rochelle, NY

I heard this story from both Hank Bauer and Virgil Trucks. Virgil played for the Yankees briefly in 1958. He was a good pitcher but played late in his career with the Yankees. He was mainly a relief pitcher and spot starter. They had two pitchers on the Yankee team, one was Virgil Trucks and the other was Johnny Kucks. During the ninth inning of a game, the pitcher got in trouble, bases were loaded, there was one out. Stengel went to take out the pitcher and bring in a relief pitcher. In the bullpen, he had two pitchers warming up, Kucks and Trucks. He told the umpire, "I want Kucks." The umpire misunderstood and brought in Virgil Trucks. Stengel was out there on the mound, and Virgil came in. He said, "What are you doing here? I don't want you." Stengel told the umpire, "I don't want this guy. I want Kucks." The umpires said, "Too bad. He's got to face one batter. As far as we're concerned, you called him in." So Stengel said to Trucks, "Go ahead and pitch to this one guy. Cross your fingers." So they went back to the dugout. Virgil threw one pitch, a ground ball, double play, game's over. After the game was over, Stengel went on the post-game interview and said, "I just had a feeling Trucks had it today."

——BILL MANGER, 56, Oklahoma City, Municipal Judge

In 1996, I was meeting a friend to go to a Yankee-Indians playoff game. It was the opening game of the divisional series. I was meeting my friend outside the Stadium Club. The Yankees went down 5-0 in the first inning. My friend was coming from work and was late.

About the top of the second inning, who comes bursting out of the doors, with a bodyguard on each side, but George Steinbrenner. He jumped into a limo and left. Another security guard came out, and I said to him, "Is he bailing out on the Yankees at the beginning of the second inning?" The guard said, "Well, the story is, he's got a business meeting he has to go to."

From the look on Steinbrenner's face, there was no way he was leaving to go to a business meeting in a playoff game in the top of the second. As it turned out, that was the game David Cone started and the Yankees ended up coming back and winning.

I wouldn't call it a hilarious story, but I thought it was funny because we always see George Steinbrenner on TV or read about him, but to see the rage in his eyes over something like this was funny. He came right out the doors of the Stadium Club, took off, and was not to be seen again. I thought it was funny that the Yankees came back to win the game, and he was either pouting somewhere in New York or on a plane to Tampa or some place.

There are myriad associations like this and the vast majority are incredibly positive. They bring you back to your youth. My life is incredibly good right now. I'm healthy, my whole family is healthy. We live comfortably. We like what we do. But still, there's a lot more to think about now than when I was a kid. Back then, when the Yankees were all-consuming, there was nothing to worry about. The biggest issue in my life was counting the days 'til the Yankee season opened.

——LEO EGAN, 43, Park Ridge, NJ, Lighting Company Owner

I was at the game when **Roger Maris** hit his sixtieth home run in 1961. My wife and four kids and I were at my mother's house one Friday night in late September, and I said to my wife, "Why don't we go to the game tonight?" I said, "Maybe Roger will hit his sixtieth. Who knows?" We sat in right field, and he hit the ball right over our head into the upper deck. The crowd was absolutely incredible, but he didn't take a bow that night. Ninety per cent of the people there were Yankee fans and wanted him to hit it. The sixty-first was hit two days later, during the Sunday day game. I thought Maris was a very great player, and certainly one of the best outfielders I ever saw.

A lot of what Billy Crystal showed in the movie *61\** about guys being against Maris and not wanting him to break Ruth's record—I never saw that. Everybody I know was rooting for Roger because we really loved this guy. He was such a gentleman. He wasn't a fanfare guy. He did his job, got clutch hits, had a great arm, and went inside the dugout. He didn't go out with the boys like Mickey did. He just did his job. There was no way you couldn't root for the man. How could you not root for a man like that?

——CHARLIE FUOCO, 68, the Bronx

On July 4, 1970, the Yankees played a doubleheader against Cleveland. Any Yankee fan worth his salt will tell you about Bobby Murcer hitting four home runs in the doubleheader.

In the first game, the Yankees pitched an old pitcher named Steve Hamilton, 6' 7", a left-hander who didn't throw very hard, but had a pitch called the "Folly Floater." He would go into his windup, and he would stop midway through and just literally toss the ball straight up

> When Roger Maris hit his 61st home run, there were 44,000 empty seats at Yankee Stadium. The attendance was 23,154.

in the air and it would rush down into the catcher's glove. The thing was if you took the pitch, it had to be a ball because it wouldn't cross the strike-zone plane. It couldn't be a strike. Tony Horton, who played for the Indians, swung at the first pitch Hamilton threw and fouled it off and motioned for him to do it again. "Go ahead, throw me another one." And Hamilton did—twice. Horton swung and missed and Hamilton struck him out. He crawled back in the dugout. It was hilarious.

Between games, somebody threw a firecracker from the bleachers that landed down on the field. There were warnings that the game would be **forfeited**. What made this game memorable was that it was the last game before the All-Star game, and Ray Fosse was catching for Cleveland. In that All-Star game in 1970, Pete Rose ran Fosse over to score a run and basically ruined his career. It was just a wild day of all kinds of funny things happening.

——**MIKE SPELMAN**, 45, Phoenix, AZ, Printing Services Salesman

When my son, Peter Jr., was nine years old, about 1966, I took him to Yankee Stadium. I got box seats right on the field, adjacent to the grass as close as you could get, past the first baseman. One of the White Sox players hit the ball over the first baseman's head on the right field line. It took one bounce, then it took another, and it was coming toward us. I grabbed my son's glove, reached over, and I made a nice catch off a short hop. Naturally, my son was screaming with joy. I stood up, showing off the ball.

*Pete Marino, Sr.*

The last forfeited game in the major leagues was on August 10, 1995 in Los Angeles. The Cardinals won 2-1.

The first baseman for the Yankees was Joe Pepitone. When I stood up, he was looking at me. With his hands he was gesturing, "Get down, get down, get down." I didn't know what the heck was going on. Finally, I saw that the fellow who hit the ball was on second base. What had happened was that the ball turned out to be fair, and if a ball is fair, you can't interfere with it. I hadn't realized that the first bounce the ball took was in fair territory.

Well, I sat down, and the people behind were saying, "You better hide the ball because the cops are coming." I took the ball and shoved it up in Peter's seat. I made him sit on it.

The two cops came over to me. They said, "Listen, are you the fellow who caught that ball?" I said, "Me? You got the wrong fellow." Sure enough, the guys sitting behind me said, "No, no, no, it wasn't him."

My kid was sitting there shifting in his seat because the ball was rolling around under his rear end between him and the seat. The cop said, "What's this kid squirming about?" I said, "He's got hemorrhoids." The cop gave me a look. They weren't sure what to do because the police don't want to get the wrong guy. They'd get sued for false arrest or such.

They went away, and Peter looked up and he said to me, "What's hemorrhoids?"

I said, "When you get older, you'll get 'em."

——**PETER W. MARINO**, 71, Manhattan

*Tom Lemme*

I got my first real, grown-up job around 1980-81, working for a private ambulance company in New York City. One day I called in sick and went to the Stadium. It was Opening Day.

That year, the Yankees introduced what turned out to be a very short-lived mascot—like the Mets had "Mr. Met" with the big baseball hat. The Yankees' mascot was an old-time baseball player with a big handlebar mustache with a head like a bat. It lasted maybe half the season, if that, but he was in the stands at Opening Day. He was walking through the stands, and who does he come upon in the sixth inning, but my friend Tommy, who has had several beers. Tommy put his arm around Mr. Yankee, or whatever this mascot's name was, and the cameras were rolling, and I gave the thumbs up. I drank a beer to Mr. Yankee, not realizing that the boys in the ambulance crew were watching the game. They saw me on TV with Mr. Yankee, drinking to his health and cheering the Yankees. I was very obvious. They said, "Oh, look, he really is sick!"

The next day, naturally, I heard about it. They docked me a day's pay and they all laughed at me. To this day, if you speak to someone who worked with me then, they'll say, "So, how are the Yankees doing?" It was embarrassing. I was three-quarters of the way in my cups at the time. It was Opening Day, the Yankees were doing well. I'd had three or four beers. With wild abandon, I waved to the cameras, imitating Phil Rizzuto. "Hey, Holy Cow!"

——TOM LEMME, 43, Garden City South, Long Island, Physician Assistant

When I was nineteen, I was in college in Boston, and when the Yankees would come to town, they stayed at the Sheraton. I would sneak into the hotel and hang out by the pool and pretend I was staying there. I would sit by the pool in my bathing suit hoping that some Yankee would come up and just fall in love with me. The only guy I met was Billy Martin.

It was probably about 1989. The Yankees were in first place and had played one game against the Red Sox the day before, which they had won. I was at the pool with a girlfriend. Billy Martin was sitting by the pool with Art Fowler, who was his pitching coach, and they were just sitting by the bar probably drinking a Bloody Mary early in the morning. I just had to go over to them. There's no way I'm not gonna go over and get his autograph. He's Billy Martin. That's a big deal!

So I went over and started talking to them. I said, "Great game last night. Great that you're in first place. You're doing a great job, and the team looks really good." I was making small talk while he was signing an autograph for me. I kept these little trivia cards and had asked him to sign one that had a Billy Martin question on it.

He asked me if I was going to the game that night, and I said I wasn't because I didn't have a ticket. He asked me if I wanted a ticket.

Yeah, of course, I want a ticket from Billy Martin. I said, "I would love to go." He said, "Well, come on up to my room, room 2620, and I'll give you a ticket." At the time, I probably said, " Okay, nice to meet you." He said, "Well, I'll see you later then." And I walked away.

I actually did take the elevator up to that floor and stood outside the room, but I never went in.

———ILENE SNIDER, 37, raised in the Bronx, SF Giants Exec. Asst.

There weren't a lot of Yankee fans in north Texas, but the Yankees were about the only team we could get on the radio when I was growing up in the 1940s and early 1950s. I think the games were tape-delayed, or rebroadcast, out of Dallas. Most of the people in my town of Denison were St. Louis Cardinal fans because St. Louis was the closest team. There weren't any teams in the southern part of the country then. We didn't have teams in Texas or Kansas City. I don't know why the radio stations there transmitted the Yankee games. You could always get the Notre Dame games or the Army-Navy games on the radio, along with the Southwest Conference.

Sometimes there was so much static on the radio that the games would fade in and out. It drove me crazy. I'd be listening to a Yankee game, and then static interfered and the signal would disappear and then it would come back again.

———RICHARD BREWER, 66, on his Denison, Texas youth

In 1999, I broke a tooth watching a Yankee game on TV. They were playing the Texas Rangers, and I wanted them to win badly because if they did, they would get to the World Series. I was very nervous, especially about Juan Gonzalez, who was a great hitter.

I was sitting in front of the television, I was eating a piece of stale rye bread with a hard crust, and watching Juan Gonzalez at the plate. I was so stressed that I chewed so hard down on the bread that I actually broke my front tooth and my post. I had to get an emergency appointment and go to the dentist the next morning. It cost me about five hundred dollars.

———JERRY FADEN, 57, Tamarac, FL, Engineer

None of us who were close to the team in the late 1960s could believe what was going on. We always thought that we would be

*Bill White, Marty Appel, Frank Messer (back to camera) and Phil Rizzuto*

returning to the top any day now. We didn't know it was going to last as long as it did. At that point, you knew some of the players on the team were other teams' cast-offs, and you'd think about how un-Yankee they seemed and wonder how could this guy be wearing this uniform? It was very depressing. Bill Bryan, a catcher, comes to mind. A pitcher like Thad Tillotson. An outfielder like Steve Whitaker. How did these guys get to sit in a Yankee team photo? It just didn't make sense.

———MARTY APPEL, 53, Mamaroneck, NY, Public Relations Executive

I was a second-year resident in training in Boston. A buddy of mine from college, John Ertman, was working for the Yankees and he got his job in an interesting way. He had been at University of Virginia Law School, and he and a bunch of his law school buddies decided they wanted to buy part of a minor league team. He was the ringleader and sent out letters to the different major league teams asking them if they had any openings for investors. This would have been in the mid-1980s.

John got a nice letter back from the Yankees saying, "No, there's nothing in that way, but we thought your letter was well written. Would you like to join up with the Yankee legal team?" John was a huge baseball fan, so he decided to sign up with them. Apparently

George Steinbrenner, as was his wont, had alienated the top five or six lawyers in the organization. So, at the ripe old age of twenty-eight, my buddy was either the second or the lead counsel for the New York Yankees. He was the guy who would fly out to Dave Winfield's house to go over Dave's contract.

I mentioned to John one day on the phone that I was coming home for the weekend, and he said, "The Yankees are in town. Why don't you go over to the side door, one of the private doors, tell them your name, and I'll leave a pass so you can come up and watch the game with me." How cool was that? So I said, "Sure." At the side entrance, there was a nice guy waiting there saying, "Dr. Philippides, come with me."

We walked past the Diamond Club and into George Steinbrenner's box, where George hangs out and watches the game. I guess he was out of town, and no one was watching, so we got to sit up in his box and watch the game. At one point, my friend, John, turned to me and said, "Hey, want a beer?" He went over to Steinbrenner's refrigerator and pulled out a beer. We're sitting there in George Steinbrenner's box seats, drinking his beer, watching his baseball team play, and then, all of a sudden somebody else came over. It was Lou Piniella, who was smoking a cigarette. He sat down next to me and said, "Hey, my name's Lou Piniella." Of course, I knew who he was.

He had a beer with us. Now the three of us are sitting there watching the Yankees and drinking George Steinbrenner's beer. There was a close play at second base in the second or third inning. John got this sort of strained look on his face, and then the phone rang. He picked up the phone and started saying, "Yes, Mr. Steinbrenner. Yeah. Yeah. Okay." He hung up the phone.

Apparently, Steinbrenner thought the call at second was bull____, and he wanted John to call the guys running the Diamond Vision and have them play it over and over to show that the umps missed the call. Piniella was just cracking up. He couldn't believe how petty Steinbrenner was being. Apparently, he did this all the time so John knew this call was coming.

That's my slice of George Steinbrenner.

———GEORGE PHILIPPIDES, 42, Boston, Cardiologist

People buy me Yankee things. My sister bought me a Yankee blanket and she just bought me a Derek Jeter Christmas ornament to add to my ornament collection. I go on the Internet and order crazy stuff. I don't have a souvenir ball, though. I never caught one, and that used to aggravate me. When I was a kid, I was so crazy I would take my glove to games and nearly break my fingers trying to catch a ball.

I have a Yankee hat that George Steinbrenner sent me. The way that happened was in 1981 or '82, I was working in Dallas as a credit manager. I used a collection agency in south Florida owned by two guys who were ex-football players. At the time, Steinbrenner and the actor **Burt Reynolds** were trying to get a new football league together. The two ex-football players would call me, knowing I was a Yankee fan, and tell me they were going to have dinner with Steinbrenner and Reynolds.

At the time, Steinbrenner was buying all these hitters but not getting any pitching. I told them to tell George that he was starting to get on my nerves because he could get all the hitters he wanted but until he started to get some pitching, he wasn't going to win. I also told them to tell Steinbrenner I wanted a Yankee jacket.

When they called me back, they said George said to tell me, "Mind your own business and stick to your credit managing and I'll stick to the Yankees." They said he wasn't going to send me a Yankee jacket, but he was going to send two Yankee caps, which he did. I gave one of the hats to a fellow who worked in my company's shipping department who was a big Yankee fan, and I kept the other one.

——**THERESA ARO**, 67, Retired, Credit Operations

In junior high school, I started checking out baseball books from the library, developing my baseball education. In the eighth grade, in 1965, New Years Day, I was quite despondent because I was feeling so stressed from all the pressure I had put myself under to perform in school. I was totally, internally, super-motivated toward school. That year was probably the most academically pressured I had ever felt. After four months of this, I felt, "I don't know if I can take it any longer. What's there to live for?" Somehow I made it to my

Burt Reynolds and Lee Corso were roommates and football teammates at Florida State University.

closet where all my baseball magazines were, and I said, "Oh, base-ball." Of course, there wasn't any baseball going on at that time of the year, so the magazines are what snapped me out of it.

————VINNY NATALE, 52, Accountant, raised in Cranston, RI

In 1962, I entered All Hallows High School, which was a block and a half from Yankee Stadium. The school was emotionally tied in to Yankee Stadium. It was a commuter school so kids from all over the city came there. It was a school full of rabid Yankee fans. We all con-gregated on the Jerome Avenue elevated train station and peeked over to watch the games.

The school didn't have any playing fields, so all our gym classes and athletic teams practiced at Macombs Dam Park, adjacent to Yankee Stadium. I was on the track team, and we had our practices looking right up at the stadium. For a month, we practiced marching for the St. Patrick's Day parade around Yankee Stadium at 6:37 in the morning.

————STEVE MASCIANGELO, 53, raised in the Bronx

About 1953-54, when my sister started dating, I was still a kid, maybe eleven. She became engaged to a guy, who is still her husband all these years later, and he was a big-time Yankee fan. He and I weren't getting along that well. He knew he was going to marry my sister, and he didn't like the fact that I was a Dodger fan. He just couldn't deal with it. Then one day, he came to our house and sur-prised me with three box seats for Yankee Stadium. He put them on the table. He said, "It's too bad you're a Dodger fan. These tickets include all the hot dogs you can eat and soda and whatever you want. What am I going to do with them?"

I was really excited. I said, "I'll go with you." Then he said, "I can't go with a Dodger fan to Yankee Stadium. Only Yankee fans can go there." I was only a kid and he had these three box-seat tickets, so I said, "Okay, I'm a Yankee fan." They played the Washington Sena-tors and lost that day, but it was fun. I had never been to the Bronx before, and to me it was like going to a foreign place, which I thought was pretty neat. So that's how I became a Yankee fan.

————JERRY FADEN, 57, Brooklyn, Florida

*Yankee fans through and through.*

*Photo credit: Courtesy of TakeHimDowntown.com*

Last season, I was at a Yankee-Rockies game, and I was sitting next to a little girl who was eight, her older sister, probably twenty, and the sister's boyfriend. Sitting in the row right in front of them was another sister, who was about sixteen, her boyfriend, and her brother, who was twelve. They were Hispanic and had driven up all the way from Pueblo, Colorado, which is much further south, almost in New Mexico. They came all that way see the Yankees. The little boy had a Derek Jeter shirt on. They had Yankee hats and stuff. It started to rain so I shared my umbrella with the little girl.

So here was this Hispanic group, not one of them over twenty, rooting for the Yankees. They'd never been to New York. I think something this shows something very special about the Yankees—that if you ask almost anyone, twenty-one or older to name one Yankee, they will be able to. The Yankees have had for decades a continuous string of big name players and managers, so everybody knows Babe Ruth. Everybody knows Mickey Mantle. I think that irrespective of all the pennants and World Series' the Yankees have won, probably more than any other team, people identify them with baseball.

——LIBBY ROPER, 52, Denver; Colorado

To me, Willie Randolph was a link to those teams in the late 1970s that were so great. His trade from the Pirates is as much a marker of the time the Yankees got good as Paul O'Neill's trade from the Reds was a marker of the time the Yankees got good in the 1990s. I remember Jim Bouton, an ex-Yankee, who did the sports on Channel 2 in New York, at the time announcing the Yankees' acquisition of Randolph, and Bouton said, "This trade is a beauty." No one had ever heard of Willie Randolph 'til then, because he was not an experienced player at that time, but Bouton was so right. The Yankees were a much better team from that moment on.

——**VICTOR LEVIN**, 41, Former New Yorker

# Chapter 10

# Hot Dates, Cool Mates

## The Promise of a Lover
## The Performance of a Husband

# I'M GONNA SWEEP HER OFF HER FEET JUST AS SOON AS I GET THIS TOILET PAPER OFF MY SHOE

### Kevin Fitzpatrick

*Thirty-six, single, and raised in St. Louis by ex-New Yorkers, Kevin Fitzpatrick has found the secret to the perfect date: taking a woman to a game at Yankee Stadium. By the seventh-inning stretch, Kevin will know whether he'll invite her to a second game, or whether he should have left her standing at the Big Bat.*

*After stints as a copywriter for the backs of Topps baseball cards, launching Major League Baseball's Web site, mlb.com, in 1995, and working at foxsports.com, Kevin and his brother now run their own Internet firm, Fitzpatrick Brothers Studios on the Upper West Side of Manhattan.*

I was working as an editor at Major League baseball's magazine in 1995 when they asked me if I wanted to start their Web site. Back then, no one was doing much on line. For the two and a half years that I ran it, I went to fifty or sixty games a year. Otherwise, I go to at least twenty-five. I grew up in the Midwest, in St. Louis, though my parents were originally from New York—Brooklyn Dodger fans no less. Ten years ago, when I moved to New York, the greatest city on the planet, I couldn't be a National League fan because I hate the Mets. I'd never seen American League baseball growing up in St. Louis, so I threw my lot in with the Yankees when they were pretty terrible, in 1991-1992.

Going to a game is a social event. I go to a lot of games with dates. I'm thirty-six and single. I always get two tickets to every game so I can bring a friend, usually a girl. I will only date girls that like baseball. The off-season stinks because a baseball game is the perfect first date. If the conversation stops, you can just watch the game. You can drink the whole time. You're sitting there in the sun. I've taken dozens of girls to games. It's a great thing.

The girls I date don't have to be Yankee fans, they just have to like baseball. It wouldn't matter to me if a girl is a Mets fan. That would spice things up. If a girl isn't a baseball fan, something is wrong with her. There's so much about baseball that's about life, about teamwork and fair play and sportsmanship and American history. And because I like the game so much and I go to so many games, if I had a girlfriend that didn't like baseball, there'd be a couple of times a week for eight months when I wouldn't see her.

> **There's so much about baseball that's about life, about teamwork and fair play and sportsmanship and American history.**

I've taken about six or eight female bartenders to games because they watch a lot of baseball on TV when they're working, and they know the game and who the players are. Also, they're usually pretty attractive. You don't have to explain stuff like pitching changes and who all the players are since they already know them.

My friends and I have certain rituals when we go to Yankee Stadium. Before the game, we almost always go to Ball Park Lanes, a bowling alley on River Avenue. There's a bar inside the bowling alley so we go there for our pre-game beers. It's packed with Yankee fans. If we don't meet there, we meet at the Big Bat. When I tell some girls who've never been to Yankee Stadium to meet me at the Bat, they say, "Where's the bat?" And sometimes they can't find it.

Sometimes these girls have lasted only one game. If they make it to two, they could be a "keeper." They tend to call during the post-season, and say, "I'd really like to go to the World Series." Yeah, right.

One time a friend and I were going to the bowling alley after the game, and on our way, we watched these two girls having hot dogs. One girl dropped her whole hot dog right on the sidewalk. It had sauerkraut and mustard and just went plop on the sidewalk. My friend bought her a hot dog and handed it to her and said, "Here, I saw you drop your hot dog. Here's your hot dog." She couldn't believe it. We'd been drinking the whole game. We went into the bowling alley, started to drink some more, and then the next thing we knew, two girls showed up, and there's the hot dog girl. Luckily for me, my friend's married, so I got the hot dog girl. It turned out she was a nurse at Columbia-Presbyterian Hospital, and I got her number just because of the hot dog incident. Whenever I call her, I say, "Is this the hot dog girl?" I e-mail her, and to this day, I can't remember her name, but to me, she's the "hot dog girl."

I had one female friend who I'd go to games with who was in love with Tino Martinez's butt, so we got our seats on the first-base side. Whenever there was something in the news about Tino, she'd always have to hear about it. She tried to deny that he was married. She was totally obsessed with him, mostly just for his butt, though.

I met three girls from Ireland who were in New York for a week's vacation. I said, "Have you ever been to a baseball game?" They said, "No." I said, "All right. We're going to go tomorrow." The next day I sent these three girls to their first baseball game. Of course, they had no idea what was going on, but they were rooting for Paul O'Neill because he had an Irish surname. Someone hit a home run and I said, "Wow, you guys are really lucky, because there aren't a lot of home runs." Well, it turned out there were four **home runs** in that game, so the girls were going bonkers.

They liked two things about being at the ballgame. One, that you didn't even have to leave your seat, and the beer man will come right to you and give you your beer, which they obviously don't do in Ireland. And second, they really liked the action. They loved the fans, the roaring, and the cheering. They all got Yankee hats, of course, to take back to Ireland. So, I guess there are some Yankee fans over in Dublin somewhere.

> Mark McGwire holds the record for longest home run at six major league ballparks...but not Oakland (Pedro Munoz).
>
> McGwire's brother Dan, a #1 draft pick of the Seattle Seahawks is the tallest quarterback in NFL history.

# SHORT STORIES FROM LONG MEMORIES

## TAKE HER OUT TO THE BALL GAME

A couple of girls I dated didn't want to go to Yankee Stadium, so if I took a girl, she really had to like me, or else she had to be a baseball fan. At reunions, I've seen the girl I dated most of high school and she remembers vividly my taking her to Yankee Stadium. She has told me, "I didn't know what I was looking at when you took me to see Maris, Mantle, Berra and all those people. I appreciate it now, but I didn't then. Then it was just a nice experience to spend time together."

Taking a date to the Stadium was kind of an acid test. "Would this relationship last," "Did they want to go or not?" That was always a big litmus test on your relationship.

——BILL MANGER, 56, Municipal Judge

If I ever took a girl to a Yankee game, it was an admission to myself that I was serious, because basically I was saying, "Meet the thing that on some level you're competing with. Here's something that I love and always will, perhaps in addition to you."

When you take a girl to Yankee Stadium, which is in the south Bronx, for Pete's sake, there's a lot you have to work out. How are we gonna get there? What does it say if you're asking the girl to get in the subway where she will be pressed up against the edge of the subway car by five thousand people on the way home? Is that really the way she wants to spend an afternoon? You have to make sure you can find a seat. If somehow an usher gets involved, you have to tip properly and swiftly. You have to be able to figure out where the right hot dog stand is. There's a lot of pressure. If you go by yourself or with guys or just with friends, who cares? You figure things out when you get there. But you want a date to go well, so you to work out these little details ahead of time.

So if I took a girl to a Yankee game, I was laying myself bare. I have done this, with varying success I might add. Some women I dated out here in California couldn't believe that somebody would expect them to get in the car, drive an hour and a half to Orange County to sit

*Victor Levin and his daughter*

for four hours just to drive back for another hour and a half. These women were always informed by the experience. These were the kind of dates on which both of us learned something.

My wife, who is from Washington, D.C., has become a fan and loves to go to games, but being in the television business, I can't always get out to watch a game, so for many years she tolerated a bit of insanity on my part. This was prior to any of those fancy recording systems like TiVo. If I got home at ten o'clock and the game was still going on and I wanted to watch it, I'd have to run a series of tapes. I'd have to stop the tape I had running, quickly throw in another one, go to another VCR, rewind that tape, play that tape, taking care not to see any live television in the process of putting the tape on, watch that tape, speed through the commercials, get to the end of that tape, go upstairs to the VCR that was still recording the game on a second tape, repeat the process with a third tape, and on and on.

Of course, I could never catch up one hundred percent. There's a mathematical limit to how fast you can go. But there are games I have that run ten tapes because it's taken me that long to catch up. Eventually the VCR is twenty seconds behind the actual game, and you realize it's pointless to continue the process. My wife puts up with this every year that the Yankees play a big game. So here's this insane man, running through the house, with videotapes all over the place, which I save, by the way. I have a garage full of them.

——VICTOR LEVIN, 41, Los Angeles

A couple of years ago, my boyfriend, Corwin, and I were on our way back to Boston from Philadelphia, and we decided to stop at the Jersey shore for a last hurrah. Labor Day weekend is the last big weekend at the Jersey shore. We were walking down the boardwalk, and we came to one of those spinning wheel games where you put down a dollar on a name or a number and one of those giant roulette wheels spin around, and they have all the major league jerseys. As we walked along, my eyes were scanning the wheel. There are a hundred and eighty different names and numbers you can choose from. As I looked, I saw "Doc," and in that instant the wheel lit up. What went through my mind was: "Doc Gooden pitched a no-hitter in 1996. Mike Mussina almost pitched a no-hitter yesterday. Doc Gooden retired this year and helped to raise the championship flag on Opening Day."

All these things went through my mind, and I whipped a dollar out of my pocket and I stuck it down. You had to press the button to spin the wheel. I shut my eyes, pressed the button and waited and waited. You have to press the button again to make the wheel stop. I pressed it again. I won!

After what had happened the day before, I thought, "Somebody's got to wear Mike Mussina's jersey." So that's how—after all these years I've refused to spend the money—I ended up with a major league baseball player authentic jersey. It's the real thing. I wear it when I go to Fenway Park. That's tough. Wearing your Yankee gear to Fenway Park is an experience.

——CECILIA TAN, 35, now living in Cambridge, MA

Being a Yankee fan can be hazardous to your social life. Before I was married, I'd had relationships with women that didn't work, partly because of my infatuation with the Yankees. The girl I took to the high school prom broke up with me, and she made a list of things she didn't like about me—kind of "How do I hate thee? Let me count the ways?" I think the second or third entry on her list was, "You like the Yankees more than you like me." She'd had it. It was summer, and I wasn't being as attentive as I should have been.

One time I was set up on a blind date, and the woman and I met for a game at Fenway Park. I got into this sour mood because the Yankees were getting blown out. I remember just being dour. The next day the girl who set us up called and said, "What is wrong with you?" My date had called the girl and said, "I thought you said he was a nice guy. He's an idiot." I ran into her at a party about a month later, and it was way too late and too little. I was a bad guy. The Yankee fan thing can get in the way. In a strange way, I wouldn't have a problem dating a Red Sox fan, but I would never date a Republican, and I would never date a Mets fan. I can somehow relate or at least sympathize with the hardship Red Sox fans have endured and the fact that they still love their team intensely despite all that. The Red Sox fans don't grate me the same way the Mets fans do.

——GEORGE PHILIPPIDES, 42, Boston

When my sister was about to be married, her fiancé asked me to be his best man. I found out that he was a Red Sox fan, and not only that, that he's a Notre Dame fan! I went to USC, and Notre Dame is our most traditional rival. I can't bring myself to root for either of those teams. I always root for whoever's playing against them.

The wedding took place in 1982 at my aunt's house. Two or three of my Yankee-fan friends and cousins were going to be at the wedding, and I found out that two or three of his best friends were Yankee fans. I cooked up this little scheme where about eight of us got together and went out and bought a Red Sox hat and some Yankee hats and I hid them. After the ceremony, I made a toast, and then I said, "We have a special little something for you to remember this."

I called all the guys up who were in on it, and the band started playing "New York, New York." We pulled out the Yankee hats and put them on, wrapped our arms around each other's shoulders and started doing the can-can. We dumped the Red Sox hat in the middle of the floor and start stomping on it as we danced around. My brother-in-law had a good sense of humor. He and my sister were laughing hysterically. He's taken a lot of abuse from me over the years. Twenty years later, and they still talk about it.

——**BOB OETTINGER**, 50, raised in Detroit

When my wife and I were engaged and planning for our marriage, I didn't want to miss any of the baseball season so I told her we could only get married after the baseball season. We got married on October 17, 1992. Luckily, the Yankees didn't make it to the post-season that year.

We had the wedding reception video taped for all eternity. There's a portion in the tape where she is handed the microphone and says her message to me, and there's a portion where I get the microphone and I say my message to her Of course, I break into the Lou Gehrig speech, "Today, I consider myself the luckiest man on the face of the earth." I did it with the echo just like in real life, "Today, day, day, I consider myself, self, self," with the reverberation. She wasn't too pleased about that.

——**STEVE LOMBARDI**, 40, raised on Staten Island, NY

# TO BE CONTINUED!

We hope you have enjoyed the first annual *For Yankee Fans Only*. You can be in next year's edition if you have a neat story. You can email it to info@theprintedpage.com (put "Yankee Fan" in the Subject line) or call the author directly at 602-738-5889.

For information on ordering more copies of *For Yankee Fans Only* as well as any of the author's other best-selling books, go to www.fandemonium.net.

. . . . I left the Stadium with my mom and dad. Before we even got to the parking lot, kids approached me, asking for my autograph. I signed about ten and then I said, "Okay, I've got to go. I'm gonna have dinner with my parents now. I'll sign more tomorrow." My mom said, "No, you don't. You stay right here and you sign every one of these autographs. We'll wait." I spent twenty minutes signing an autograph for every single kid because my mom said I had to. . . .—Jim Bouton, Ex-Yankee Ace

. . . . It was so strange when The Mick died. There's a radio in the bathroom, and I always turn it on. I hit CBS at the top of the hour, and the first thing I heard was that Mick had died. I sat on my bed and . . . I'm crying now, because I was crying like a baby that night. You feel attached to these people. It's hard to explain. I'm not part of their life, but, for sure, they were part of mine. . . .
—Mark Rollinson, 52, Yonkers, NY

. . . My wife, Linda, is a huge Red Sox fan. She's a big believer in the Curse of the Bambino mythology. A couple of years ago, she set up a shrine in our kitchen. It consisted of a photograph of Babe in a Red Sox uniform. Underneath, she set a little candle and every Friday she would light the candle. Every Friday, she would also go buy the Babe a cigar. These weren't cheap cigars either. After about six months, I told her that the Babe had been dead for over half a century, and I really didn't feel like spending five bucks a week on cigars for him anymore. . . . —Mark Jurkowitz, Yankee Fan